Dying for a Change

"An amazing story! We don't have to [...]
from the important revelations movin[...]
as he confronted drowning in the sea. [...]
any doubt that there is an energy force out there ready to help us find our
way…we need only listen."
Susan Jeffers Ph.D
Author of 'Feel the Fear and Do It Anyway' and 'Embracing Uncertainty'

"Riveting! Prepare to read in one sitting. William has given us a modern
parable for our times. It will inspire you, provoke you and ultimately,
get you thinking about your own life."
Fiona Harrold
Britain's best-selling author of Be Your Own Life-Coach

"This is a rare, exciting, brilliant and entertaining read. Once started, I
wasn't able to put it down. It is the raw story of how a man, dominated
and driven by ambition, finds himself in a life-and-death crisis, wrestling
with a storming, freezing ocean, and in the midst of drowning and
fighting for survival, is shaken up and transformed by startling insights
and illuminations about the true nature of life, delivered to him by an
unseen but immensely wise presence. Readers who have loved books
like *Jonathan Livingstone Seagull*, The Paulo Coelho and Dan Millman
books – or just a thundering readable adventure story – will greet *Dying
for a Change* as a modern classic and bestseller."
William Bloom
**Author and founder and co-director of The Foundation for
Holistic Spirituality**

"In his book, *Dying for a Change*, William has brilliantly captured that
single thing that every great Sage seeks; the epiphany. The reader is
transported to a place where heretofore only the prophets have been.
There you experience the wonder of human transformation as William
reaches into his soul and somehow magically conjures the words that
allow us all to feel the events that changed his life; that fateful moment
when he stood at heavens door."
Bill Mosher
Award-Winning TV producer and founder of *Visionaries, Inc.*

"For most people death is a fearful ending to a journey not fully realized. For William Murtha the prospect of his own death in such an unusual way was a blessing in disguise-not just for William and his family but also the world. It is through his book, *Dying for a Change*, that each of us has a chance to once again awaken to possibility, opportunity and the realization that our lives matter, our voice counts and that what shall be for our lives is up to us."

John St. Augustine
Author of *Living an Uncommon Life* and Host and Senior
Producer of Oprah Radio on XM

"With *Dying for a Change*, William Murtha offers a powerful and moving testimony of his near-death experience and how it radically changed his world view. This thought-provoking and insightful book addresses the very essence of the nature of reality. A must read for anyone who wishes to reflect on the human condition and beyond."

Evelyn Elsaesser-Valarino
Co-author with Kenneth Ring of *Lessons from the Light*

"A thoroughly enjoyable, challenging and profound read. This inspirational book will make you sit up and take greater notice of all those small yet often meaningful coincidences in your life."

Gay Hendricks, Ph.D.
Author of Five Wishes and co-author, with Dr. Kathlyn Hendricks,
Conscious Loving and Spirit-Centered Relationships

"William Murtha's portrayal of his life, with his fears, challenges, and family recollections, is laid bare through the telling of a dramatic, life changing experience. The insight, understanding and awareness which were given to him in his moment of desperation demonstrates that the Grace of God is ever present in our lives, and reveals itself in wondrous, mysterious ways. A compelling journey that will inspire while simultaneously giving pause for inner reflection and contemplation."

Audrey Kitagawa
Author and UN United Religions Initiative

"*Dying for a Change* demonstrates the invincible power of the Divine Spirit within. William Murtha is a teacher of great inspiration, and his book confirms that there is no death. You must read it".

Sonia Choquette
Intuitive and author of *Trust Your Vibes*

"*Dying for a Change* illuminates the power of the human spirit, the nature of transformation and the mysterious force that binds humanity and shapes our collective destiny. William Murtha came out of his terrifying ordeal to become a luminous embodiment of the emerging global consciousness."

James O'Dea,
Past President of the Institute of Noetic Sciences

"As a physician, I've often wondered if there is a way we could all benefit from a Near Death Experience (NDE) without actually having to go through one. In *Dying for a Change*, William gives us just that- the unique chance to vicariously experience a dramatic NDE- and live to tell the tale. It is my hope that this book will be a wake up call for all those who, like William, are dying to make a much-needed change in their life's direction. It's all the inspiration you'll ever need."

Christiane Northrup, M.D.
PBS Host and Author of *Women's Bodies, Women's Wisdom and The Wisdom of Menopause*

Dying
for a
Change

Survival, Hope and the Miracle of Choice

William L. Murtha

Transformation Media Books

Transformation Media Books

Copyright © 2009 William L. Murtha

Published by Transformation Media Books, USA
www.TransformationMediaBooks.com

An imprint of Pen & Publish, Inc.
Bloomington, Indiana
(812) 837-9226
info@PenandPublish.com

www.PenandPublish.com

ISBN: 978-0-9823850-8-1

Library of Congress Control Number: 2009931550

This book is printed on acid free paper.

Printed in the USA

Thanks and Gratitude...

This book would never have happened had it not been for the unquestionable love and support of several beloved friends and family members, each who contributed massively in their own miraculous ways. My special thanks go out to my gifted editor, Susan Heim, who through grace and sensitivity, managed to chisel my manuscript into the story I always knew possible.

To my best friend in the world, Simon Pearson... who was the first person I ever trusted to hear my incredible true story. And to Paul Lillycrop, for the countless conversations and support on the phone. Thank you both for finding the space to listen openly without criticism or judgement. Your endless patience and understanding will be forever appreciated- so thank you.

To Katy Clarke...the first living and breathing angel I had ever encountered. Your unwavering belief in my raw talent, coupled with your meticulous teaching skills and love, enabled me to discover my true 'writer's voice.'

To my three beautiful daughters, Jenna, Olivia and Kitty...thank you for allowing me to experience what it truly means to be a father.

To Nathan Swindlehurst, the man with the telescope, who, thankfully, listened to his gut instinct. I wouldn't even be here today if it were not for your quick thinking and decisive action, so heartfelt thanks.

To my great friend and publisher, Ginny Weissman...thank you for believing in me and my book, and for making a dream come true in getting *Dying for a Change* out there in the world.

And finally, thank you to my loving parents, Pat and Bill Murtha... who have both taught me numerous life lessons in tenacity, forgiveness and empathy.

Prologue

Without warning, a wave crashed over the top of the seawall, hitting me full in the face. The water was ice cold, and I was thrown backward off my bike by the force of the wave. I banged my head on the wall that separated the coastal pathway from the railway line. Shocked and dazed, I scrambled up on one knee. I was soaked and shivered violently. Embarrassed, I looked around. Thank goodness nobody was there to see me. I laughed and imagined what I would say to Alison.

Suddenly, a second wave slammed into me and caught me off balance. Thrown backward by the force, I was knocked against the wall again and landed on my back. With nowhere for the water to go, it hit the back wall before rushing back into the sea. My bike was scooped up and disappeared over the edge. Panicking, I scrabbled frantically at the hard ground, desperately trying to grab something, anything to hold, but there was nothing. Then I knew for sure: I would be next. In that instant, I was swept over the edge of the seawall by another wave.

Those next few seconds seemed like an eternity. Falling twenty-something feet, I imagined the worst. Directly below me were jagged rocks. Then I hit the water. Every muscle flinched. My left leg thumped into the bike frame, sending a shudder through my whole body. The shock of hitting freezing water was like an electric current. A putrid stench overwhelmed me. I had landed close to the sewage outlet pipe. Coming up and gasping for breath, I instinctively punched the air. I was okay, at least for the moment.

My elation was short-lived, though, and I knew I was in trouble. Frantically paddling water and struggling to breathe, I instinctively stretched out and touched the menacing seawall, which was covered in algae. I had no way of seeing over the wall, and I was in the shadows. Nobody could see me. Nobody would find me. I started yelling, but the crashing waves drowned out my cries for help. I soon gave up. Shouting was useless. As I turned to look at the dying sun, a huge wave hit me full in the face. Gagging, I struggled for breath again. My lungs filled with contaminated water, and I threw up. The smell of sewage was overpowering. Then another wave threw me hard against the wall. And then another. And another.

Still swallowing sewage and seawater, I couldn't stop being sick. I wondered if I were drowning. The waves were powerful, relentless. The noise was deafening. The smell disgusting. Wave after wave pummelled me against the wall. My eyes were stinging, and everything was a blur. Thrashing around, I was struggling to stay afloat.

Shaking violently in the bitterly cold water, I began to convulse. Crying and whimpering, I felt weak and pathetic. Pumping my legs madly to keep my head above water, I could feel them giving way beneath me, as if heavy weights were attached to them. I wondered how much longer they would hold out. All I wanted was to be at home and warm, with my wife and children. Safe and in the company of those I loved most.

For a brief moment, I considered giving up, but the thought of my family lifted something deep inside me. In a split second, I knew I had to keep fighting. An unexpected surge of optimism raced through me. It was an energy surge like I'd never felt before. My whole body felt lighter, stronger. I actually believed that somebody would find me and save me.

I stopped crying and tried to pull myself together. I let wave after wave belt me in the back of the head, which was now throbbing. I rubbed my stinging eyes and cleared seawater from my nose. But rationality soon returned. I knew it was hopeless and sank back in despair. Nobody would be out walking around here after dark. For the briefest of moments, I held onto the fragile belief that my wife Alison would raise the alarm. Perhaps she'd realize that something was not right, and then call someone out to search for me. But I soon realized it would be useless. After all, I could be anywhere along my five-mile bike route. And even if the emergency services were alerted, I'd be dead well before they could find me. It was up to me to save myself.

Battered up and down with the waves, I desperately tried to kick myself away from the wall, but I was barely moving anywhere. I stared up again at the high, oppressive seawall. It felt like my prison. Is this where my life would end? I had never been so afraid. Never been so cold. Never felt so utterly alone.

The thought of dying petrified me.

One

*C*ontemplating the existence of my soul was the *last* thing on my mind as I set out that evening.

After a hard day at work, I was out on my bike ride heading toward home. Before I left, I had hurriedly pecked my wife on the cheek and tucked my two daughters into bed. It was a stunning but cold April evening. The skies were clear. The sun was sinking into the sea, and a full moon was rising. Cycling along the coastal path that seemed to stretch on forever, I mulled over the words of a writer I'd heard on a radio show earlier that day. I had been out driving, selling to customers, and listening to the radio. The writer's comments had angered me, and I couldn't stop thinking about them.

Agitated, I tried blocking out my thoughts by pushing my body harder, but it was useless. No matter how much I tried to forget, his words kept rebounding back to me. Unwanted thoughts often have a nasty habit of sticking around, especially when we try to ignore them.

To empty his voice from my head, I frantically pedalled away my stress from the day. My bike, like my life, was now going faster and faster, but when the writer's words still refused to leave my mind, I gave in and tried to make sense of them. He'd been talking about life after death, a subject that had fascinated me for many years. He mentioned how western society ignored death; nobody wanted to face up to the prospect that none of us is immortal. He mentioned that opinions and beliefs were radically shifting within the scientific community. He implied that science would soon have to rewrite the very laws of nature as new research uncovered substantial evidence that matter was not quite what scientists once believed it to be. This quantum shift in perspective was also affecting today's society, he said. Ever-increasing numbers of people were now looking into the possibility that the world was alive with consciousness. In his worldview, he no longer believed we were all separate from one another or from the planet. He believed we were all connected, joined by an invisible thread of universal energy.

He concluded the interview by saying that Britain is the most non-spiritual nation in the entire world, which could be linked to the fact that we work longer hours than most other westernized countries. This overwork leads to increasing levels of exhaustion and aggression, relationship breakdowns and spiralling debt. When he added insomnia and an ever-increasing dependence on alcohol and drugs, my blood ran cold. This could be my life he was describing.

Running late for my sales appointments that day, I'd nonetheless pulled off at a service station to listen to the radio program. At first, I wanted to take down the name of the writer's book before I forgot it. Even though I hadn't read an entire book in more than twenty-five years, I wanted to read his. I had a gut instinct it was important.

Oblivious to the lunchtime madness all around me, I turned up the radio. I heard how social conditioning causes us to act in certain ways, even though we know subconsciously it is against our better nature. The majority of us waste huge parts of our lives chasing material possessions, including big houses, new cars and expensive holidays. The point was made that we should try living within our means. We should live up to our *own* expectations, rather than those of others.

A shudder went down my spine. This was *me* he was talking about. I was incensed. I didn't want to listen to him anymore, but I felt compelled nonetheless.

Finally, the speaker challenged listeners to spend more time re-evaluating their lives, to look around and notice how many others also seemed miserable and unfulfilled.

Sitting in the car, I looked all around me. Every other car at the service station had someone like me at the wheel. Businesspeople were frantically talking on cell phones, grabbing lunch between appointments. Everyone was rushing, and they all appeared ill, preoccupied or stressed. We all looked as if the life force had been sucked out of us.

The memories from lunchtime gripped me more fiercely as I rode toward home along the coastal pathway. I was still reeling. Cycling hard, the writer's words were like a toothache I couldn't ignore. The inner conflict and restlessness that he'd identified in so many people, I now realized, had been growing inside of me, simmering for a very long time.

Pushing myself to the limit on my bike, head down against the wind, I suddenly recalled what had irritated me most about the radio program. The host had challenged his guest to sum up what was missing from our lives. "How can we find more meaning and purpose to our increasingly fractured existence?" he had asked. Without hesitation, the writer had replied, "Spirituality. We need a more spiritual dimension to our lives."

The writer's reply threw me completely. Having been with him most of the way, I became annoyed. It was as if he was suddenly talking a foreign language to me. None of it made sense. He'd added that creativity, meditation and prayer were essential if we wanted to attain a more balanced sense of well-being. That was the point where I had switched off. The whole thing was like a shower that left me cold. Whereas before I had listened intently, now I felt like the mat had been pulled from beneath me. In my opinion, spirituality, prayer and meditation meant religion. And, to me, religion meant nothing more than hypocrisy and control.

Now seething, the word "spirituality" rang loudly in my ears as I pedalled faster along the seawall. My legs were aching, and I had a stitch in my side. I ignored the physical pain because it was doing me a favor. It obliterated my emotional and psychological pain.

For as long as I could remember, religion had implied to me that I obey others' beliefs over my own. For me, all religious teachings were dictatorial and unhealthy. Because of traumatic childhood experiences involving religion, the whole "spiritual thing" petrified me. Ignorant societal attitudes toward opposing beliefs made me wary of all religious groups. I was deeply suspicious of organizations that preached to me; those groups that wished to exert their influence over others. I was deeply suspect of fundamentalist religions that preached that *their* way was the *only* way.

When I'd heard that we should meditate and practice prayer more often, I mentally switched off. My confidence in the writer's words had been shattered. I didn't take down his name or the title of his spiritual book. In disgust, I changed the station.

Switching over to another radio program was one thing, but switching off my irritation was something different altogether. My evening cycle rides usually enabled me to forget pressures, deadlines and what had gone on throughout the day. They usually allowed me the time to unwind and forget about those things that caused me stress. But this time, my bike ride was different. The speaker and his spiritual theories wouldn't budge from my mind.

I began cursing the writer from the radio show. His cozy spiritual concepts were fine for him; he didn't have to live in the real world, I told myself. He didn't need to fight over orders, keep customers happy or race around in traffic. He didn't have a hundred problems to solve, budgets to put together, salaries to find or staff to keep happy. And, to top it off, I knew he didn't even have a family to support. It's easy to become "enlightened," I snorted, without these daily pressures.

I was fuming at his wild assumption that we could all change and improve our lives at will. He'd said that *we* are the ones in control of creating our own future. We are the ones who cause everything that happens in our lives. It was all nonsense.

The light was fading fast. The narrow path that stretched ahead of me was deserted, empty of the usual people out for a stroll or walking their dogs. I could hurtle along on my bike without fear of colliding with others.

I was mindful of the sheer drop into the sea to my left. There was no railing along this three-mile stretch, so I concentrated hard. Occasionally, I'd glance up and catch the stars as they slowly started punching their way through the twilight blue sky. Looking back at the sea, a strange sensation suddenly overwhelmed me. For the slightest of moments, it felt as if the sea was linked to my emotions. This serene feeling briefly calmed me and somehow relaxed me. It felt as if the water and I were somehow connected. The blood running through my veins felt like the very same "stuff" that made up the sea. It was an awesome feeling, but it suddenly vanished, just as quickly as it had arrived.

Mystified and confused by what had just happened, I yanked on the brakes and ground to a halt. At the same time, a train hurtled by on the railway tracks next to the path. The ground under me shook, as a sudden gust of cold wind blew through me. The noise was deafening. Pausing, I looked up at the tall cliffs behind the railway track. The dying sun was staining them a deep, earthy red.

Motionless, I tried to make sense of what had just happened. Rationally and logically, I wanted to ignore it. Shut it all out. I wanted to put it down to an overactive imagination, but I couldn't. A deeper part of me knew that I should hold on to that extraordinary experience. Something profound *had* happened. I knew it had. I felt as if something had shifted inside me. Torn between two conflicting thoughts, I set off again and tried to ignore them.

Racing along the open stretch with the cold wind blowing in my face, I smiled briefly. It was April—the end of another fiscal year. An enormous bonus would soon be filling my bank account. It was an annual bonus that I had grown accustomed to all too easily.

Over the past few years, it seemed that the more money I earned, the more I spent. And the more I spent, the more I needed to earn. The whole thing had rapidly become a vicious circle, one that was growing way beyond my control.

Yet again this year, I had overcooked my credit cards. I had taken out a consolidation loan attached to my home. In the short-term, my bonus would pay off all my debts and bring my large mortgage up to date, but I knew that big bonuses and an increase in the value of my home wouldn't be there forever. Ultimately, something would have to give.

The company where I worked as a director supplied materials to a booming construction and development industry. We were benefiting from the property upturn of the late nineties. Thanks to record profits, we had shared sizable bonuses. But the sacrifices had been severe. The more successful I became, the less time I had to enjoy with my wife and two daughters. The more profit I made, the higher my quotas for the following year. My whole life felt as if it was spinning wildly out of control, and I didn't have the time or energy to find the stop button.

Working late every night, I was always tired, forever stressed. I missed out on the important things in my life, including the girls' swimming lessons, meetings with their teachers, Christmas plays and summer carnivals. Because of the time spent travelling, I only saw my daughters, Jenna and Olivia, for brief moments during the week. In an attempt to make up for it, my wife Alison and I tried to give them everything they ever wanted. We spent small fortunes trying to guarantee their happiness. This year, I hoped I could make up for my absences by treating the family to a big holiday abroad, paid for by my bonus. But deep in my heart, I knew it was never enough. What the girls really *wanted* was our time, love and affection. What they desperately *needed* didn't cost a thing.

Keeping my personal and family life separate from my professional life used to be easy. It had been no problem when I was younger, but more recently, keeping the two separate was becoming impossible. As the workload increased, I had less control over my temper. And as my inbox grew more cluttered, my patience shortened. I'd recently found myself snapping at the children for no apparent reason. I'd fall out with people over the most ridiculous things. This erratic behavior soon became normal for me.

As I pushed ever-harder on my bike, I began wondering where my happiness had disappeared to. I used to be so energetic and full of life. I was once so imaginative and creative, without a single care in the world. But over the past few years, I had grown anxious and miserable. I was becoming grumpy and detached. With staff to look after and a huge mortgage to maintain, I felt isolated and trapped. Everyone wanted a piece of me. My time. My attention. My decisions. But I never left anything in reserve for myself.

I chided myself for being so ungrateful. After all, I'd achieved so much in my life. I was fortunate. I had a lovely wife. Two great kids. A huge house. But I was greedy. I wanted everything. Bigger. Better. I always wanted more.

An active social life, close friends and a challenging career should have fulfilled me. Made me happy. But they didn't. Somehow, there was still a huge hole left in my life. I didn't know what it was or even how to fill it, but I did know one thing: this was not where I wanted to be.

Racing along, I tried to make sense of the gap that was clearly opening in my life. Why hadn't I explored these feelings before? And why hadn't I ever found the courage to do something about it? Nobody had a clue as to how I was feeling because I never shared what was going on inside me. I always kept my emotions to myself. It was a man thing; I didn't want to be thought of as weak. If ignoring my true feelings didn't work, I could always numb my irritation with alcohol and drugs. But I hated myself for being weak, for hiding my emotions. I'd spent an entire lifetime pretending to other people that everything was fine in my world. I'd always painted a rosy picture that my life was great. But now I realized that much of my life had been spent living an illusion.

I had a sudden urge at that very moment to sit down with Alison and finally tell her what was bugging me. I wanted to share with her how I was feeling, and I desperately wanted more time for us to talk. To listen. More opportunity for us to connect on a much deeper, more meaningful level.

I also wanted more integrity, more truth. At work. At home. I wanted to believe in people again. I wanted to believe in myself. I demanded such high standards from others, yet I rarely lived up to those standards myself. I had blatantly lied to my clients earlier in the day. When I had been late for my appointments, I had blamed the traffic. But it hadn't been the traffic. It was me. I was at fault for pulling off at the service station. It was me who'd wanted to listen to that radio program. I had nobody to blame but myself. Being late, losing orders and making up feeble excuses were all becoming bad habits, and I despised myself for being such a hypocrite.

I slowed down on my bike to a point where the path narrowed. Beginning to see everything with greater clarity, I acknowledged that my deep restlessness was probably there for a reason. I realized I couldn't keep running from the intuitive voice at the back of my mind. Sooner or later, I had to face up to my truth and listen to what my conscience was saying.

As I pushed down hard on one of the bike pedals, my foot slipped. I hadn't been concentrating. My ankle jarred against the chain, pain shot through me, and I shuddered. My anger and self-loathing intensified.

Despising my own weakness, I threw both hands on my head and let the bike steer itself. I knew it was a reckless habit of mine, but I didn't care. One false move meant I'd be crashing into the sea, but this was my only chance to be daring, challenge my fears and push my limits. The adrenaline rush of risking all was mind-blowing and made me feel alive again. I could understand why rock climbers need to climb and race-car drivers need to race.

There was a small break in the seawall where the coastal path ended suddenly, and then a drop of twenty feet to another path, almost level with the sea. Cyclists usually carry their bikes down several narrow steps to this lower walkway before rejoining the cycle route where the steps head back to the higher sea path.

I gingerly edged sideways down the battered, slippery steps with my bike hooked over my shoulder. I was panting and sweating despite the cold. While I usually took off my padded jacket at this stage, for some unknown reason, I decided to keep it on. I rode the short distance along the lower path, dismounted and then climbed slowly back up the steps. Reaching the top, I paused for breath. By now, I was aching and exhausted.

A sick, uneasy feeling filled the core of my stomach. It was different from anything I'd felt before. It was more than the usual fatigue of a strenuous bike ride. Ignoring my discomfort, I sucked in a breath of sea air and pushed off again. I could just about see the town center a mile away. I was only five minutes from home.

Then the wave hit.

Two

I'd only been in the water for a few minutes, but the back of my throat burned, and my nose was blocked. Swallowing more and more water, I began choking. I put two fingers into my mouth and made myself sick. I couldn't see clearly, and I was gasping for breath. If I was going to live, I knew I had to think quickly. But I couldn't think. Fear paralyzed me. I considered screaming out again, but I couldn't. I was losing my voice. My heavy clothes were dragging me under. I was gradually being pulled farther out by the tide and drifting into the mouth of the estuary.

When I realized that the waves were less fierce away from the seawall, I knew with utter clarity what I had to do. Ignoring the waves, I took in long, drawn-out breaths. With each in-breath, my optimism grew.

I lunged forward, desperate to reach the break in the seawall. I used every last possible ounce of energy to move, but it was hopeless. I was going against the tide. My fleece coat was saturated, and every bone in my body ached. Gasping for air, shivering, I collapsed and gave in. The waves could take me, I thought. It was easier than fighting.

By now, the last rays of sunshine burned the back of my head. I knew this was my last sunset. Another wave hit me straight in the face, and I gagged. This time the water went deep into my lungs, and I was immediately sick. I thought about taking off some clothes to make myself more buoyant, but I suddenly heard an insistent voice in my head telling me to keep them on. I ignored it and started to pull off my fleece.

"No!" the voice boomed emphatically. It was authoritative. "Keep it on." The tone startled me.

Then my entire body convulsed. Shock had kicked in. My arms and legs were moving wildly in one last, frantic scramble. I couldn't seem to control them. I was losing the fight, going under. Swallowing even more water, I became light-headed. My chest was tight, on fire.

A cramp in my forearms reminded me of when I was learning to box as a boy. Keeping up my guard in the last round was always sheer agony, and now I was going through a similar experience. Only this time, it was life or death. This was my last round.

Crying hysterically, a clear image shot into my mind. It was my wedding day. Alison and I were coming out of the church, laughing. The air was filled with confetti. It was the happiest day of my life. Then, a wave slapped me in the face, robbing me of this happy image. Coming back to my present reality, I remembered that I was only one week away from my tenth wedding anniversary.

But the memory of Alison had renewed my resolve to stay conscious, connected to life. I didn't want to die. Not without saying good-bye. At the age of thirty-four, I wasn't ready to give up on life.

More images began to flood my head. Snapshots. Memories. I could see Alison again. My girls. Then my mum, dad, brothers and friends. I pictured holding my oldest daughter, Jenna, at the very moment she'd been born. That thought made me sob uncontrollably. It had been the proudest day of my life.

Then, bizarrely, I recalled the contents of a television program that had featured a life or death rescue. The images were vivid. A man had been washed out to sea and survived. He'd said that even good swimmers drown because they panic and forget to breathe properly. I could hear him saying that the first thing to do is to stay calm. Not to panic.

Although I was certain I was going to die anyway, I felt compelled to follow his advice. Snatching air between waves, I built up a rhythm. In. Out. In. Out. Every breath injected me with renewed confidence. Breathing slowly and deeply made me more alert. I was more conscious of my thoughts. Of my feelings. More conscious of myself.

My body began to feel different somehow. Lighter. Energized. All of a sudden, I felt my body lift up higher in the water. I wondered if I was dreaming. Floating horizontally, I moved on top of the waves. I was now moving *with* the waves, not fighting them. It felt surreal, yet more real than anything before. The more deeply I inhaled, the lighter my body became. The calmer I remained, the more positive I felt. All tension ebbed away. I wondered what was happening to me. Was this the end? Was this what it was like to die?

Every cell in my body was communicating with me. Every muscle, every atom of my being, seemed to be talking *with* me, encouraging me. I wondered briefly if I was going mad. I pinched my arm hard. It confirmed what I already knew. I *was* still fully conscious.

My senses were heightened. I was tuned into everything around me and everything inside me. Something was communicating with me, guiding me. Telling me not to panic. Reassuring me that I'd be fine.

I knew that I was infinitely more than just my body. I don't know how I knew; I just did. A calming presence washed over me, and all fear evaporated. I was no longer freezing cold. Nothing ached. I couldn't feel anything but a complete sense of freedom and peace. Even the waves hitting my head were now only a minor irritation. I was in a state of sheer bliss. All loving. Unconditional. There was nothing left for me to do but relax and go with the flow, to be at one with this awesome, incredible power. This presence. I didn't want this sensational feeling to come to an end.

Lying on my back in the water, with my arms stretched wide, I waited to see what would happen next. Looking up, I watched the white vapor trails of planes against the darkening sky. It was an uncomfortable reminder that nightfall would soon arrive. Would this be the last setting sun I would ever see?

My thoughts drifted with the waves. I remembered what Alison and I had told the girls recently. We'd always promised them that when they were old enough, we would take them to Florida. To Disney World. The holiday of a lifetime. I had only recently booked that dream trip. It was to be our first big vacation abroad as a family. The first time in many years that Alison and I could both get the same two weeks off.

But then an overwhelming, crushing feeling suddenly filled my chest as I realized I would never be there to see that dream through. And I'd probably never see my family again. That thought alone horrified me. It felt as if someone had just pulled the plug on my life. All sense of serenity dissolved. Clenching and unclenching my fists, I tried to keep the blood circulating in my fingers. They were blue. I felt so helpless and stupid. How the hell did I ever put myself in this fatal position?

In the distance, I could see the lights coming on in town. I could just make out the church spire close to my home. The girls would be fast asleep by now, and Alison would be watching television, or catching up on paperwork for the tea shop she owned. Nobody had a clue where I was or what I was going through. I felt so utterly desperate and alone.

My children would grow up without me. I wouldn't see them graduate. Or learn to drive. I wouldn't watch them leave home, lead their own lives. I wouldn't be at their weddings to give them away. Someone else might even be in my place, standing in my shoes. What if Alison was to meet someone? My girls would have another father. Someone else to call Dad. And, as time passed, they would remember less about me. They would forget how much I cared for them. How much I loved and cherished them.

I tried to remember my last words to Alison, but I couldn't. Then I realized I hadn't said anything. Not even good-bye. Just a quick peck on the check, a kiss that meant nothing. I had dashed off, rushing as usual, and had only waved half-heartedly as I'd passed the window. I loathed myself for that. What sort of husband was I? Useless and pathetic. Forever busy and rushing around. Permanently exhausted. I had barely allowed myself any time for my family throughout the week, and even when I did spend time with them on the weekends, I couldn't relax. I would feel guilty, preoccupied or stressed that I wasn't doing something for work. I'd be concentrating on what I had to do Monday morning. My mind would be someplace else.

If I died, Alison would be able to cope without any problem. She was used to me being away and having the girls on her own. It was Alison who usually read the girls a bedtime story. She was the one who held their lives together. Not me. I just turned up and paid for it.

I had recently taken out a large life insurance policy. It would cover everything, all of it. Alison and the girls would be well-provided for. The mortgage would be paid off, the credit cards cleared. At least my debts would die with me.

For a brief moment, there seemed to be an upside to this mess I was in. I was worth more dead than alive. In that second, I knew I had to put "my house in order." Satisfied that my family would be taken care of, I submitted. I gave in. I was gradually coming to terms with the inevitable. This was the end of my life. A deeply unfulfilled and unappreciated life.

Submerged between a twilight zone of acceptance and self-pity, I suddenly sensed that the world around me was evaporating. At first, it was as if someone had turned down the contrast on a television screen. All of my physical senses began falling away. Colors blurred. Noise faded. I was no longer in touch with my feelings, my body or my environment. I couldn't hear the crashing waves or the squawking seagulls. There was no sense of the water, the biting cold or anything else. It was as if my mind, body and consciousness were shutting down. They were in another time and place, somewhere in the past.

Three

Sweets in one hand and football magazine in the other, I am sprinting down the hill toward the iron bridge. I can't keep up with my friends. My eleven-year-old legs are aching, my heart thumping. It feels as if my lungs are about to explode. My two friends have been taunting, teasing and fighting me all day in the classroom, but still I am determined they are not going to leave me behind. With my school bag flapping madly, I race after them.

"Watch out!" I hear one of my friends yelling as I shoot across the busy road in front of an oncoming car.

For a split second, I can't move. Time freezes. I lock eyes with the woman driver. The horror on her face is agonizing. I actually feel her pain as if it is mine. Then there is nothing but darkness. I can't feel, see or hear anything. I can't sense any pain. I wonder if I am dead, but then a calm feeling spreads over me and sweeps away my fearful thoughts.

I sense a friendly presence close by, but it's not a physical presence. It isn't a person. A knowing comes from inside my body. I feel it in my veins. In every bone. Every cell. Something or someone is talking to me. Assuring me, telling me that everything will be fine. It instructs me not to panic. Not to worry. All will be well.

I should be upset, but I am not. I think about my parents, my brothers. They don't know yet that I am dead. I want to let them know. Send a message to them saying I am fine and I love them.

As I think about my mum and dad, an image of their faces appears. They look older, a lot older. They have been crying, and for a moment it makes me feel sad, too. I feel their suffering. It is intensely painful. But I am not ready to say good-bye to them. Not yet. Not now. Their faces suddenly vanish, as quickly as they'd appeared.

It would be easy to give up, especially with the wonderful feeling I now have. The presence is warm and protective. It makes me feel alive in a new way. A different way.

There are no lights or tunnels. (I'd read about them in Dad's books on the afterlife.) It's just peaceful. I know somehow that I am safe. Protected. This is a love I have never felt before.

But I am not ready to die yet. I am thinking of my family. My friends. The life I haven't lived yet. All the things I love about my life. This love is making me fight back and hold on.

Suddenly, a woman's voice breaks through the silence. My peace shatters. I can hear her sobbing. I can't see her, but I know it's her. The woman who knocked me over.

I feel sick. Dizzy. Then I realize I am picking up her feelings. She is terrified. Her anxiety pierces me. I want to yell out, to tell her that it's my stupid fault. I try speaking, but the words are stuck in my head. There's more wailing. I try to shut it out. I hear a siren.

A man's voice shouts, "Leave the boy alone! Don't move him!"

I want to tell them that I'm okay, but I can't. I hear a vehicle screech to a halt. Yelling and screaming. Doors slamming. People shouting.

I am confused. Please, someone, anyone, tell me if I'm still alive.

My whole body feels strange, tingly. It reminds me of the time I received an electric shock when I was helping Dad fix a socket at home.

I suddenly feel a warm hand pressing on my wrist. It tickles. I don't know why, but I like this person. I know that it is someone caring and gentle, loving and kind. The same person is brushing a hand against my cheek, forehead and neck. My heart races. I feel alive again.

Intense pain washes over me and, at the same time, the warm presence abruptly leaves me. I don't want it to leave. It is reassuring and all-loving. But it is gone.

I feel my neck aching, then a jolt in my back. It feels as if every part of my body is on fire. I am now conscious of lying in the road. My body is shaking, and tiny, jagged stones are drilling into the back of my head. Then I slowly open my eyes. Everything is a blur. Glancing sideways, I notice a wheel close to my face. I try to turn my head, but I can't. Someone is holding it tightly. I'm scared. I don't know what to do.

Focusing, I notice a crowd of people hunched around me. They are all staring. Nobody speaks. The driver is the first person I recognize. Her eyes are red. She has been crying, and her eye makeup is streaked down her cheeks. She doesn't need to say anything. The relief on her face when our eyes meet again says it all.

Later, I learn that I don't have a scratch on me.

Four

*A*s images of my childhood accident fell away, my physical senses returned. Shivering, the hairs on my body were standing on end. My muscles were tense. My toes numb. I glanced at the darkening horizon. I was fully conscious of being back in the sea. It took me a few moments to gather my thoughts and to try to work out what had just happened.

It was as if I had been back in time, actually at the scene of the accident. I had lived everything again. Only *this* time, it had been different. *This* time, there had been another dimension. I had experienced deeper insight and understanding.

I wondered how I could have forgotten about that childhood accident. Perhaps I hadn't wanted to remember it. Perhaps it suited me to forget. But I *had* been back there, touching that very moment when I thought I had died.

Why was it only now that I grasped the real meaning of what had happened? Reliving that whole scene again allowed me to sense what others had been feeling at the time. I felt their pain and concern. I was locked into their fear, anxiety and emotions. It was as if I was everything and everybody, all at the same time.

My head was spinning. I wasn't sure what was real anymore. I tried to convince myself that my imagination had run wildly out of control. Perhaps the cold had affected my psychological state. Perhaps I was delusional and had made up the whole thing in my head. Yet I couldn't let go of the extraordinary scene. I knew I had been back there, reliving it and re-experiencing it for a purpose.

Two distinct dialogues were going on in my mind. Two separate selves contradicting each other. Questioning one another. On one side

17

was my rational, logical self that tried to ignore all that had happened. It struggled to acknowledge anything it couldn't properly explain. This was the side that I had previously let rule my thoughts and my life. But now I became acutely aware of another side, a deeper, more loving and calm sense of self, in tandem with an undeniable, all-knowing intelligence. A simple, yet powerful presence. These two selves struggled for control, and my attention bounced back and forth between both parts of my mind.

Refereeing the two opposing selves was draining my energy. The doubting, questioning, rational self was like a whining child. It wouldn't keep quiet. It niggled, condemned and chipped away. I was aggravated and tired of listening to it. At that moment, I chose to give in to the undemanding, loving part of me—the side that had lain dormant for so long. I allowed it to expand, and this serene and deeply peaceful essence suffused my being. It became a conscious part of me. I was aware of being reconnected to something.

Somehow, I knew it had always been there, but I hadn't been aware of it for a very long time. This was the part of self that I felt at home with, the essence that I trusted. It was that part of me that had felt the pain of the woman who hit me with her car. Her suffering had briefly belonged to me, been part of me. And after reliving it all again, I knew precisely what I had inflicted on that poor woman. I was appalled with myself. Everything was my fault. I was the one who had caused her to suffer all that pain.

Heart racing, I stared up at the stars that were slowly bursting through the darkening sky and tried to shut out my torment, but it was impossible. I remembered the sheer anger and frustration I had felt just moments before that car had hit me. My two friends had been running away from me. They were to blame for the accident.

Renewed contempt for my friends bubbled up inside me. It started from my heart and fanned outward. I pictured the road again. The car. The accident. Then my whole body began to stiffen in the water. I was paralyzed by a heavy energy that seemed to be clogging my arteries. It was a negative, life-sapping emotion that had been trapped inside me for all these years. At that moment, the old negative part of me had the upper hand.

But, then, my whole perspective shifted. The loving, calm sense of self that I had just brought to life in the water took over once again. I felt my repressed anger release, and a warm presence filled the void. It was the same presence I had experienced when I'd been knocked down by the car.

Wanting to re-engage with it, I shut my eyes. I barely heard the crashing waves or felt the cold in my body. Pointing all conscious attention inward, I sensed that this presence had a valuable lesson to teach me. "Forgive" flashed through my mind. I could feel the *vibration* of the word.

I began to forgive my friends. I no longer blamed them. Or even hated them. They hadn't pushed me in front of a car. I had run into the road myself. It had been my fault.

Then, a blurred image of a woman came to me. Instantly, I knew it was the driver from the accident. Only this time, she looked radiant and glowing. She smiled softly at me. Instinctively, I knew what she needed from me. She had come back in search of forgiveness. She wanted release and redemption. She wanted to move on.

Looking into her eyes, her pain engulfed me. I felt her misery, suffering, all of it. I crashed into the center of her pain, like a car slamming into a wall. It was raw. Unresolved. A neglected pain that had come to be healed.

Something inside told me that this woman was no longer alive. I intuitively knew that she had been dead for many years. In what seemed to be a fraction of a second, I learned everything about her. Her life, her past and, especially, the part she had played in my accident. That accident had changed her life. It had changed both of our lives.

For a short while after the accident, she'd struggled to regain enough courage to get back behind the wheel. Thankfully, as time passed, she had gradually built up the confidence to drive again. But things were never the same for her. Not a day passed when she didn't revisit that terrifying moment when a young boy had unexpectedly shot out in front of her and been knocked to the road.

Like a stain that wouldn't wash out, she eventually learned to live with her terrifying ordeal, but things had never been the same for her or her family. I started to loathe myself for the pain I had inflicted on them. I was deeply ashamed and angry. I had blocked the incident out of my mind. In all the years since, I had never once given a thought to what my stupidity had meant to that woman's life.

Without warning, I became two consciences, both hers and mine. Sharing dual perspectives and experiences, I observed the entire accident all over again, but this time it was through *her* eyes.

I see the whites of his eyes as a boy suddenly steps into the road in front of my car. My heart thumps wildly as I desperately try to swerve around him. I hear someone scream a warning from the side of the road, but the boy doesn't move. Petrified, I watch as he just stares ahead, frozen to the spot.

In the fraction of a second, I press my foot hard on the brake. I can't bear to watch, and I close my eyes. And then . . . I hear a loud, hard thump on the windshield.

As if in slow motion, the car skids to a halt. I smell burning rubber, and my face is now resting on the steering wheel. Shaking uncontrollably, I bite my lip and taste blood. Slowly coming to my senses, I realize there is now mayhem all around me. Other cars have stopped, and people are running everywhere. I hear shouting, yelling, screaming. I see people run over to where a body is lying in the road. There's no sign of movement.

What should I do? For a brief moment, I hope and pray that this is all just a bad dream. But then it hits me. This is no dream. This is real. I just killed someone. A little boy. Somebody's son.

I feel sick. My stomach churns, and my head throbs, but somehow I stagger from the car and collapse onto my knees beside the still and silent boy. I plead with him, "Tell me you're okay... Give me a sign... Anything... Please!"

MY GOD, I'VE KILLED HIM... I'VE KILLED HIM... WHAT DO I DO?... WHAT DO I DO?... PLEASE... IT'S NOT MY FAULT... I PROMISE... IT'S... NOT... MY...FAULT!

The sound of a siren shatters the air.

PLEASE. GOD. HELP ME... PLEASE DO SOMETHING... ANYTHING.

With a shaking hand, I touch the boy's head. A man shouts, "Don't move him!"

An ambulance pulls up a few feet from the body, but all I can do is sob. What have I done? I barely notice as they take the boy away. I can't bear it anymore.

I'm suddenly aware of being right back in the freezing cold water. Closing my eyes in an attempt to forget about everything, I prayed for forgiveness. Redemption. Anything. As long as it would take away the guilt.

To my amazement, I realized the woman's face was still there, even though my eyes were now closed. She continued to beam the most peaceful, compassionate and unconditionally loving smile I had ever seen. It was a sheer vibration of love and forgiveness. It was so strong and pure that I could feel it running through my veins. But I felt undeserving. Even though I could practically touch this infinite love projected toward me, shame wouldn't let me accept it. I wanted *her* to forgive *me*, not the other way around.

As our eyes met again, I knew she forgave me at the very same moment I forgave her. The agonizing feeling of shame that had been tugging at my stomach suddenly vanished. The tightness in my chest loosened and fell away. It was as if a heavy, dark, emotional cord was being cut. I was finally free, and so was she.

Five

*T*he whole experience of seeing the accident again jogged my memory. Shaking from the cold, I remembered how I'd become more sensitive in the following months. At times, my body had sensed something beyond my natural five senses.

If I was standing close to someone who was angry, I'd feel my stomach tighten. My shoulders would tense. There would be a sharp pain in my head, and I'd feel uneasy around the person. Sometimes, I would even get angry for no particular reason. Other people's emotions seemed to be rubbing off on me. Affecting me.

It was as if my intuition was radar. I could plug into the thoughts and feelings of other people. The more emotionally connected I was to someone, the stronger the vibration. These vibes were most evident when I was with my mother. My entire body seemed to be an antenna. I was the receiver, and I picked up her thoughts and feelings.

Only a few weeks after the accident, I decided to play a game by trying to guess what my mother was about to say. I wanted to figure out what she was thinking and how she was feeling. I couldn't believe how often I was right, and it completely freaked me out. I was only eleven. I was scared, and I didn't understand what was happening. So I pushed it away and blamed everything on my overactive imagination. But, before long, it was occurring so frequently that I could no longer ignore it.

Soon, my sensitivity to other people heightened even more. This wasn't happening just around my mother. I started to become really good at guessing how my friends felt. I could tune into people's moods before they even came to my door. I soon realized that I was receptive to not only angry and prickly emotions, but also to feelings of peace and calm. It was incredible. The more I listened and empathized, the more I tuned in to their feelings. Their moods. Emotions. Thoughts. Fears.

My sensitivity was even more vibrant when I shut out my own thoughts and feelings. I imagined that my mind was a huge blackboard, and my thoughts were written on the board. If I wanted to tune into another person's feelings, I would picture that blackboard being wiped clean. It worked every time. After that, I had no problem picking up on someone's emotions.

Every now and again, I would begin to doubt my abilities. I'd go through periods when I would stop believing. I would either try to find a rational explanation or convince myself that I had a blood clot or something on my brain. In moments when I was most afraid that there something was mentally wrong with me, I would completely shut down all of my extra senses.

I never shared my experiences with anyone. I *wanted* to explain to others that I knew what they were feeling, but I couldn't pluck up the courage to tell even my own mother, although I was most sensitive to her feelings. If she was in pain, I felt the pain, too, as if it belonged to me. But I couldn't say a word. I didn't feel secure enough. I was quiet and afraid of my own shadow. I was shy. Anyway, who would listen to an eleven-year-old boy? If I ever did pluck up the courage, what would I say?

At that age, I was too petrified that people would think I was crazy, even though a strong gut instinct always told me I wasn't. I knew there were other people like me. I had read about them in some of the books that my father had brought home. I may have struggled to fully explain why and how this had come about, but somehow I knew that what I was feeling was instinctual and natural. The calm, peaceful part of me knew I wasn't insane.

The sea was bitterly cold. My neck was stiff. My toes and fingers were so numb that I was afraid they would snap off.

Shivering uncontrollably, I couldn't stop the dam burst of memories and thoughts from pouring into my mind. Why was it only now that I was thinking about the immediate aftermath of the accident? Why was I so locked into the time when I was eleven years old? A time when I'd experienced an incredible connection to a sixth sense?

As a child, why had I thought that no one would ever believe me? What had led me to think that nobody would be interested in what I was going through? And later, as an adult, why had I never found the courage and self-belief to share my experiences with others?

When I was fifteen, my parents announced, out of the blue, that the family was moving. They'd made a sudden decision to escape from the rat race of London. They wanted a quieter life for my two younger brothers and me. A move out into the country. Somewhere that wasn't so crowded. They chose Devon, where life would be much slower, cleaner and healthier.

The move gave me the perfect opportunity to forget about the after-effects of the accident. Without being chained to the past, I could wipe the slate clean. It almost felt as if I was starting my life all over again. I felt an incredible sense of freedom and joy. Happily settled in Devon, I didn't look back or share my earlier experiences with any of my new friends. I didn't want to. Nobody needed to know.

Years later, as a young adult, I met my future wife, Alison. I never shared what had happened to me as a child with her either. I was living a new life and doing well for myself as a successful salesman out on the road. It never seemed relevant to think about or discuss what had gone before. To me, it wasn't important anymore. I had left all that life behind. I certainly wasn't going to trawl it up all over again, even though Alison was my wife.

Now, alone and freezing in the sea, I had finally unlocked a secret that had been dormant for more than twenty years. Only now, it was too late to share my incredible story with anyone. I would die in this sea and nobody would ever have a clue what I had been through as a child. My secret would go down with me.

Dying for a Change

Six

*P*icked up by the swirling currents, I was being swept farther out to sea. The wind grew stronger as night fell. Cold spray skimmed off the waves and whipped my face. My eyes stung, and I kept rubbing them. I wanted to see the last strands of sunlight against the night sky. But, more than that, I wanted to be at home, warm and safe, with my wife and children. I just wanted to see them again.

All chance of survival seemed to be slipping from my grasp. A deep feeling of utter hopelessness filled me. I felt bitter, angry and resentful that my life was ending this way. I made a solemn promise then and there that if by some miracle I did survive, I would tell everyone about my gift of insight and intuition. All of it. No more secrets.

Suddenly, I had a blinding headache. A searing pain shot down from my head and all the way to my shoulders and back. My vision blurred, and my hearing became distorted. Shaking from the cold, I could feel the muscles in my stomach and legs tighten. Perhaps this was the beginning of the end. I struggled for breath. How much longer could I survive in the freezing water?

From early childhood, I had experienced recurring nightmares about drowning. I would wake up in a sweat, with an overwhelming sense of dread. In one dream, I was trapped in the hull of a ship. Rising water had left me with no means of escape. Panicked and fighting to stay alive, I'd take my last breath before water engulfed me. At that point, I usually woke up, choking for air.

Now, it appeared that my nightmares had become reality. Weak and exhausted, I closed my eyes to try to block them out, but frightening images still flooded my mind. I saw my body washed up on a beach, close to where I lived. Then I saw a snapshot of my funeral. People were crying and standing around my grave. Afterward, I saw my family and friends living their lives without me. I saw my children, sad and alone.

My mind was filled with terrifying thoughts about my life coming to an end. The floodgates were open to every fear I'd ever had about dying. I had the sensation I was falling, no longer in control of my body.

I remembered that the body's organs shut down in extreme cold. I'd heard that the lungs would seize and the body would stiffen. I felt a pain in my back and rubbed it. Perhaps my kidneys were failing and this was the end.

Paranoia took over. I believed my organs were shutting down. The worst pain was in my chest. I massaged the area over my heart. I put my hand on my stomach. I touched my head. I knew that the brain was the last organ to stop functioning, which horrified me. I would feel everything. All of it. Right up to the end. I just wanted it over as quickly as possible. I was ready for the end to come.

And yet, another part of me wanted to hang on, whatever the physical pain. I had fought so hard to stay conscious. I couldn't give up now. I had too much to live for. I knew I needed to think more clearly and quickly if I wanted to see my wife and children again. I needed to find hope, but how?

Drifting farther and farther out to sea, I was shaking more than ever. My teeth were chattering, and I kept biting my tongue. I opened my eyes and stared up at the full moon. Charged from the sun that had since set, it had an orange glow. The burning orb seemed to warm my thoughts momentarily. I don't know how or why, but it injected me with a new sense of hope and belief.

My adrenaline pumped again. I wasn't ready to surrender, to give up on seeing my family again. I had to push away all my fears and somehow ignore the all-consuming terror that I was about to die. My emotions intensified, and my will to live grew stronger. I raised a clenched fist in the air and shouted. "I will survive! I will see this through!"

Exhausted, I let the waves sweep me along on my back. I shut out the pain from the cold and tried to focus on my breathing. After a while, a warm sensation started to build in my chest and spread quickly through my body. The feeling of cold was replaced by an intense heat that raced around my heart. An overwhelming feeling of love, compassion and serenity washed over me, lifting and inspiring me. It filled me with such joy that I forgot where I was. My body felt lighter. Less tense. In that moment, I knew I was more than just my physical body. I was infinitely more than just my mind. I felt connected to something greater than me, something larger and infinitely more loving than I'd ever known before.

Seven

I'm kneeling on a chair, combing my mother's hair. She's asked me to brush out the hairspray. I never refuse to help my mum when she asks for something because I know she needs all the help she can get. The attention helps her to forget about the constant arguments with my dad and her worries over money. It relaxes her and makes her feel better.

Standing on tip-toes, I pull the brush down hard. My mother winces but doesn't complain. I continue until my wrists and forearms are numb. She takes a long drag from her cigarette. She is tense, but I already knew that. I have begun to feel her tension inside my own body. I desperately want to tell my mum what I feel, but I can't. I don't know where to begin. I'm not even sure that she would understand. I'm not fully sure I understand.

Resting a hand on my mum's shoulder, a thought suddenly fills my mind. But it's not my thought; it belongs to my mother. I know she's mad because an angry feeling also bubbles in me.

Leaning into my mum's back, an image of my father pops into my mind. I've never seen him in such a rage, and it frightens me.

Another image shoots into my head. I see a football match, and I'm standing with the crowd in an enormous stadium. Everyone is cheering. The noise is deafening. Then, the scene vanishes. I try to make sense of it, but can't. It means absolutely nothing to me, but then it's always like that. It's not until later that everything begins to make sense.

Still struggling to get the hairspray out of my mum's hair, I continue to feel angry thoughts coming from her. She's furious with my father for drinking away the money that we so badly need. She wants him to stay home and not go to the pub.

31

In my mind, I see a match being struck. A huge flame flares up. My stomach flips over, and my chest hurts. It feels as if my strength is being sucked away. I know what this means. My mother's emotions are overwhelming her. I can feel it. Her anger is like poison flowing through my veins and invading me. It's suffocating me, and I want it to stop. I want to say something to my mother, but I'm afraid she'll dismiss my thoughts as my imagination.

Another snapshot shoots into my head. This time, it's a shovel burying air bubbles in the ground. I realize later that this represents my mum's trapped emotions, and that she's hiding from her pain, just as she always does.

I badly want my mother to know everything. I want to explain that I feel what she is feeling. I want to tell her that ignoring the trapped anger is bad for her body and could make her ill. Sometimes, I even feel how she is feeling when she is not near me, before she gets home from work.

I wish she could trust me. I know she hasn't got any close friends. Perhaps she could share her worries with me. I wouldn't mind. At least it might stop her from bottling it all up.

Suddenly, I was conscious of being in the freezing water again. I scanned around, trying to get my bearings. I saw the seawall and the railway line above it. A train thundered past, and I could just make out the lit carriages. The noise of the train helped bring me back to reality, to make sense of what I had just experienced.

I had been right back there with my mum again. It had been so real. I was certain it was more than just a memory. I *had* actually been there, reliving and feeling every emotion.

Eight

I looked over toward the path on the red headland that jutted out on the edge of town. It made me think about my parents. They had come to visit us only a few weeks ago. It was a Sunday, and the whole family had taken Jenna and Olivia out walking on that same path. I remembered being miserable that day. I had other things on my mind. Problems at work. Troubles with finances. I had been quiet and subdued all day. I'd hardly spoken to my parents. They had played with the children. And now I would never see them again.

Angry and bitter, I lashed out. Like a madman, I began punching the water. Again and again, I let the waves hit me full in the face. I allowed my rage to spew out. But it was exhausting. I felt like I had fought for hours. I kept sinking down under the water. Every time I came back up, I launched one wild punch after another at the waves. I imagined them to be a real person, someone who was robbing me of my life.

Although I was exhausted, angry and fuming, it felt good to unleash the full force of my fury. But it was burning me out. Like a car running out of fuel, my energy soon stalled. Every muscle in my body stiffened. I was spent.

But though my body was shutting down, my mind was still very much active. I began thinking about the things I had always promised myself. I had planned to do so much with my life. I was going to *be* so much, but I had always taken my life for granted. Tomorrow would be soon enough, I told myself. Or the next day. Or the day after that. I'd always imagined there would be plenty of chances. Once my busy life was under control. Once I had more time. Once I had more money. Once the mortgage was paid off. Once the children had left home. I'd been saying these things to myself for the past twenty years. I had believed that my life would be controlled by *my* timetable, that it would take off when I chose. But it was too late for that now. I had blown it.

Racked by an overpowering guilt that I had hidden behind my dreams, I was devastated. I had let myself down. I had let everyone down. And now, there would be no more dreams.

Why had I not been more daring throughout my life? Why had I not made the most of it? Why had I not made every day count? I had taken so much for granted. And now, with blinding insight, I could see I had committed the ultimate sin. I had squandered and wasted my life.

I plummeted into self-pity and cursed all the times that I had let something trivial annoy me. Why had I wasted so much time worrying about work, meeting targets and paying bills? Or the many other times I had fretted over something ridiculous? Something pointless?

On numerous occasions, I had come home late from work. The children had long since gone to bed, and I ate my dinner alone in the kitchen. Struggling to stay awake, I'd watch the late news. And sometimes, if I was lucky, I would catch up with Alison before she went to bed.

A whole week could pass without seeing my children. I was gone before they awoke and back when they were asleep. Even when we managed to go on holiday, something always cropped up. An emergency at work. A problem with a client. I spent half my holidays on my cell phone. My family had deserved far more from me.

With the waves slapping me in the face, I started to cry like a baby. I felt useless and pathetic, as if I had been sleepwalking through my entire life. As I looked toward the town, I could just make out the church spire close to my home—the home that had financially stretched us to the limit. We had lived in a tiny, two-bedroom house when Jenna and Olivia were born. We didn't have much money then, but we had been content. Alison and I had time for each other and our children. We were happy.

I thought about the promises I had made when the girls had been born. Moments after they'd come into the world, I had held them tightly in my arms. They looked so perfect. So innocent. I promised they would never experience the difficulties I had had as a child. I would always be there for them. Loving them. Supporting them. I would never let Jenna and Olivia feel abandoned or unwanted, I vowed.

I wanted to be all the things that my dad had struggled tirelessly to become. In his mind, he'd done his best. But I had memories of being with my brothers, stuck in the car, while Dad drank in the pub. We'd been left on our own in beer gardens for hours on end. I knew he could have done much more. He could have *become* a whole lot more, which he realizes now that it's too late. But history doesn't always repeat itself. I was utterly determined that things were going to be very different for *my* children. I was going to put them first in my life.

But it never happened.

Floating aimlessly with the tide, I was ashamed. I loathed what I had become. I tried to tell myself that all the sacrifices I had made were for my family's benefit. I was working so hard so they could have a better life, but it wasn't all true. I knew that chasing success and winning big contracts were also propping up my ego. I wasn't doing it just for the kids or for a more affluent life. I was doing it to bolster my self-esteem. To show that I was successful. To prove that I was somebody. I wanted to show the world that I was a winner.

But had I really been a winner? Or was I just hiding behind apparent success to cover up a deep sense of insecurity? Perhaps I was hiding from the demons of the past. Looking back, it all seemed hollow and empty.

Perhaps I didn't deserve to live. I closed my eyes. I just wanted to sleep.

Nine

*I*t's the middle of the night. I can't get back to sleep. The silence is making me edgy. My mother is pacing up and down in the living room. I creep from my bedroom and peer next door into my parents' room. It's empty. Dad isn't home yet.

Heart racing, I tiptoe across the hall to the living room. Mum doesn't know I am awake. She is smoking again. I wish she would go to bed. But, as usual, she's up and ready for a fight.

I can feel the tension in the house. I'm exhausted. I have a test at school tomorrow, and I need to get some rest. But I can't sleep.

I creep back to my room and climb into bed. Both my younger brothers are fast asleep. I reach down and grab my new alarm clock. It has a special dial that glows in the dark. It's three in the morning.

I sweep back the bedroom curtains and look up the road. There is still no sign of Dad's car.

Cigarette smoke wafts into the bedroom. I hate the smell. Everything in the house reeks of cigarette smoke, but I'd never dream of upsetting my mother by telling her. I love her too much. I may be only eleven, but as the oldest boy, I try to watch out for her. She has so much on her plate. Mum needs her cigarettes like I need to play football. It's our escape. It helps us to cope with Dad, especially after he has been out drinking all night with his friends.

I've had trouble sleeping ever since my accident six months ago. If Mum stirs during the night, I wake up, and I'm immediately tuned in to how she is feeling. I wish Dad would get home soon so he and Mum could have their fight. Get it over with. Maybe then I could get some sleep.

I hear the click of the cigarette lighter. Mum's asthma is acting up, and her breathing is heavy. I just wish she'd go to bed before Dad gets home and they have another fight. A tight, nervous pain rips across my stomach. I know she won't. Not until she's settled her score.

The faint hum of a car engine breaks the silence. I know it's Dad's car. I yank the bed sheets over my head. Burying my face in my pillow, I pray that this time, maybe just maybe, everything will be fine. There will be no argument. No fighting. No swearing. But I know there will be.

The hum grows louder. I press my face up against the window until I'm blinded by the headlights. Dad's car is sweeping into the driveway, but I'm sure he hasn't seen me.

Dad turns off the engine, and then he does what he normally does. He just sits there. Waiting. I hate this part. I know what he is doing. He is making up his feeble excuses. He knows that Mum will still be up. Waiting for him. Ready for him.

Dad sits there for a minute or two, but it feels like forever. Finally, he stumbles out of the car, drunk as usual. I can hear that Mum has stopped pacing, and Dad is fumbling for his keys. Eventually, he gets the right key in the lock and slowly pushes open the front door. At the same time, I see Mum dash past my bedroom in the hallway. I hear a punch, and then Mum screams at him. I put my hands over my ears in a feeble attempt to block it all out, but it's no good. I still hear Mum shouting.

"You bastard! You inconsiderate bastard!"

My bedroom door is wide open. I jump out of bed and peer down the hallway. Dad is cowering in the corner by the front door. Mum is punching him relentlessly. He doesn't attempt to fight back. He knows he is in the wrong. He takes Mum's punishment. She's furious, like something possessed, hurling a torrent of obscenities at him.

Both my brothers stir. I lean around the door and hold my finger up to my mouth. In shock, they look at me, but say nothing. Frightened by the noise, Peter jumps into Terry's bed. They both begin crying.

Mum soon burns herself out. Exhausted, she draws back, but not before kicking Dad. I want to cry, but I don't. I need to be brave for my brothers.

Without acknowledging me, Mum stomps past my bedroom. I don't think she even sees me. The door to her room slams. Dad suddenly notices me in the doorway, but doesn't utter a word. He grabs a blanket from the hall cupboard and settles down on the sofa. Exhausted, my brothers and I finally drift off to sleep.

Ten

*I*t is the day after the fight. At nine in the evening, we're still waiting for Dad to return home from the office. He should have been back at teatime. He was supposed to be looking after us tonight.

Mum needs to head off to work. It's dark, and her nightshift at the factory begins at ten. She has to catch the bus and can't afford to miss work again. I can feel her anger building. She hasn't said anything, but I know she's fuming.

I've had an edgy feeling at school all day that I can't explain. I just don't feel right. Even more oddly, I have smelled wafts of kerosene all day long.

I've really struggled to concentrate at school lately, and the worst day is always Wednesday, when I have a double English lesson. I hate it. The teacher always picks on me. I have to stand up and read aloud to the whole class. The teacher makes me keep reading until I am told to sit down—which isn't until I am word perfect. I have a problem reading. Miss words. Add words. I sometimes skip whole lines. The words seem to jump all over the page. Why can the others read well, but I can't? It doesn't seem fair. Sometimes, the girls at the back of the class start snickering at me. This only makes me feel worse.

The teacher thinks I'm screwing up on purpose, but I'm not. Some days, I stumble more than others. I don't know why. I know my teacher thinks I should be in the lower-level class because I overheard him talking to another teacher one day when I was passing by the teachers' lounge. When my English teacher is angry, I usually look him straight in the eyes and try to work out what he's thinking and feeling, just like I do with my mother. But all I ever sense is someone who is intensely bitter and angry. Someone who doesn't want to do what he is doing.

There was a time when I loved reading. It was everything to me. I could take my time when I read on my own. There was no one there to ridicule me. And the words didn't jump about so much. Sitting alone in a corner somewhere, escaping to other worlds, was fantastic.

Last Wednesday, English was hell. The dismissal bell rang while I was reading to the class. Everyone expected to get up and race home, but the teacher just stood there with his arms tightly folded, telling everyone they had to stay until I'd finished. Those extra ten minutes felt like torture. The more frustrated everyone got, the more I panicked and messed up. Everyone was fidgeting and glaring at me, including the teacher. Out of pity for the others, he eventually let us go. But he told me I must read the same passage again at the next class—and I had better do it perfectly.

Mum's still rushing around getting ready for work. I can't figure out why Dad isn't home yet. I stay in the living room, curled up the sofa, holding my reading book from school. I keep reading the same pages over and over again, determined to learn them by heart. But it's difficult to concentrate. For some reason, I can smell the kerosene again.

From where I'm sitting, I can see right through to the kitchen. Mum is slamming the cupboard doors and stomping around. She knows she must get away soon and catch her bus. My brothers have already gone to bed, but I'm waiting up to see what will happen.

The back door suddenly swings open. Mum and I stop what we are doing as Dad breezes in. He smiles as if nothing is wrong. His breath stinks of drink.

The uneasy silence is awful. Dad just looks at me. Nobody says a word. I don't think my parents have spoken since their fight last night. Mum glares at Dad. She barges past him and then mutters something under her breath. I can feel her hatred. With a stupid smirk on his face, Dad grabs Mum's arm. It's his way of apologizing, but Mum pushes him backward.

"Go away. Don't touch me, Bill."

"Come on, Pat," he slurs. "Forgive and forget."

Mum looks as though she's about to explode. "So where the bloody hell have you been this time?"

"It's only a couple of pints," he smiles, turning away.

Mum gets in front of him and slaps him across the face. Shocked and surprised, Dad rocks backward, his smile giving way to fury. I keep my head down, pretending that I am reading my book, but from the corner of my eye, I can see my brothers peering around the corner.

"You know I'm working tonight, you selfish bastard!" Mum yells. "But you never think about anyone but yourself. I don't know why you don't piss off and leave us alone. You'd rather be off with your mates anyway."

"Pat, come on," Dad says, trying to make up. "Don't be stupid." He reaches for her again.

"Don't…touch…me…Bill."

Mum slaps him a second time. I notice an angry red mark on his cheek.

"I'm telling you, Pat, don't do that again," Dad warns.

Mum slaps him a third time. He finally snaps. Now he doesn't look like my dad. His face is bright red, and he's charging around like a maniac. I've never seen him this way before. He frightens me.

Without warning, Dad rushes back and pins Mum up against the wall. He is shaking with rage. Suddenly, he throws her against the wall, screaming in her face. He then barges past her and goes through the doorway into the kitchen. He crashes into the kitchen table, sending it flying. The back door almost comes off its hinges as he charges into the garden. I look at Mum in horror.

"Has he left us?" I ask. Mum grabs her handbag, snatches a cigarette and lights it. She's shaking and crying. Her makeup is running.

I notice my brothers crying in the corner. They are wearing their pajamas. I want to cry as well, but I can't. I want to show that I am strong.

Suddenly, without warning, the back door flies open and slams against the kitchen wall. Dad bursts in, dragging a large can of kerosene into the living room. I can't understand what he is doing. We all look at one another in confusion and fear. It's summer. The heaters don't need firing up. Dad starts tipping kerosene everywhere—over the carpets, the furniture, everything. The smell of kerosene fills the house.

Mum tries to grab Dad's arm, but he's too strong for her. He pushes her away from him and against the wall.

"Bill, don't be stupid!" she shouts, tussling with him.

I am terrified. I can't be strong anymore. Now I am crying and shaking.

"No, Dad!" I yell, getting up from the chair. "Please, don't!"

Nobody can get near him. He's emptying the whole can onto the plants, carpet and walls. The television. Table. Fireplace. The smell is disgusting.

"Dad, don't!" I scream again.

It's as though he can't hear anyone. Perhaps he has gone mad.

Mum jumps on his back and starts scratching him, but still he carries on.

I don't know what to do. It feels as though everything is moving in slow motion. Dad throws Mum off his back and pours the last of the kerosene onto the curtains. He snatches a box of matches from the mantelpiece. Nobody dares to move. We are petrified. He's going to strike a match and set the house on fire. We're all going to die.

"No!" everyone yells at once. For a split second, everything seems to stop. Dad stands there, motionless, holding the matches. He looks confused, as if he has just wakened from a dream.

Eleven

*A*ll images of my father and our home in London vanished as I suddenly became aware of the freezing water. Being back there again, seeing Dad cracking up, had brought back memories that I thought I had locked away. I had forgotten about that evening when he had nearly burned down the house. And all of us with it.

As I struggled to breathe, I wondered why key moments from my childhood were being replayed. Why now? And why did I have a distinct feeling that I was reliving them for a purpose?

Treading water, I tried to compose myself and relax both my mind and body. I needed to concentrate on staying afloat and filling my lungs with air. But I kept remembering all the times from my childhood when my parents seemed to be forever arguing. During the summer of 1976, there was a water shortage. Sadly, what I recall most about that scorching hot summer weren't the long, drawn-out evenings or playing in the garden. It was watching my parents constantly bicker. A niggling, tense feeling always hung around the house. It was toxic. We could all feel it and sense it, and I hated being close to it. It hurt to see the two people I loved most in the world rip themselves apart. When they fought, I could literally feel their anger as if it belonged to me.

One day, during that brutal summer of '76, my mother moved out and went to stay with Gran. With Mum away and Dad cooking, the evening meal was a greasy fry-up. I think it was the only meal that Dad knew how to cook. The atmosphere in the house without Mum was completely different. Not better, just different. Dad would let us run riot. We could do whatever we wanted. Go to bed late. Eat when we chose. But Mum's absences usually only lasted for a few days. Then she'd come back home, and things would return to normal. Until the next time.

The cold sea was making my body stiffen. I was being tossed back and forth by the changing tide. My extremities were numb, but my mind was more active and clearer than ever. Closing my eyes, I thought back to when I was fifteen. We finally moved out of London, which meant that Dad would no longer be within driving distance of his friends, who'd been such a bad influence on him. When we finally settled in our new home in Devon, he still liked to indulge in a social drink, but it was nothing like before.

For some time after our move, I found it difficult to forgive Dad for his past behavior. I wanted to know exactly why he'd put drinking, friends and socializing ahead of his family's needs. Perhaps he was a product of his past. I knew he'd had a colorful childhood in East London, and I loved when Dad would share his fascinating stories with me about growing up during the Second World War. Dad had been born to older parents. His mother had been married before and already had other children, but they were much older than Dad, so he had been raised as if he was an only child.

His brothers were adults by the time Dad was just starting school. They rarely had space in their lives for their much younger stepbrother. And on the rare occasions they did look after him, it was usually because they had no choice. Dad remembers being carted around from one smoky pub to another, and from one seedy club to another, when he was just six years old. Sometimes, he still had on his school uniform.

Alf, one of dad's stepbrothers, was always dressed in a sharp pin-striped suit, tie and polished shoes. He would tell Dad that no matter what he saw or heard when they were out together, he had to keep his mouth firmly shut. Dad saw things that children his age were not supposed to see.

An intimidating man, Alf was built like an ox. He was a heavy gambler and an illegal bookmaker, and he travelled all over London. Alf hung around the most notorious villains of the time, including the infamous Reggie and Ronnie Kray. These characters, with their unpredictable behavior, were an everyday part of Alf's violent world. It was what he had grown up with and what he was used to, but to a small boy, it was frightening.

But if Alf hit a winning streak, my dad would see a very different side of life. Alf would take him to eat in the best restaurants in London. Together, they would travel first class on the train. Those were the times my dad remembered best.

Despite all I'd intended, I hadn't been a better father to my own children than my father had been toward my brothers and me. But, considering his upbringing, I knew it was unfair to see my dad only in a bad light. Away from drink, my dad could be the most loving, compassionate and caring person I knew. I lost count of the times he would bring a complete stranger home from the pub. He always felt sorry for those who lived alone or had little money, so he'd often invite them to join us for tea.

Even though I was freezing, I smiled to myself as I remembered Christmases at our house. Dad always slipped out for a quick drink at lunchtime before the whole family sat down together, which incensed my mother. She believed that Dad should give up the pub for at least one day of the year.

With Christmas dinner becoming overcooked, Dad would roll in late, usually with a stranger in tow from the pub. Taking my dad into the kitchen, Mum would go berserk. It meant that she had to stretch what food she'd cooked. But, at the same time, I sensed that she quite liked the idea that we were giving someone worse off than ourselves a real family Christmas. Even though she initially protested about the whole thing, deep down she loved that Dad was helping others.

But then there was the other side to my dad. A much darker side. A side I didn't like very much. It would erupt and ignite every time alcohol was involved.

In many ways, my dad had been an irresponsible father, but though our upbringings had been different, much of my life had mirrored his. I had also let work and alcohol come before my family. I, too, had kept my emotions locked away. The only difference between us was that Dad's faults were out in the open for all to see. Everyone in our family was aware of Dad's drinking. They knew that he preferred to go out with his friends on weekends. But I was living a big lie. I led two separate lives: a home life and a work life. I could hide my drinking under the cover of business.

At least my father had had the courage to be truthful about his drinking. He had been brave enough to tell Mum how he'd blown all the housekeeping money. But I had been dishonest. I may not have told lies, but I didn't tell the truth either.

I belonged to a tight-knit "secret society," a small group of colleagues, clients and friends who all hid the truth from those back home. Most of us were drinking heavily and some, like me, were also taking drugs. Like a child in a candy shop, I was trying everything, including crack cocaine and heroin. So much of my life had been hidden in the shadows.

Alison always knew what city I was staying in and she at least had some idea what clients I was taking away on business, but she never suspected what was really going on. Alison trusted me. She knew that the trips allowed me to develop strong client relationships. We both accepted the sacrifices. My not being there was part of the job. I don't think she could have imagined that I was capable of behaving in such an irresponsible and idiotic way. I was living a double life.

By now, Alison was running her own business—a successful teashop in the town where we lived. She worked long hours, and when I was away (which included many weekends), our children were looked after by their grandparents. Alison took all this in her stride, accepting that we hardly saw each other. We thought it was worth it because I was generating more business, and more business meant more money. A better lifestyle. Our combined salaries put us in a very affluent income bracket. We had grown used to living a very comfortable life. But it was nothing more than a façade.

Spending way beyond our means, my bonuses were being swallowed up by our hectic lifestyle. It was like pouring money into a black hole. To compensate, we would both work longer hours, which meant little time together and with the children. We swept aside the separation as being a temporary blip, both naively believing that sometime in the future, things would ease up. But they never did. Working obsessively to keep our heads above water had become the norm.

Thrashing around in the water, I was furious with myself. How could Alison and I have been so stupid? How could we have believed that living up to a certain lifestyle was more important than spending time together? We had given away irreplaceable time with our children in favor of working ridiculous hours. We had put money and success ahead of nurturing Jenna and Olivia, and now it was too late to change anything.

The wind picked up. The sea became rougher. Even though I was being thrown around by ferocious waves, I was thinking more clearly than ever. I saw all my mistakes, my shortcomings, my greed and my dishonesty. I clearly saw it all. Alison and I had used materialism as a substitute for everything that was lacking in our lives.

Over the years, I tried everything I could to borrow more money. I needed to stay afloat and to pay off the huge mountain of credit card debt we had accumulated. On several occasions, I had spoken to our mortgage lender about increasing our home loan. There was a sizable amount of collateral wrapped up in the house, so that meant I could borrow whatever extra money we needed to keep our heads above water and live a life we couldn't really afford. I was treating our home as an inexhaustible bank resource. But it simply added to our ballooning mortgage. It didn't seem to matter, though, because the value of our home shot through the roof every year.

But I was lying to myself. It *did* matter that I was living on borrowed time. Within a few years, our re-mortgaged loan was outstripping our original home loan. We were sliding deeper into the red. It was a vicious cycle. The harder and longer we worked, the more we needed to spend to pretend it was all worthwhile. And the more Alison and I spent, the more we needed to earn.

My trips with business clients had become a much-needed escape. I was able to leave all my financial problems behind. It allowed me breathing space. I could forget about the pressures of an eighty-hour week, or the demands of business clients and sales targets.

I was becoming addicted to those drink- and drug-fuelled trips away. People were beginning to ask questions. I was losing weight and looking ill. I didn't care. Part of the excitement was choosing new places to visit. My "secret society" of clients and friends liked to push the boundaries as much as we could. We were constantly vying with one another, each of us trying to find more daring and dangerous places to go.

Most trips were funded from our huge corporate expense account. The building industry was buoyant, and a large entertainment budget was available. In my region, we were doing exceptionally well. This gave me the perfect "alibi." More success meant more time away with my top clients, where I could hide my addictions. But things were rapidly getting out of hand. Sometimes, when I was out of the country, I was plunged into an unfamiliar world. I'd wake up in some dirty backstreet bar in a city I barely knew. I'd buy drugs from anywhere and anyone. I was often reckless and fearless. All common sense had deserted me. I was irresponsible and no longer cared for my own safety or well-being.

After a heavy night out on the town, I would often stumble back through dimly lit back streets trying to find my hotel. When I did eventually get back, often just as the sun was coming up, I would collapse in a heap on the floor. Drugged to the eyeballs and exhausted, I would sleep it off until lunchtime. And then I would meet up with the rest of the gang, and we would start all over again.

Every trip was the same. Deep down, I knew I was killing myself. I knew that it couldn't go on. My life had been a complete and utter failure, and I deserved to die.

I shivered uncontrollably from both my rage and the cold. I had taken so much of my life for granted. Right on cue, another wave hit me full in the face. This was the harsh reality.

I continued to beat myself up as the waves battered my body. Why had I always chosen to run away from my problems? Why had I deceived myself and Alison? And why had I never plucked up the courage to share with her how I was truly feeling?

When I was younger, I used to stay with older relatives a lot. I was often told to sit still, be quiet and read a book. It was drummed into me that men and boys should be strong and keep their feelings to themselves. But I didn't want to. I wanted everyone to know exactly how I was feeling. I wanted my truth to be seen, listened to and acknowledged. I wanted others to understand what I was going through. And I especially wanted to tell everyone about the unusual feelings I picked up from others. By the time I was a teenager, I was sick and tired of pretending, but I didn't have the courage or confidence to share my feelings with anyone.

Being petrified of sharing my heightened emotions with other people stuck with me throughout my adult life. Constantly worried about what others would think of me, I would mask my anger and frustration by using drugs and alcohol. Or I'd go on a mad spending spree, buying anything from new clothes to holidays. I was running away from a lifetime of unexpressed emotion and pain. But no matter what I did or how much money I threw at it, nothing made it any better. It only made things worse. I had hidden my true self from Alison and then complained that she didn't understand me. I suddenly realized it was me who didn't understand myself.

I closed my eyes, clenched my hands together and prayed. I didn't have a clue who I was praying to. I wasn't even sure what I was praying for. It was instinctive. I wanted redemption. I wanted forgiveness. Forgiveness for my recklessness. For my ignorance and stupidity. Nothing was going to wipe the slate clean, but I needed to say I was sorry. However, the past kept rearing its ugly head, intruding on my desire to make peace with it.

Twelve

I'm lying facedown on my bedroom floor, crying like a baby. I just want to be left alone. I can't believe what happened today. I should have put two and two together. I'd had a strange feeling in my stomach since I got up this morning. I knew right away that something was wrong with Mum, but I didn't pay attention to my feelings.

Last night, Mum told us that, as a special treat, she will take us to the seaside the next day. We are so excited. It will just be Terry, Peter, Mum and me. Dad will be at work all day.

I am glad to be going out. I'm getting nervous about starting secondary school next week. The summer holidays are nearly over. Mum says I'll be fine once I settle down at the big school, but I'm not as certain. So much has happened in the past six months. I'm no longer sure who I am or what is real anymore. Some days, I wonder if I am going mad.

This morning, we set off on the train for Southend-on-Sea. The train is so packed, we can hardly move. Everyone is going to the beach. There aren't enough seats, so my younger brother, Peter, has to sit on my lap all the way there. But, despite the mayhem going on around her, Mum seems preoccupied.

When we arrive in Southend, we walk along the packed seafront. It is boiling hot. Mum gives us some pocket money to play on the penny falls in the arcade. Then we have chips for lunch and an ice cream on the pier. Later, while we are on the beach, playing and laughing, I look up, expecting to see Mum laughing with us. But she is staring blankly out to sea, smoking a cigarette.

My brothers and I are tired but happy as we head back home. On the way to the train station, a street photographer comes over to us. He makes me laugh and takes a photograph of me, telling Mum it will be ready the next day. Desperate for Mum to say yes, I ask if I can have one. Suddenly, Mum grabs my arm and yanks me away. To my horror, she yells at the man to leave us alone and physically pushes him away.

Back on the train, I realize I shouldn't have been surprised by Mum's reaction. I'd been feeling uneasy all day about Mum, but I would never have believed that she would overreact and carry on like that. I watch Mum as she smokes and stares out of the carriage window. I suddenly remember that when we were leaving the house this morning, I had seen her stuff a letter into a drawer. I wanted to ask her about it, but I'd been afraid it would annoy her. She seemed to have enough to worry about.

Exhausted, we arrive back home around teatime. A massive bundle of papers is sitting on the doorstep, and a large sticker is stuck to the door, which Mum rips off. When we trudge into the living room, I can't believe my eyes. Everything is gone. Every piece of furniture. The stereo. Dad's record collection. Everything. There is nothing left. At the thought that we had been robbed, my brothers and I begin to cry. But Mum doesn't. The truth is written all over her face. She had been expecting this all day.

I want to ask what's happened, but I am frightened that Mum will tell me something I don't want to hear. Maybe my dad has left us and taken everything with him. I know it has something to do with Dad. I can feel it in my stomach.

Still lying on the bedroom floor, with my tear-stained face pressed into the carpet, I hear the front door suddenly slam. I jump up and run into the hallway.

"Dad, you're back!"

I throw my arms around his waist. I'm so happy. He hasn't left us! Dad looks sad, and he is as white as a sheet. He says nothing and rushes into the living room. I follow him. I can smell that he has been drinking. Staring at Mum and looking distraught, Dad also seems to have known something we didn't.

"Billy. Terry. Peter," he says finally, blowing his nose. I sit cross-legged on the floor and rub my eyes. My heart is thumping, and my stomach is going berserk.

"We haven't been burgled," Dad says slowly. "The bailiffs have been here. Somehow, they got into the house."

"What's the bailiffs?" I ask. I am confused. I look at Mum. I can tell she's furious with Dad.

"They get a warrant. That means they take away things from our house," he stutters. His words echo around the empty room. For a minute, we are all quiet.

"But why?" I ask reluctantly, breaking the uncomfortable silence. Dad stares across at Mum. Arms crossed, she's smoking another cigarette.

"Go on," demands Mum. "Tell him."

Dad pauses.

"It's...when you haven't paid your bills," Dad says, looking down at the floor.

It doesn't make sense at first. Mum and Dad have always had enough money to smoke and drink, yet they don't have enough money to pay the bills? I don't get it.

"But why, Dad?" I ask. "Why haven't you paid the bills?"

My father just stares at the ceiling. Close to tears, he is too choked up and embarrassed to speak. But he doesn't need to say anything else. I've already guessed why the bills haven't been paid. The money's all been spent at the pub.

Thirteen

*M*y father's distraught face faded away. I was back in the sea, floating on top of the choppy waves. Every single bone in my body ached, and it took me a moment to gather my thoughts. My heart was still pounding from the shock of reliving the day when our home had been emptied. But *had* I really relived it? Or was it just my imagination playing tricks on me? Somehow, I knew I wasn't dreaming. It had been like a time trip. I had revisited that day.

A sonic boom thundered overhead, scattering my thoughts. I glanced up at the aircraft. As I stared at the melting vapor trail, I immediately thought of the holiday to Disney World in Florida that Ali, the girls and I were booked to go on later in the year.

It wasn't fair that I would never see Ali and our daughters again. I loved them so much. I had too much left to say to them. Too much life to live with them. I tried to "see" Jenna and Olivia's faces, but for some reason they wouldn't come to me. Panicking, I desperately scrabbled for an image of Ali. My parents. My brothers. My friends. But, annoyingly, my mind was a complete blank. What was happening to me? Was I losing my grasp of reality? I really didn't want to, but I knew I had to block all thoughts of my family out of my mind to protect my sanity. It felt like my heart and soul were being ripped out.

I had to refocus on the situation at hand. Although I was aching and riddled with cold, I managed to get myself more upright in the water, with my legs straight down below me. I couldn't feel my feet or toes, so I started to kick my legs around, trying to get the circulation going.

I noticed a swirl building on the surface of the water. I knew from friends of mine who were fishermen that swirls happen just as the tide is turning and signal a time when surging undercurrents will be most active. It may have looked calm on the surface, but I knew there was a strong riptide underneath.

I realized I was no longer being washed farther out into the mouth of the estuary. Instead, the force of the tide was slowly pulling me around in a circular motion. I was being carried along by the strong current.

Suddenly, I felt a gentle tug on my legs. And then another. And then several more. Then, without warning, I was yanked under the water. I popped back up and resurfaced immediately. Shocked and gasping for breath, I tried to compose myself. But I didn't have time to think. The riptide pulled me under for a second time. Only this time, it was for longer, and I was dragged farther down.

Gasping, I held my breath. My lungs felt as if they would implode, and there was a painful tightness in my chest. Swirling and tumbling, it felt as if I was in the spin cycle of a giant washing machine. Disoriented, I was dragged by the force of the undercurrent. I opened my eyes to try to see the surface, but I saw only air bubbles in front of me. Then, all of a sudden, I burst to the surface like a cork flying out of a champagne bottle.

Dazed and choking, I managed to snatch a few breaths. I had just managed to fill my lungs with air when I was grabbed for the third time. I frantically flapped my arms and legs in a desperate fight to stop myself from being sucked under again, but it was useless. Like a vast bathtub being emptied, the powerful undercurrent tugged me deep beneath the waves. This time, the force was even stronger. I expected to burst to the surface again, but nothing happened.

Like a rag doll, I was yanked in all directions by the riptide. Terrified that I wouldn't resurface again, I began to count in my head to distract myself. *One, two, three...* I stopped fighting and went with the current. Protectively, I threw my arms around my body and squeezed as tightly as I could. I kept counting.

By the time I reached *ten, eleven, twelve,* my eyes were firmly shut. I swallowed a mouthful of vile seawater and choked. I kept hoping, praying that I'd come back up. Water went up my nose and into the back of my throat. All I could taste was salt. *Twenty, twenty-one...* "Hold on," I kept thinking. "Stick with it." By the time I reached *thirty,* it was all about survival.

Forty... I felt sure my lungs would rupture and collapse. I needed to breathe. I needed air. *Fifty...* Tumbling in the mixer of surging water, I was shaking violently, convulsing. My head was throbbing, and I struggled to stay connected. I was losing consciousness. I screamed in my head, and a million images seemed to flash in my mind all at once.

Sixty... Now there was abject fear. Horrified, I realized I wouldn't be coming back. My body stiffened. I dug my nails hard into my arm. I wasn't ready to let go. *Seventy...* I wasn't ready to die.

In sheer desperation, I instinctively flung out my arms as I spun around under the water. My own elbow caught me under the rib cage, winding me. I couldn't take anymore. My chest wanted to explode. *Eighty...* This was what drowning felt like. What dying felt like. And now I knew how I would die. Every cell felt as if it would erupt. *Ninety...* I couldn't hold on. My lungs were bursting. The pain was unbearable. This was it. This had to be it.

I wanted my family.

Then, just as I reached *ninety-nine*, finally, unexpectedly, I burst to the surface. My eyeballs felt as if they would pop. I immediately threw up. Gasping for air, I took in several short, sharp breaths in case I got pulled down again. Shaking violently from the shock, I opened my eyes. The first thing I saw was the full moon, perched high above the cliffs. It was magnetic, drawing me to it. Reassuring. Healing. It calmed me.

Everything seemed to slow down. I could still hear the waves driving into the seawall and the loud hiss of the water as it drew back, but something had changed. Inexplicably, all fear had left me.

Treading water, I looked back up at the cliffs and toward the moon again. I was captivated. It was the most stunning sight I had ever laid my eyes on. I surprised myself by smiling. I was filled with the most intense sense of love, joy and appreciation. I burst out crying at the magnificence of it all. The brilliance and perfection. A flood of deep-rooted emotion swept through me and out of me. I instinctively knew that it was a lifetime of trapped, unexpressed emotion.

I was alive, and it felt wonderful. I stared up in sheer amazement at the beauty of the night sky. Its vastness filled me with peace and serenity. It was awesome. Infinite. And I was part of it.

Staring up at the stars, I remembered how the wonder of the universe had always fascinated me. In the past, no matter how frantic my life was, I would still find the time to snatch a moment and look up at the constellations. It had been a deep passion of mine since I was a boy. Many times, I would let my imagination run wild and make up fantastic stories. I would pretend that we had all come from the stars. I'd convince myself that each and every one of us had originated from some faraway galaxy and time.

Full of warmth, love and gratitude that I had survived, I was intoxicated by the sense of wonder I was experiencing. Everything looked different, clearer. It felt like the first day of a new life, as if I was seeing everything around me through all new eyes.

Then, I had the most peculiar fleeting insight that I had had this drowning experience before—and that I would have it again. This certainty of knowledge momentarily threw me, but I calmly brushed it aside. I didn't want to think about death or dying. Not now.

Something significant in me had shifted. I had never felt more truly alive than I did at that moment. More present. More conscious. More aware of my surroundings. I couldn't figure out *why* this had happened, but I knew it had everything to do with being dragged under the water. I was part of something larger than myself. More than my physical body. More than my mind.

I didn't want this moment of bliss to end. I desperately clung to it, like a newborn baby clings to his mother. A feeling of love overwhelmed me and filled me. I felt I was touching the very essence of my being. The only time I had ever been remotely close to similar feelings was when I had taken drugs, which had briefly amplified my sense of wonderment and joy. For a little while, the high would make me feel that everything in the world was perfect. Connected. That somehow everything was joined to one vast web of life.

A wave caught me full in the face. Strangely, the ice-cold water no longer troubled me. I could barely feel it. Perhaps my body had grown used to the cold. Maybe I was becoming numb to it. A different sensation swept over me, like an energy racing through me. But it wasn't anxiety or fear this time. This loving, all-embracing energy was empowering, liberating and inviting. I felt fearless and light. Warm and protected. I wasn't alone. I was aware of an all-powerful, loving presence being part of me.

The more I kept telling myself I didn't deserve this extraordinary feeling, the more I received. The more I tried pushing it away, the more it flowed freely through me.

I was perplexed by the sense of calm I felt. I slowly began to piece together what I had gone through. I had just been dragged under the water by the force of the current. It was the most terrifying ordeal I'd ever known. I thought my time had come. So, why was I so calm? If it was the worst experience I'd ever had, why was I so unaffected by it now? It didn't make sense. The prospect of death held no fear for me now.

Fourteen

Relaxed and drifting with the waves, I looked up at the stars, which jogged my memory. I remembered the many evenings when I would camp out in the garden with my younger brother, Terry. As children, we were inseparable. We'd do everything together. Ride bikes. Play football. Build camps. We didn't have much money for new clothes, so Mum or one of my aunts would make them. To our horror, they always knitted us matching outfits. We hated it. Our friends made fun of us. But it didn't matter. We stuck together. We were a team.

Terry and I would build clubhouses in the back garden made out of plywood, discarded doors and corrugated sheeting. We'd find old, abandoned carpeting and drag it home on the back of our bikes. In the summer, we'd build a huge camp out on the lawn. And at night, we would sleep in our clubhouse. We loved it. Along with a dozen or so of our friends, we'd stay up half the night, playing cards and telling scary stories by flashlight.

It was exciting being outside at night on our own. There were all sorts of strange noises. The darkness played tricks on us. But it didn't stop us from crawling out in the middle of the night, lying on the grass and staring up at the stars in the clear night sky. It was magical.

Now, as the waves lapped over my face, it was as if I was staring at the same night sky I looked at as a child. The thought made me sob out loud, but my tears weren't from sadness. They were tears of overwhelming appreciation for the close bond Terry and I had shared. We had been through so much together. But even allowing for all the fighting between Mum and Dad, Terry, Peter and I still shared fantastic childhood memories. All of our friends' parents fought, too, so we all thought it was normal. We didn't know it could be any different. We assumed everyone's father drank and struggled for money.

To my regret, Terry and I had lost touch as adults. We had just drifted apart, and I knew it was partly my fault. Why hadn't I tried harder to stay in touch with Terry? Why had I let our relationship fizzle out? I was the oldest. I should have known better. I could have tried harder.

But instead of feeling self-condemnation, all I could feel were love and gratitude for all the wonderful times Terry and I had shared as children. My chest felt as if it might explode. The warmth emanating from my heart fanned out and engulfed every part of me. I was happy, ecstatic. If I had died right there and then, I would have been at peace. I would have passed on as the happiest person alive. Memories engulfed me once again.

It's the last weekend before I start secondary school. I'm awakened by Terry jumping on my bed.

"Billy, come on, time to get up!" he shouts, yanking back the curtains. "Have you forgotten that we're going out on our bikes today?"

The sunshine is pouring into our bedroom. It's glorious outside, just as it's been every day this summer holiday. We hurriedly get dressed and race into the kitchen. Mum, Dad and Peter are still fast asleep. We're going to meet up with several friends. "Our gang," we call them. We gulp back our breakfast and then make up a picnic for the day. As usual, there's nothing in the fridge, so we raid the cupboard and make do with jam sandwiches, a packet of Rich Tea biscuits and a large bottle of watered-down orange juice.

Excited, Terry and I head off and meet up with our friends at the local park. We're late. They are sitting on their bikes waiting for us. They each have their backpacks and sandwiches with them. Except Ritchie. As always, he's forgotten his.

Ritchie's brother, Ryan, has the best bike in the gang. It's a brand-new Chopper, and we're all jealous. Julian, the newest in the gang, is trying to bribe Ryan with candy so he can have a go on the Chopper. Frankie is there, too. Frankie is one of my best friends. Everyone likes him. His parents own the candy shop on the corner.

As a treat, Frankie has smuggled out handfuls of chocolate bars, football stickers, sweets and whatever else he was able to grab from the shop. He shares the treats with us, as always. We kick off and speed along the country lanes on the edge of town.

The sun is baking, and before long we're dripping with sweat. Stripped to our shorts, we cycle for hours. Our backs are sunburned, and we're plastered in dust. Peddling fast along narrow, winding lanes, we stop close to a reservoir. We throw our bikes against the fence, clamber over and scramble up the steep hill. I race Terry up the bank. Reaching the top, all six of us scream and jump feet-first into the water below. It's cold and immediately cools us down. We're all splashing one another and messing about. We play in the water for hours.

Afterward, we lie on the grass drying off under a clear blue sky. Exhausted but content, we polish off what food we have left and swig back warm orange juice straight from the bottle. It is disgusting, but nobody cares.

We promise that the gang will always share secrets with one another, and that we will never lose touch when we grow up. We will always be friends. As Terry and I lie on the grassy bank together, in the warm sunshine, I'm seized by a sudden, unexpected feeling of dread. I feel uneasy, and there's a strange tightness in my chest. I don't quite understand what I'm feeling. I try to ignore it by thinking about something else.

Later, as I throw stones into the water, I think about how lucky Terry and I have been to spend every day of the summer holidays together. I've enjoyed spending time with him. Even though he is two years younger than me, Terry's happiest when he is hanging around with our older gang. Mum's told me a million times that I must take care of Terry, but it feels like the other way around to me. He isn't scared of anything or anybody. I'm nothing like him. Terry is able to talk to anyone and stand up to them, but I hold back. I hate trouble. I don't like arguing and fighting.

Every one of us in the gang is different, but we get on brilliantly together. Looking around, I realize how lucky I am to have such great friends. We do everything together. We look out for each other. Our gang is solid, like a family. It's wonderful knowing that we can all trust one another. We can tell each other anything. There are no secrets between us. I am part of something special. I belong.

Frankie and Ryan are prodding each other with sticks. Ritchie is teasing Julian. And Terry is trying to wrestle a melted bar of chocolate from me. I know I will always remember this moment.

When I'm with my friends, I forget all about Dad's drinking or the fighting between my parents. I forget about my accident and all the weird things that have happened to me ever since. My friends make me feel safe and protected.

From nowhere, the restless feeling I'd had rumbling inside me earlier suddenly erupts like an almighty volcano. Overwhelming dread and panic fill my chest. My stomach tightens, and I feel sick. Then it hits me. I have secrets. Secrets that nobody else knows. Flustered, I look around at my friends. I know now that I can't carry on living this lie. I'm a fake. I don't belong here with the gang. The secrets that I have kept from my best friends all summer shoot into my head all at once. I remember the out-of-body experience I had after my accident. I remember the feelings that I pick up from my mother.

Terrified that I will be found out, I drop the chocolate bar and just stare at Terry. He stares back at me. He's not stupid. He senses that something is wrong.

"What's up, Billy?"

"Nothing," I lie, turning away.

I want to tell Terry everything. I pause and take a deep breath. A cold shiver runs down my spine. Here goes… I turn around to face him, but fear grips me. I freeze. I keep my mouth firmly zipped. Terry just looks at me.

"What's wrong?"

"Nothing," I lie again.

It's no good. I can't go through with it. If I do tell Terry, he probably won't believe me. He might tell all our friends, and they will think I am mad. I can't do anything that will threaten my place in the gang.

I wish I had Terry's courage to just come out with things. But I'm not Terry. Suddenly, I feel like the loneliest person on earth.

Fifteen

I know the moment I wake up the next morning that something strange has happened. The dream I'd had felt so vivid, so real. I jump out of bed and pull back the curtains. Sun pours in, but it looks chilly today. Lying back on my bed, I start piecing together my dream. I had been in the crowd watching a soccer game. I knew we were in a foreign country because everyone was talking in a language I didn't understand. The fans around me wore blue shirts and waved banners madly. Some people held flags with three stripes of color on them—red, white and green.

I don't always remember my dreams, but this one is different. I remember every single detail. Closing my eyes, I again see myself standing on tiptoes among the crowd, close to the halfway line. The noise of the crowd is deafening. Then both teams come out. I recognize the team members in white right away. They're from England. Following them out of the tunnel is the home team in the blue shirts. The stadium erupts to the chants of "Italia!"

I jump out of bed, realizing the significance of my dream. It is the soccer match that England is going to play later today against Italy. The score in my dream had been 2-0 for Italy. I can still see it vividly. I see the goals, the scorers and the end result.

Excited, I run into Dad's bedroom. I want to tell him all about it. He often has dreams that come true. He's always putting money on things at the bookmakers if he's had a dream. But this is my first dream that we can bet on.

"Dad!" I shout, jumping onto his bed. "I know the score of the soccer game today. We lose 2-0."

Still half-asleep, Dad mumbles, "What do you mean? They don't play until later today."

"No, I mean I've dreamt about the result. I saw the goals. One in each half. And Italy won the match in the end." Hearing this, Dad comes to. He is always interested in other people's dreams, especially if he can put a gambling bet on them.

"Are you absolutely sure?" he asks, quickly getting dressed. "There's no doubt?"

"I'm positive, Dad. I was there, cheering on England. Italy scored one goal in each half. One of them was from a corner. It all felt so real."

Dad doesn't need any more persuasion.

"Come on," he says. "We're heading down to the bookmakers. I just hope you are right."

That scares me. What does he mean by that?

Dad snatches his keys, then reaches up toward a high cupboard shelf and gets down a pint-glass, which is full of money. He empties it and stuffs all the bills in his trouser pockets. I freeze. What is he doing? This is Mum's money for the food and bills. "Come on, Billy," he says. "Grab your coat. We're going for a drive."

I feel sick. I wish I hadn't opened my stupid, big mouth.

Driving to the bookmakers in the next town, I am quiet. All I can think of is Mum finding out. If Dad loses all our money, it will be my fault. I shouldn't have said anything.

We're both sitting down with my brothers, watching the game. I can barely concentrate. Dad hasn't just put all the money on Italy to win. He's stupidly put it all on the result to be 2-0. What have I done? I've let Mum down. I know I have. She'll never forgive me. She'll never trust me again. She'll think I'm no better than Dad.

I can't bear to watch the game. It's torture. England has nearly scored several times already. If it does, then we'll lose everything.

Against the run of play, Italy scores. One-nil. I can't believe it. It's exactly as I saw it in my dream. Ecstatic, I almost jump up out of my chair. Dad looks across and smiles. I smile back at him. Half-time arrives. It's one-nil to Italy.

The second half begins. Italy scores another goal. We jump up together. Two-nil.

Waiting for the final whistle is agonizing. I keep praying that England won't snatch a late goal. I want them to lose. Finally, the match ends. We go mad. I can't take it all in. Dad has won his bet. More importantly, my skin has been saved.

Sixteen

I knew that I was nearing the end of my life. I closed my eyes and waited for death to overtake me. I had dreaded this moment, but now that it had arrived, I actually welcomed it. Alison and the girls would be taken care of financially, and they would be looked after by family and friends. The love I had shared with Ali and the girls could never be taken away. I instinctively knew that unconditional love was constant and eternal.

I no longer feared death or what awaited me. I was totally at peace. Drifting in and out of consciousness, I held on to all the love I'd been blessed with throughout my life. I imagined myself to be soaring upward with the wind. I knew that I was outside of my body. I was *more* than my body. Higher and higher, I was flying like a bird. All I could feel was the spray of the waves below me. I was without physical limitation. I was free, detached from everything, and yet part of it all.

I could no longer smell anything, and I could barely hear the sea. It was nothing but a distant hum in the background. My senses were failing, and I knew this was a sign of the end. I began crying as the full realization of what was happening engulfed me.

I managed to force my hands together even though I could barely feel my fingers. I prayed with all my heart and soul once more for forgiveness. The urge to pray was instinctive even though I had little belief in the existence of God. I knew in my heart that this was my last chance to redeem myself. I didn't care who or what I was praying to. I needed to release all the negative emotion that I had carried with me for years.

"God, forgive me," I sobbed. "Forgive me for not being the husband or father I should have been. And forgive me for taking my life for granted."

I knew without question that I had not lived up to my potential. I definitely hadn't given it my best shot. That hurt more than anything. Like driving a stake through the center of my heart, the pain was unbearable. So many of my hopes and dreams, promises and aspirations had been left unfulfilled. I had wasted so much of my life. I didn't deserve to live.

Filled with self-loathing, I drifted with the waves. I wanted it all to be over.

I was ready to die.

In your heart, do you honestly and truthfully imagine your life to have been a complete failure?

Shocked by the softly spoken male voice, my mind stopped. All thoughts of dying suddenly emptied from my head. My mind was devoid of everything else—*except* the voice. I was mystified. The voice and the words that I heard didn't belong to me. It wasn't my voice. They weren't my thoughts. The words were authoritative, controlled, but loving. For a fleeting moment, I wondered if my mind was playing tricks on me. But I knew it wasn't. There was an *absolute* knowing. I *had* heard that voice. The words had been whispered, as if spoken inside my head. Too petrified to reply, though, I kept my eyes firmly shut and tried to ignore the voice. Maybe it wouldn't come again.

I'll repeat what I have already said. Do you truthfully imagine that your life has been a failure? And do you really feel in your heart of hearts, in the depth of your soul, that your time on earth has been wasted?

This time, the voice was louder and more urgent. Now, it seemed to be spoken from every part of me, not just my head. Before I had time to think, I replied out loud.

Yes, as a matter of fact, I do.

Then please, please, think again and change your mind. For I tell you these absolute truths: No one person's life is ever wasted. No one person's life is deemed a failure, regardless of how long a lifetime is lived. If a human soul incarnates for but one hour, then its life has brought a profound meaning to the world. Your time on earth has not been wasted. Far from it. Your life expressed has had an enormous impact upon other people's lives—more than you could ever imagine in your wildest dreams. And that is true for every single human being, regardless of how insignificant their lives may appear.

Before I could formulate a response, the gentle but clear voice continued to speak.

In your heart and soul, in the depth of your being, do you honestly believe that you are a complete failure? Do you truly imagine that fate has dealt you a cruel card? What if I told you that everything in life is being drawn to you, by you? What if I said that everything you are now experiencing in the sea, has happened for a purpose? Would you take on board that belief? Could you even begin to fathom what that truly means? I will share with you this undeniable fact: Everything that you have ever experienced, are experiencing, and will ever experience have all been created and manifested by only one person on this planet. You.

Me! Why on earth would I create situations in my life that draw me toward pain and suffering? And why would I ever wish to threaten my own life? I'd have to be out of my mind to intend that.

Exactly. That is exactly what you are doing right now. You are totally out of your mind. Put another way, you are in a place of "no mind." And for the purpose of this conversation, that's good.

Now, please try to keep a clear mind. Clear away all negative thoughts and judgments from your head because that's how you, or rather we, are having this conversation—by your conscious choosing to be out of your mind. Only then can you create a gap in your consciousness wide enough for us to communicate.

Let me explain more clearly. When you are fully conscious (which really means, fully aware), and when you are not flooding your mind with fear, unnecessary thoughts or sensory data, you effectively create a clear space in your thinking. Let's imagine that clear space in your head as a clean, white-washed board on the wall. Now, if the board is wiped clean, what can come in to fill the space?

Other thoughts.

Nearly right, but it's not what you literally think. Yes, it is "thoughts," but not those thoughts from your own mind because you are no longer thinking. Remember, you are now outside of your mind. You have side-stepped it. So what other thoughts are they? Where do they originate from? What is the source?

Perhaps thoughts inspired from other people?

Warm. You are half-right. They are the inspirational thoughts coming to you from four prime sources. In truth, there are many more sources than four, but for now, I will focus on these.

Number one is the most common. It is as you intimated—the thoughts that you pick up from others, especially those people you are emotionally attached to, be it work colleagues, loved ones, family and friends.

So we actually do pick up thoughts from other people then? Somehow, and I don't know why, I've always sensed that to be true.

Your initial gut instinct was correct. Of course, you can tap into the energy of other people. Everybody can. Unfortunately, few people believe this, let alone use the wonderful inherent abilities they have within them.

For most of your life, you have made the most common basic error. You have assumed that your imagination is playing tricks on you. The moment an inspired thought suddenly enters your head, you immediately deny your initial instincts. You kill them off before they even have a chance to flower. Most of your life, you have ignored your first impression, your gut instinct. You have believed what life has taught you, rather than what your gut instinct demonstrates to you.

Nurture over nature. That's what you are implying here, is it not? That we go with social conditioning rather than the characteristics that we are naturally born with.

Yes. Instinct, feeling and intuition are all natural gifts that everyone is born with. They are your "radar" in life.

Our radar? What do you mean by that?

Intuition is your true compass throughout life. It enables you to navigate your life journey. Intuition acts just as radar would when you are lost in the sea of life. It helps you to navigate through those tricky, narrow straits without hitting the rocks. Intuition helps you to find your way in the fog.

So intuition is a type of support system? It helps us to see what is coming up in our lives.

Yes. Intuition is a tool that gives you insight and guidance. It is your internal guidance system.
You get to feel a situation and try it on for size before you choose to own it. Unfortunately, so few people accept that their intuition is real. If you knew the real potential of your intuition, you would never take it for granted. You would constantly use it to guide you through choppy waters.

I know this to be true. From my own life experiences, my gut instinct has told me one thing, and my head another.

So which one have you always chosen?

It would be fair to say both. But sometimes my gut feeling seemed so irrational and off the mark that I ignored it and went with what my head was telling me.

The reason you continued with this behavior was that you didn't wish to challenge your thinking. You didn't want to contradict what your head and collective thoughts were telling you. Yet I shine this truth inside you: Always go with your intuition first. Listen to your body. Your initial instinct demonstrates, through bodily feelings, what your truth is. When you follow your head, you are following your collective thoughts, which have been assembled from the beliefs of others. Therefore, when any life situation arises, always challenge your own thinking.

Always challenge my own thoughts. I like that.

Challenging your own thoughts is the most important step to becoming more conscious.

Do you mean more aware?

Yes, more aware of what is going on inside you. Don't just observe your outer reality. Give equal attention and awareness (consciousness) to your inner universe and what your body is showing you. Feelings always lead you home to the truth because they are your truth—manifested.

When you tune into the energy of another, you are using your emotions as a bridge. The emotional state of empathy enables you to feel what another is thinking and feeling. Empathy is the ability to tune into someone outside of you and literally feel his or her emotions as though they were inside you. By being open, you create a channel and tune into someone.

Similar to what I did with my mother when I was younger. I picked up her angry vibes, her repressed fury toward my father.

Yes. You tuned into her channel because the emotional frequency you dialed up resonated with you both. Your mother and you shared an important emotional bond—you both wanted your father to change his drinking habits. You wanted things to change. And here's another fact about that particular situation. You both respected one another's resilience. It is this respect that propelled your emotional connection. Dual respect creates a mighty emotional force.

When two or more are gathered . . .

Precisely. When two or more are gathered in the same passionate cause, an immeasurable force is unleashed. That can work in both positive and negative causes. When the energy of emotions bond together, the sum is infinitely greater than the parts.

So if we tune into someone we are close to, a strong emotional bond develops.

Not just emotional. A heightened psychic bond develops, too. You experienced this frequently with your mother.

I know, and I didn't really appreciate what was going on when I was only eleven years old. I thought I was going mad.

You were most definitely not going mad. The madness is that these feelings and natural-born gifts are allowed to be continuously denied by most of society. That is the insanity of the situation. Know that this ability has always been present. It is part of what makes us all human beings. The madness is on humanity's part to keep denying these beautiful gifts. They are real. They are not just a figment of our overactive imaginations.

Remember, to tune into another person and experience the glory of human connection, you have to concentrate. Clear your mind completely of any unwanted thoughts. Let go of the static, and then tune into the right frequency. Apply these childlike principles, and your life experience will multiply beyond comprehension. You will literally go beyond mind, and in doing so, tune into the real person.

You are heavily emphasizing *tuning* in. Can you please expand on that principle more fully?

Tuning in essentially means sensing fully what your feelings are trying to show you. Your feelings interpret what somebody else is thinking. That's possible because emotion is the channel of communication. It is the glue, the bonding agent that connects us all together.

When we emotionally connect, we literally feel what others think. We cannot think what another feels because that is an objective action, empty of emotion. It is emotion-less. To be void of emotion means that you are disconnected from not only your own feelings, but also the feelings of others. And by others, I mean all other life forms on this earth, as well as humans.

You can only love others to the degree that you love yourself. The world is a perfect mirror of your innermost thoughts and feelings.

I think I get what you are saying. There have been many times in my life when I felt deeply disconnected from others, including those closest to me. I've felt detached and alone, confused and afraid. I've made the mistake of blaming others for this disconnection, this feeling of isolation and loneliness. I have accused others of being insensitive, unthoughtful, uncaring. Reading between the lines, perhaps I'm the one who was to blame. It is my fault that I haven't opened up and been honest with my emotions. Perhaps I should have loved myself more.

Please do not cast blame on yourself. You did what you did—what most people do. That is life. To heap regret and recrimination on yourself misses the entire point of what it means to be human. We all fail at one time or another. We all fall short of our own teachings and beliefs. We all make mistakes. That is because we are all human. Know that you are normal to fall short of your own grand vision, and you will inherit a valuable life lesson. That's what life is for. It creates a framework for us so that we can learn from our mistakes. Of course, there are no mistakes if we use these experiences wisely. Every mistake carries within it the seed of true wisdom. The mistake is that you give yourself a hard time over it. The mistake is that you don't learn from your mistakes. The mistake is that you let fear stop you from trying to be more. If you do not fail, then you have not tried...

Seventeen

I repeated the words over and over to myself, savoring them. *If you do not fail, then you have not tried…*

That is beautiful. I like that. I totally agree. That has been my mantra, I guess, throughout my whole working life. To keep on trying no matter what shows up.

Yes, I know, and it is a good philosophy that has served you very well. It has helped you to take risks. And it has taught you that mistakes are only stepping stones on the path to success. And here's another fact: The amount of failure you experience is directly proportionate to the amount of success you experience. The two are mirrors of one another. They are two different sides of the same coin.

Another gem. I love that expression, too. It is so poignant. I *have* failed and been hit hard by so many events in my life. There have been countless occasions when I've thought to myself that I can't take anymore. I was certain that I didn't have the energy to get up off the mat. There's been many a time when I've thought that this must be the final knockout punch.

You have demonstrated great courage and will. You have shown to yourself that the fight in life is worth pursuing. Yet I tell you something else: Life does not always have to be a constant fight. It doesn't have to be one long struggle. Even the language you choose to describe your struggle demonstrates your addiction to the fight. This is not the only way to live. It is an illusion. Wouldn't you much prefer to live a bigger part of your earthbound experience in harmony? Harmony is where all your energies (your vibration) correlates with the rest of life. That way, you truly create a more balanced, full and inspired life.

Fighting doesn't always have to be the only way. There are other ways of living. Better ways.

But I had to fight. There was no choice. Things were showing up in my life that wanted to put me on the floor. Without fighting for everything I have, I would be in the gutter. I'd have nothing. No, I don't agree with you. The fight must always go on.

When I haul myself out of bed every day, I see the whole process of life as one big fight. In my present sales environment, I either get there first for the order, or I miss out and lose. We all have to fight for what we have achieved. We must all struggle for what we have. That's what life is about, isn't it? Fighting for what you believe. Fighting for what you want.

What if I told you that fighting for everything isn't necessary? There is always enough in the world. There are always enough sales orders, food, housing and clothing. There's an abundance of water, shelter, love and compassion. The question is never about whether there is enough. It is about whether people want to share what they hoard. Please do not make the mistake of believing that life should be one constant fight and battle from birth till death. When life is approached in that way, it will be empty of the joy you are so desperately seeking in the world.

And, please, do not confuse passion with fighting. They are direct opposites. One leads you to disconnect from both your heartfelt dreams and other people. The other leads you, wonderfully, to a place of fulfilment. A place where you discover what it means to truly be a human being.

Passion leads to freedom. Fighting leaves you imprisoned.

But what you are implying completely tips up on its head what I have always believed. I'm sorry, but I cannot accept that we do not have to fight for everything.

Do you believe that you must fight for everything, or have you been taught it? Do not become entangled by what culture and the society have demonstrated to you. History is not always a good example. Fighting is fighting, whether it is for sales orders or countries. The act of fighting is a learned response. It is in direct response to a feeling of lack. There isn't enough, so I will fight for it. All fighting evolves from the misguided belief that there is not enough in the world...of anything. That is why you had to fight for your business, fight for your orders.

I'm really confused here. How can we relate fighting for countries with fighting for sales orders? That is just stretching the point too far.

Is it? Let me say this: The way most people fight for the everyday things in their lives perfectly projects how countries also fight for land, for oil, for resources. One is a perfect mirror of the other. Remember, we are a microcosm of the world in which we live. Just as the universe is a macrocosm of our lives. How we act locally is demonstrated globally. There is no difference. The beliefs and behaviors are identical, only on a far different scale.

Let me ask you a question. On your sales budgets, how did you fare against your sales targets?

Sorry! I don't get the connection. Why are you asking me that? That has nothing to do with it.

I think it has. Let me show you. Please play along with me for a moment. How are you presently doing with your sales targets against budgets?

Ah, I suspect I'm achieving around three times what I'm expected to do. Yes, that's probably right. Three hundred percent of budget would be a fair assessment.

You have just answered my question.

How do you come to that conclusion?

You're fighting for orders, and hard work has helped you to achieve three times what is expected of you.

Here's something to make you think. If you have two-thirds more than you need, who is losing out? Who is going short? If you have three times the amount of business needed to make your company profitable, what other company is suffering?

Oh, I see what you are driving at. I never thought of it that way.

Exactly. When we fight for something more than we need, it surely makes sense to realize that another is missing out somewhere. Can you not see the connection? Can you not join the dots? This doesn't just apply to your world. This applies to everything in the world, be it food, water, clothing, shelter, oil…

What I am demonstrating is that need and want are not the same. And neither are passion and fighting. Fighting is usually grounded in the misplaced and fearful notion that there is not enough to go around. It is buried in the false belief that life and the universe will not deliver to us what we need. So, instead, we constantly fight for everything tooth and nail.

Yet life will always deliver us what we need. It always has. This is demonstrated throughout the natural kingdom. Do birds starve in the winter? Do wild animals go hungry in the spring? No, so long as nature spreads its bounty around, everything is supported. Nature has an inherent, built-in belief that there will always be sufficient to share.

Unfortunately, there is one species on this earth that forgets this wonderful dance going on. There's only one dominant species that imagines it is going short. Humanity. Humans confuse need with want, and passion with fighting. Passion is born in the heart. Fighting derives from the fear of lack.

Let me change the topic and pose another question. What inspired you to dust yourself off, pick yourself up, and come at life all over again when the chips were down? When you said earlier that you had to fight for everything, what motivated you to carry on? And what made you believe in yourself?

I'm not exactly sure. I suppose I had a gut feeling deep inside me that everything would be fine in the end. Call it hope, fearlessness, stupidity, ignorance. It was like a deep knowing. It somehow just felt right. I had an unwavering belief in my own ability. I had a feeling, or impression, that I would get back up again. When

I was going through a dark period in my teens, I felt this deep sense of belief that somehow got me through the fog. I can't fully articulate where this belief originated from, or why I went along with it. I suppose it was an intuitive sense. A strong feeling inside me that whispered, *Don't worry, you will be fine.*

That is wonderful insight that you have demonstrated. You were wise to listen to your instincts. Always go with your first impression because the impression you paint for yourself will always portray what's happening on the canvas of your outer world. Remember, you are constantly painting your own picture of life. You choose the brushes, the colors and what light to use. You could also say that you are the paintbrush itself, constantly choosing what to create.

I love that interpretation. It is so poetic. I am going through life painting what I want to portray.

Your life demonstrated on the external world is a direct expression and portrait of your inner world. Know that in every moment of your life, you are the one constantly creating. You are the artist of both your inner and outer worlds. But instead of brushes, you use thoughts and feelings. Instead of colors, you use words.

And instead of light, we use actions. This insight is incredible. I am blown away by all of this.

I could not have put it better myself. And here's something more. The insight becomes deeper, richer and more profound. The canvas you are painting in life is actually a mirror. And the color you inject into your physical world is a direct representation of what colors you mix up in your inner world.

So the feelings I have inside of me reflect back into my outside world?

You have it. What you think and feel, you literally create. The colors you choose decide the picture you see.
Do you not see the perfection in the design? Do you not appreciate the simplicity of creation? You, and nobody else, are creating the life

you experience. And if you want to develop another picture of your life, simply choose again. Change what is happening inside of you. Swap the colors. Change the brushes. And if that still doesn't work for you, then change the light.

Change the light?

Change how you are looking at the picture. See it from another angle, another dimension.

Or choose another perspective.

Good, you are playing the game. If nothing else works, change the perspective. Look at your life through a new lens. See it through a different light. A new perspective enables you to see situations in a new light. It will give you insight.

So always be conscious what you wish for. That is why it is imperative that you constantly monitor your thoughts. Always be aware of what you are thinking. Be alert to what you are saying and doing. These are the artist's tools that are coloring and creating your life. And please remember that you cannot create the right picture without the correct colors. You cannot see beauty if the light is distorted.

Eighteen

I was beginning to understand the role I had played in creating my own experiences—in designing my own life. I wanted to learn more…

This insight is spinning me out. What you are saying makes total sense to me. Yes, I understand it now. What I think and feel, I *have* always created. That's true. And what I've believed in my gut has always come true, too.

Remember, if you sense it, then it's right. Always trust your inner senses. They will always point you toward your inner world. Your inner senses will reflect back to you what you see and feel inside.

What are our inner senses? Do you mean the five senses?

No. Our inner sensory perception is different. The outer senses of smell, touch, taste, vision and hearing enable you to interpret the outside world. They help to bring the outside world inside of you and make it real. However, the inner senses do the exact opposite. They help your inner world manifest into the outer reality. They enable the unseen and hidden potential that lies deep within you to express and manifest itself.

Let me get this right. We have another sense other than our five senses? You are clearly talking about the extra sixth sense, aren't you? I always thought that this was true.

No.

Oh, sorry. I could have sworn that we all had a sixth sense, an extra sense that helps us to perceive things that sit outside the known five senses. I always imagined that this extra sense enabled me to intuit and perceive the feelings going on inside my mother. I thought this sixth sense was an intuitive sense, one that enabled me a glimpse into tiny parts of my future. I'm shocked that it doesn't exist.

Way too much has happened to me to just explain away unusual phenomena as mere chance. There have been countless times when my gut instinct has led me to truths that I couldn't possibly have just guessed. I'm really disappointed.

Let me rescue you before you throw yourself down a hole.

There is no sixth sense as such. But there are several other senses that cannot be defined by scientific instruments or analyzing or measuring. These other, inner senses could be termed as ESP (extra sensory perception) because that's precisely what they are. These senses are extra to your normal perception. They are hidden senses that you perceive and become aware of as you gradually increase your awareness. Your consciousness. When you become more conscious, you throw a new light onto everything. You see more. You feel and perceive more.

That's a very good way of putting it. I like that.

Good. And perception is nothing more than a combination of all these hidden, inner senses brought together as one. So, in a sense, they could be referred to as pure, channelled senses. They are innocent, pure and free of corruption from the physical, outer senses.

You could say that these extra senses should really be your first sense. They should be the senses that you feel first because they interpret data before the known five senses kick in.

Perception and intuition are tools of the right brain, the artistic and creative side of the brain.

Can I ask you something? Why do you keep referring to them as hidden senses?

The inner universe of your inner world is hidden away. It is contained within you. Not outside of you. That is why another cannot measure this other world. It's subjective, and it is hidden from the rest of the world.

Nobody else can see this inner world or take it away from you. It is private to you alone. That is, until you choose to express it out into the physical world. Then you have shared it with others. You have poured the light of consciousness onto it.

Know that this inner world I am describing is connected to you at all times. It is within you and permeating through you.

Remember, life can not do for you what is not allowed to do through you. To do this, you must first be open to your inner universe. This hidden, inner universe connects all of you and everything. You may see it better in your mind if you visualize a gigantic web.

Yes, I can visualize it as one huge web.

That's it. An invisible web that connects, links, weaves, permeates and touches everything in not only the physical universe you witness, but also in the inner, unseen, unmanifested universe.

Do you mean parallel universe?

Yes, you could see it that way.

I think I'm spinning here. This inner universe that you describe, how does that relate to the inner senses you mentioned?

My dear, dear friend. The infinite possibilities of the universe lie deep within you in all ways and at all times. I wish you could realize that. Your inner senses are the channels that link who you think you are, in this physical world, to the infinite and abundant inner universe. It is this inner universe, your higher self, that is the real you. You are infinitely more than just a physical being.

But what *is* the inner universe?

The inner universe is a field of invisible energy and infinite potential that holds the physical universe in place. Deep within you, buried in every cell of your body, in every molecule of your being, in every atom of your brain, is a universe so vast, large and infinite that you could not comprehend it properly within your present earth-based understandings. It is the source of all creation and inspiration.

For now, settle with these concepts. The inner universe contains within it the creative seed of every possibility. You truly possess within you infinite capabilities of a magnitude that are hard to conceptualize. The inner senses you are gifted with at birth are simply the bridge to this inner universe of source energy.

You presently have several inner senses that link up your inner and outer worlds. They bridge your outer world (reality) with the inner world (infinite possibility). These inner senses are directly connected to the field of energy that vibrates through every living and non-living thing in the universe.

In both universes, the seen and unseen.

Yes, in both universes. The manifested and the unmanifested. Now, what the inner senses channel to you from the unmanifested, unseen and hidden universe is pure energy in the form of light, which, for the purpose of this understanding, I will simply term as inspiration, creativity, love/truth, imagination, insight and intuition. Of course, the universe is infinitely more complex than this simplistic terminology. And just as science is discovering ever new dimensions, so will more inner senses develop as we all evolve. But for now, it suits, within the construct of what I need to express, if we focus on these senses alone.

So intuition *is* a form of sixth sense then?

Yes, as are the other inner senses. Now, what these inward pointing senses channel to you, once you become conscious of them and call them forward, are fragments of energy from the unseen world. Let's call them essences.

Sorry?

It is easy to become bogged down in terminology here because words are so restricting in trying to explain the laws of the infinite. Therefore, I will keep this explanation as straightforward and as simple as possible.

Good, because this is beginning to confuse me.

An essence is the pure, concentrated element of the whole. It is but a fragment of source. The tiniest, yet most important element in the entire process of creation.

So, in your context, what is source?

Source is the infinite, creative energy of the universe. It is the unseen. The unmanifested. The divine. It is the infinite potential of the universe in energy form.

Let's use some visual images here that may help you to paint a more defined picture of creation.

Now, first of all, try seeing source as a larder that houses all the ingredients you would ever need to make every single possible meal imaginable. This larder is attached to a gigantic kitchen.

You could describe it as a kind of super-kitchen, with every kind of food available, where every meal is possible.

Good interpretation. But remember, not only are all the ingredients available, but also all the tools and kitchen utensils you would ever require. This enables the super-kitchen to cook up and create every conceivable dish. Everything is on the menu.

No orders turned down.

You have it. Now, the inner senses I have already described are all vital components in this process of creation. You could say that these senses are your serving staff. They bring these delicious orders right up to your table. You order it and hope, if you are aware, it will be delivered.

Of course, after half an hour waiting, you are so hungry that it matters little who actually serves you. You have ordered your meal, waited patiently, and now you just want to enjoy it. You don't care whether it is insight, creativity or inspiration that serves it up.

And you hope they deliver you exactly what you ordered.

Very interesting that you mentioned that. I will come back to that later.

As you are fully aware, due to occasional problems, your meal doesn't always turn up to your complete satisfaction. There are several things that can go horribly wrong. For example, you may not have conveyed your wishes succinctly or clearly enough to the waiter. There may be a slight misunderstanding between you and the person who has taken your order. Or, something may have been lost in the translation.

We may have forgotten to mention something. The steak I had ordered may have been undercooked because I forgot to inform the waiter that I hated blood spewing out.

There may be several reasons why your order has turned up wrong. Inevitably, it always comes down to a lack of communication somewhere between you and the restaurant server. Somewhere in the chain, not enough information has been exchanged. You may have presumed something or guessed that something will happen.

Or it may be my fault for ordering the wrong thing.

Yes, that's a possibility.
Now, what these six inner senses, your servers, do is act as the channel, the go-between. They bridge your intentions and orders with source, the kitchen. They link up, fetch and manifest your order. Not immediately, but in time.

If my intention has been correctly conveyed, the kitchen will create what I have ordered.

Yes, so long as everything comes together. But remember this also: The speed with which your meal is delivered depends solely on how complicated your meal was.
Now, try to imagine that every order you have ever given to the waiter is a thought or intention. Your thoughts are now your orders.
Let's for a moment lose the metaphor of a kitchen and replace it with the process of creation. We'll come back to it. Instead of a kitchen reproducing your orders, I want you to visualize the universal source delivering your intentions.

Yep, I have got it.

Now, ask yourself these questions: Would I ever order a meal that I couldn't stomach? Would I ever intentionally waste my time and money ordering something that I didn't wish to eat?

Of course not. Only someone out of their mind, or not concentrating properly, would do that.

Exactly. So, what would you think if I told you that most of your life has been spent ordering something that you unconsciously didn't want? What if I said most of your orders and intentions were made without any real idea of what you were ordering?

I would probably think you were mad. Why on earth would I order something that I didn't consciously want? It wouldn't make sense, would it?

I didn't say consciously want; I said unconsciously want. There is a profound difference here.

Well, why would I *unconsciously* order a meal that I didn't desire?

Because you were not fully aware that you had ordered it. Maybe the waiter had to guess what you wanted because you had not been present while the order was being taken.

I'm sorry. I don't follow where this is going.

Let me try to explain it another way. For the purpose of this explanation, I need you to use your imagination. Please picture yourself in a restaurant that serves food, whether you order it aloud or in your thoughts. If you are at the table when the waiter takes your order, then fine. You get to choose your exact intentions. The correct meal turns up. But if you are not present, the waiter throws an order in the kitchen on your behalf and asks the staff to create whatever is being dished up for everyone else. If you're not fully present, you don't get to choose.

87

Somebody else does. So the kitchen gets to decide?

Not entirely true. You are half-right. Yes, to a degree, those in the kitchen do decide what to create. But it is largely based on the intentions of everyone else in the restaurant. The conscious choices of other more conscious diners, unfortunately, determine your unconscious choices.

But if this happens and a meal turns up that I hate, it's obvious I simply wouldn't eat it.

Ah, but what if your life depended on it? What if this was the only meal to keep you alive that day? What if you had to eat what turned up?

Well, that's different. Then I would have to go along with the flow. I'd have to eat what everyone else had chosen. There would be no choice.

That is right. There would be no choice on your part.
Now imagine that this same scenario kept playing out. How long would it take you to realize that you must be present when the waiter comes and takes the order? How many times would you be prepared for others to make choices for you?

It wouldn't be long before I tired of eating other people's conscious choices.

It would certainly make you more conscious to look out for the waiter, wouldn't it? It would make you concentrate more and become aware of his movements.

Too right. Eating food that somebody else had picked wouldn't be my idea of free choice. I detest relying on others to make choices for me. It boxes me in and takes away my decision-making. I like to be in control.

I know you do.
What if I shocked you and said that you have not always been in full control of your life up to now? What would you say if I told you that

many other factors are influencing your life?

Substitute orders in a restaurant and replace them with thoughts in your head, and this is exactly how you have been ordering up your life intentions. You've been oscillating between full consciousness and unconsciousness. Awareness and no awareness.

You have occasionally been present enough to order what you wanted and have gotten the results—your intentions. The majority of the time, source energy has dealt you up what other people have ordered. You have had to digest the thoughts and intentions of others. And why? Because you were not fully present when others were placing their intentions.

That's how the majority of your life has been lived so far. It is not that you have always been making the wrong choices. The mistake, if you could term it that, is that you have sometimes not made any conscious choices at all.

Dying for a Change

Nineteen

*A*ll of my life, I thought that I had been the one in control. The decision-maker. The master of my own destiny. I could hardly believe what I was hearing.

Do you mean that I have gone along with the flow?

Yes.

No. I'm sorry. I dispute that profusely. That is simply not true. I always make my own decisions. I choose what to think, what to do and how I do it. I am the one in control of my life. I've even overheard some people say that I'm slanting toward being a control freak. I like to control the reins to everything. That is how I have achieved so much professional success—by calling my own shots.

Are you really in total control of your life? Do you really create every part of your reality?

Yes. Nearly all of my daily choices are *my* choices. At work, I decide what clients I am to visit and what orders I am to chase. I decide on business strategy, what my sales team is doing…

And what about the little time you spend with your family? Is it you who consciously decides what you will be doing with Alison and the girls on those weekends when you are home?

Well, no, not exactly. But then, I am frantically rushing around all week. I'm usually away. So it's left to Alison to arrange our social life. I just go along with the flow.

From what you are saying then, you only consciously choose the events of your daily working life?

Yes. I think that is fair to say.

So what about your sales clients around the country?

What about them?

Don't they have a strong pull on where you travel throughout the working week? Don't their intentions for you have a major influence on your days? If a top client, spending a million pounds a year, rings you up, don't you usually drop everything for him?

That's different. The business generated from taking their orders is directly attributed to keeping our company afloat. I have to maintain that business at all costs. It's everything to my office, and I do a great job looking after my clients. That's why I pull in so much work. Anyway, dropping everything for them is what makes me a good salesperson. They trust that when a problem arises, I'll always be there to resolve it. I'm reliable, and they know it.

Look deeply at your own language. The essence of truth imbued into your message can be depicted from only a few of your chosen words.

Sorry?

Scrutinize the words that you choose carefully because the language we "put out there" and the tone we use very often contain a hidden, more succinct message. You could say there is another, deeper meaning between the lines to everything we say.
In your own words, you told me that you were "taking their orders." Flip that statement around and extract another meaning from it. Does

that not now imply that the intentions of others are pulling you in an alternative direction?

That's not fair. We all, at some time in our lives, have to go along with the intentions of others. We have to follow the intentions of other organizations, people, governments, the company who employs me…the list is endless. And isn't a huge part of our lives dedicated to giving service to others? Helping and assisting them? We are serving their intentions for a good reason then, aren't we?

I agree. We do live most of our lives honoring the intentions of other people. Compassion, love and empathy are good examples of how we react to the needs and intentions of others. In fact, if we did not follow our intuition and are sometimes led by the intentions of others, life would become meaningless. We would soon become detached from the world.

I'm not disputing that we must, at some time, be led by the intentions of others. Service to another is a key element in what it means to feel human. It is the glue that holds humanity together. My point is this: Do we constantly challenge where we are being led? Do we continually question the underlying intentions of others? Do we let our emotions, and those of others, manipulate our lives? And, finally, do we analyze where our beliefs originate from?

Oh, I get what you mean. You are asking whether we are fully conscious of our life choices. You are asking me to consciously question *my* motivations and intentions, in the context of other people's intentions. Have I got it right?

You are fully conscious and correct. That is exactly my point.

Ask yourself, in all ways, am I fully aware of the true intentions all around me? Am I being conscious of what is inspiring those intentions? These are two vital questions that you should constantly be reassessing.

Never just accept what another's truth is showing you until you have filtered it through your own feelings. Your own truth. Question everything. All of it.

But if I constantly questioned everything that was ever said to me, I would go mad. I need to have some trust in the world.

You misunderstand my point. I'm not saying that you should not trust another. Trust is the bedrock of a compassionate, sane and civil society. I'm asking you to contemplate this: Whenever a statement or truth is given to you by another, do not swallow it whole. Digest it first. Look at it. Analyze it. And then, if it feels right, make it part of your own truth. Embrace it into your own heart.

I like that. Never swallow it whole. That is a very good point. You are so right. When I was younger and very impressionable, if I trusted people implicitly, I tended to swallow whole everything that they were telling me. I made the mistake of not filtering it first. Because I respected and admired them, I believed everything that they told me. But it is easy being drawn in by someone you love, trust and respect.

It is because as human beings we need to trust certain elements that make up our world. We need to believe that certain truths are sacred. That certain wisdom is universal. Trust and love are the pillars that bond us together and instill hope.

But here is a fundamental truth that belongs to everyone: Believing and trusting the inherited beliefs of others without first running those beliefs past your own "filter" is a blasphemy of the highest order. It is a blasphemy that robs and suffocates your own power and your own intentions.

Blind faith does not mean giving away your power and integrity. It doesn't entail handing over your truth to anyone, no matter how much you love, trust and respect him or her.

Therefore, always go inward first. No matter how reliable a source appears, first listen to your own inner voice.

What do you mean by "inner voice"?

The still and calm voice of your conscience. This is the most accurate guide you have. It is your compass. Your truth-teller.

Always listen first to the voice in your heart, and then go with your instincts.

Instincts and intuition are one of the same. They lead you to your truth and not the truths of others. They demonstrate this with the vibrations in your body, your emotions. This is your absolute truth.

Now here is something that will shock and astound you: Do not believe anything I am saying here…

Pardon? Do not believe anything you say? That is a very strange statement to make. What am I doing wasting my time if I am not to believe anything you say?

I have not finished.

Do not believe anything I am telling you until you have first run this wisdom through your own internal filter. Only then will new emerging truths become your truths, and not just inherited truths.

Remember, "truth" is subjective. As I have already intimated, truth depends on where you are standing in any given situation. It is dependent on your perspective and how you see the world.

There are six billion human beings on this blue planet. In the forthcoming 21st century, there will be more than eight billion. That is eight billion windows on the world, each with a completely different perspective on life.

Know that no one person's thinking is ever the same. We all see life in many different ways, and yet we are still one of the same. The very same matter that is in trees, air, nature, the earth and fire is exactly the same composition that is found within you and me.

I believe much of what you are saying. Truth depends on where we are standing in the equation at any given time.

Good, but let me add this: Do not believe it. Feel it.

Feelings will always lead you to your absolute truth in any given life situation. And if you cannot feel it, go deep inside yourself and listen to the voice of your conscience. Shut out all outside influences and run it through your filter. Then gauge, from your own feelings, how another's truth feels. Does it feel life-sustaining, light, loving and right? Does it have a ring of truth to it? Or does someone else's truth feel heavy, dark and manipulative?

Always apply this principle to everything. Remember, respect your internal space. All ways. Do not let anyone infect your energy. Honor your energy and space by filtering everything that comes into your life. Become conscious of what truths you are making your own. Be the conscious gate-keeper. Be alert, and let nothing past without first scrutinizing it.

Practice this often and, before long, you will become intuitive to what truths to let into your space. You will learn to trust your own inner guidance. You will become a master of discernment.

And then we will know what truths to make our own.

Beautifully put.
Please understand what I am shining a light on. Challenging, analyzing and questioning are not the same as doubting. It simply means that you first trust the internal compass of your own conscience, ahead of anything else.

But there are many established religions and institutions that don't want their "truths" questioned. They don't want their truths held up to the light and scrutinized.

That has been true for many millennia. That has been the case throughout history.

And look where those ideologies have taken us. They've subdued much of what is beautiful about the human race. Ideology has robbed individuals of their own minds. It has driven us down dead-ends, where every religion believes its way is the only way.

This is linked to what we are talking about here. When people learn to go within and listen to their own wisdom, they empower themselves. When they honor their own truths, ahead of the truths of others, their lives blossom.
True freedom is freedom of the mind, not just the body.

I'm now beginning to understand that I don't control my life like I first imagined I did. I'm beginning to wonder how much of my own life I *actually* have controlled in the past. This revelation is pretty frightening. Those who are weak-minded could easily be manipulated like puppets on a string. They could feel disempowered, lost and confused.

I now see how easy it is for some people to be swept along with the flow. If someone claims to have the ultimate truth, then it's easy to be carried by the surge. I know because I have done it myself.

Always be wary of those claiming to own the absolute truth. Truth is subjective. It is a personal practice. That is not to say that one truth cannot vibrate throughout a whole race. It simply means that all truths should be filtered and tried on for size.

If ever in doubt, always ask yourself: How does this truth feel for me?

Twenty

I needed to clear something up, to get more clarity on all this "truth" business.

How can we decipher what voice is leading us to our own highest truth? Like most people, I have an inner dialogue going on in my head, telling me what to do. Some of this dialogue is needy and wanting. It criticizes and condemns.

Yet, other times, my inner dialogue is compassionate and loving. It is supportive and caring. How do I know which voice will lead me to *my* truth? How can I differentiate between good guidance and bad guidance? It is hard enough to decide what outside influences to take in and believe without wondering what inner dialogue to choose. Please help me out here.

The static, or mind chatter, that constantly rolls through your head is a combination of all your thoughts, feelings and beliefs. Some of the thoughts are positive and feel good; others are self-criticizing and negative. Some of these thoughts empower you. Yet many others make you believe that you are inadequate and small.

The key, when listening to this inner dialogue, is to watch for how it makes you feel. Be conscious of all the feelings in your body. By conscious, I mean become aware. Scan your awareness all over your body. See what vibrations, or vibes, your body is giving out or picking up. If you hear a negative voice rolling through your mind, go deeper into it and watch for the associated feeling. All thoughts mirror and project a corresponding feeling in the body. This is because all thoughts are energy, and this energy is being imprinted on your cellular system.

So that's how we pick up sensations in the body then. The cells inside of us are being stamped by the energy of a thought.

More than stamped. The imprint of energy entering your body and energy system is actually vibrating your cells. It is causing the energy to vibrate at great speeds, and in doing so, it triggers off a message.

A bit like a bell ringing?

Well-described. That is a great image to use. I like that. Your cells are chiming to a different vibration, depending on what frequency your thoughts are moving on.

This is all fascinating. You are explaining it so a child could understand it. I wish I could be as articulate.

You are. You are the one filling in the gaps here. It is you who are partnering with me and making sense of this. You and I are one of the same. We are but two essences of the same whole. There is no separation between us. We are joined and yet also separate. We are two, and yet, at the same time, one.

You are not making sense here. I feel like I am going around in circles.

Please be patient. There is nothing wrong with going around in circles. Life is one huge circle. The seasons follow a circle. There is a paradox going on here, which I will explain further into our delicious conversation. For now, I will leave you with the knowledge that you and I are connected. Know that we are one totality of two separate fragments.

You have got me thinking.

Please, do not think. It is better to feel. Feelings are your truth. Thoughts are everyone else's truth.
I want to pull in the thread. So, whenever we internalize a truth, watch to see whether you feel anything inside your body. Observe your senses, your emotions and your feelings. Look for a subtle change in your energy flow.

You mean, watch for the ringing bell.

Yes. What you are observing is to see whether the cells are resonating throughout your body. This may appear as a shiver down the spine or a sudden cold sensation in the body. You may even sense an instant hit of elation or joy. It may feel like an "aha moment."
Does what I am saying make sense to you? Resonate with you?

Yes, perfect sense. I know what you are describing. I feel it.

Good.

I'll give you an example. There have been plenty of times when I have been bulldozed over by a truth that I categorically know to be true. Don't ask me to explain how I know. I just do. It's as if every cell in my body is shouting, "Yes!" I know that to be absolutely correct. You are right. When this "aha moment" suddenly happens, I must admit, it freaks me out. I don't know what to make of it. It's as if every bone and cell in my body *is* ringing a truth bell.

But hang on a moment. Didn't you say that we should always use our discernment? Didn't you imply that we should be careful, that we should filter all truths first? If I accept the truth from another without thinking it through, then I am not honoring my own truth.

Now here comes the miracle of this whole process: Your feelings are your filter. That is what informs you whether a truth resonates with you. When you have that "aha moment," your body, through your feelings, is really saying to you, "Yes, I know that to be true." There is no question whatsoever.
Now, there is only one thing that can sabotage this extraordinary sixth-sense perception. There is only one faculty that can make you doubt what you have felt inside your body.

Thinking. My thoughts usually kick in at this point and begin questioning, doubting, criticizing. "Ignore that initial hit," they will say. "Let go of that instinctual feeling."

You are right because your thinking is based on information collected from past experiences and from other people. Your thoughts view any new data coming in as suspicious. So, if they do not resonate with any previous thought patterns, they will want to ignore any new information.

Intuition uses your hidden senses to communicate energy data, and it is the vibration of cells in your body that leads you toward a new truth.

Know that your body is one huge receiver and transmitter. This is what we are talking about here, the extraordinary ability we all have to transmit and receive energy—in the form of tiny, light data particles. The cells that make up your energy system are all communicating with one another. They are blending, exchanging and swapping.

So our bodies are not a set of chemical reactions all firing off? We're not just an evolutionary accident?

No, of course not. Did you really think for one moment that everything you see in the world is a biological accident? Do you honestly believe that the universe is nothing more than dead matter, a lifeless, detached, unintelligent cosmic soup that has evolved by sheer chance?

I don't know what to think. When I was at school, I felt very uncomfortable with the notion that the universe was viewed as a machine. I remember being taught a very lifeless form of science, which had led me to believe that everything in the universe had evolved by chance. It taught me that the universe, which included earth, was nothing more than a combination of well-oiled, separate parts. I know that this forms the basic tenet of science, but I just couldn't agree. To me, this meant that we were completely separate from everything that was going on throughout the universe.

Needless to say, I flunked most of my science papers at exam time. And when it came to leaving school at sixteen, I never even collected my results.

Can you remember your science teacher?
Yes, vividly. I can picture him now.

What do you remember most?

A few things come to mind straight away. On the first day of the term, he made a point of sharing his personal beliefs with the whole class. I think it was his way of putting a marker down in the sand. One of the initial things he said was that the universe had to be viewed as a machine, and that everything contained within this machine was a separate object. This, he said, was how science had formed a solid foundation to build on. Then he said something extraordinary that really annoyed me, something that I just felt in my heart was not true. With conviction and without flinching, he said that all humans sat outside the fabric of the universe. He said that we looked in on the universe and were detached from it.

I remember being incensed. After several of the experiences I had had as a child, I simply knew this wasn't true. How could we sit outside the universe? That belief was ridiculous. We were part of the cosmos, not separated from it. We lived in it, not just observed it.

I think my curiosity and interest for all things scientific died that day. I couldn't re-ignite the passion I once had for science. It all seemed so clinical, cold and detached. Everything I was being taught seemed so empty and passionless. I simply couldn't go along with his lifeless interpretation. Even the experiments were sterile. They demonstrated nothing to me about why we are here or what our ultimate purpose is in life.

You should have spoken up for your truth. If you felt strongly enough about your beliefs, you should have dared to challenge your teacher's theories.

Hiding our truth in the shadows and never bringing it up to the light always makes us feel small. And, in time, if that same truth is not expressed fully, it will manifest itself into rage, resentment, hatred and anger.

Always remember that our inner feelings have a voice that cries out to be heard and acknowledged. Contain that voice, and you contain yourself.

Believe me, I tried to challenge our science teacher at first, and so did two other girls in the class. They both had similar feelings about science to those of my own.

In our first few lessons, we tried confronting that teacher after the class had finished. We wanted to put our point across. We wanted our questions answered.

And what did your science teacher say? Did he listen to how you all felt? Did he respect what you all had to say and then debate the theories with you?

Not likely. He was arrogant to the last and said that it was not right to bring mysticism, faith and the supernatural into a classroom of science. He said that religion, God and miracles had no part to play in the debate. Only then could science get down to the "proper" work. His final comment on the matter was very peculiar. I can recall it as if it were only yesterday. He stated that science shouldn't ever grant religion a foot in the door of inquiry because if it did, who knows what would happen.

And what impression did his attitude leave on you?

Confusion. I was confused and horrified that our teacher was so narrow-minded. I know that he was honest from the very beginning by stating that he was an atheist. But I was still shocked by his lack of desire for debate. He just wasn't interested in listening to the opinions of three inquisitive fifteen-year-olds. His excuse was that the curriculum didn't afford the time to open up our searching questions for debate. We thought that was very strange, especially considering that since day one, our teacher had lamented how science should be built on open-minded inquiry, measurement and observation.

I honestly don't think he realized that he was demonstrating the very same behavior that he venomously opposed. He criticized fundamentalists and religious leaders for bigotry, and yet he was replicating the very same principles. By dismissing the morals of others without examining the facts, he put himself on the exact same level. My friend had a nickname for him: the scientific fundamentalist.

It was good that you stood up for what you believed. Honoring your true feelings will always empower you. It will always lead you to the truth inside of you.

That whole experience left a deep impression on me. I may have been only fifteen at the time, but the teacher's arrogance got me thinking. What if all other science teachers were also closed-minded? Did that mean that any alternative questions, challenging the status quo, were to be ridiculed? Would that mean that no new opinions would be listened to and respected? The whole idea horrified me. It all seemed so constricting.

You were perfectly correct to challenge the existing paradigm. Always analyze the truth of everything, regardless of how long that truth has been set in stone. A truth borne from yesterday does not necessarily mean it is a truth for today. Truth is no different from all other forms of evolution. It changes and alters over time. It is not a fixed state.

Twenty-One

I was beginning to get a little clearer on the whole concept of "truth," but there were still some things that were a puzzle to me.

I've given you a great example of when I *did* stand up for my truth as a child, but it wasn't always that clear-cut. There were plenty of other times when I *didn't* express my truth. I was afraid of what others may say, so I kept my mouth shut and said nothing. Looking back, I now wish that I would have had more courage to speak up for myself. I wish I'd found the confidence to share some of my extraordinary experiences with others. Who knows, some of my friends may have had very similar life experiences.

I feel as if I have let myself down badly. I shouldn't have pushed what happened to me to the back of the file. It was wrong to run away from my experiences and deny them. But I did. And now I'm deeply ashamed of my actions.

Let me pour all the love I have onto you. Let me shine a torch onto your path. Please, do not give yourself a hard time. And certainly don't pour shame all over your actions. You did what you did. You are who you are.

Nobody, I repeat, nobody is perfect. And even if a person was, what would be his or her calling in life? What would be the purpose to his or her life if there were no hurdles to overcome? The most profound and educating growth comes at those times when we face adversity.

Please take this divine truth to your heart. Embrace it and hold it close to you. We are all here in physical form to remember our own magnificence. We are here, on planet earth, to grow and evolve as human beings.

Real growth of the soul can only happen when you are challenged with obstacles to overcome. Growth does not blossom from the safe and mundane, nor does it flower from the seeds of fear. Remember, all growth begins on the edge of your comfort zone. That is where your potential opens up. That is where the spring of your life begins.

Thank you for that. I know that I shouldn't be so hard on myself. I have always been my own harshest critic. In some ways, it has driven me on. It has motivated me to reach for the skies. But, in other ways, my self-condemnation has made me feel deeply inadequate. The tiny, critical dialogue in my head has constantly chattered to me that I must strive to be the best. That I must fight for everything. That I must constantly stay ahead.

And tell me, how does that make you feel?

Exhausted. I am becoming more irritable and tired. Fighting to hold onto everything I have achieved, literally, wears me down. It was fine when I was in my twenties, but recently, I feel like my whole body is beginning to burn out. I feel like a nervous wreck. I'm constantly anxious and stressed.

I'm struggling to continue to keep up with all the obscene hours I have to work. I'm finding it more and more difficult to concentrate. What's particularly shocking is that my enthusiasm for the job is ebbing away. I no longer have the passion I once had for my career.

I don't know what to make of this sudden change. Hating my job is so not me. I've always been the one who is married to his work. I'm the person who is out the door early and back home late.

I'm running scared that my life is beginning to come apart at the seams. I feel so afraid and paranoid. I feel so disconnected and alone. I'm not sure who I can turn to.

Have you openly talked about how you feel? Have you brought your real feelings up to the surface and discussed this with friends or close colleagues?

No. And what's even more frustrating is that I haven't even had the courage to tell Alison how I am feeling. She's busy with the children and her own business. The last thing I want to do is burden her with even more worries. And, anyway, I'm not so sure that I could articulate my true feelings even if I tried. I've had so many years of repressing them that I'm not certain where to begin.

If you cannot let your own wife know how you're feeling, who else is there?

No one. I have a couple of really close friends, but even so, they are male. My great fear is that they may not understand. In my profession, it is not the done thing to empty out your inner world. Clients and friends wouldn't want to know about *my* problems. They want to see a happy-go-lucky, cheery me. They like to know that there is someone close to them who is balanced and holding it together. That's why many of my clients like me calling on them. I listen to all their problems and give them an alternative viewpoint. A few top clients have even said that I would make a great counselor. They tell me that I am a very good listener.

So the world pours their problems out onto your lap. Yet who is there to help heal your emotional blockages? Who is there to listen to your problems?

Nobody, so I choose the only alternative. I keep it all bottled up. I try not to think about it too much. I think that's why I have become more addicted to the drinking and taking drugs. They help me to calm down. They enable me to accept my life situation and shut it all out.

And do you really accept the way it is? Are you happy for this denial to continue?

No, but I have no choice. I have to grin and bear it. There are orders to find and bills to pay. Anyway, that's what I do best. Grin and bear it. I put up and shut up. I just get on with living my life.

Please, let me assure you of one undeniable fact. There are always conscious choices to be made. There are always solutions. Healing is only ever one step away. Putting up with your life situation in this manner is definitely not living your life. It is certainly not life-fulfilling or life-sustaining. Living and existing are not one and the same. Merely existing disconnects you from your emotions. Living abundantly taps you into your emotions.

Do you not realize that denying how you feel traps negative energy in your body? It blocks your life flow and makes you ill.

Know that hiding how you feel under a smiling face is only a temporary cosmetic fix. I know that you are a positive thinker. You always have been, but positive thinking is only one level of your everyday reality. And if positive thoughts are not built on a solid foundation, then they are nothing more than an illusory veneer.

You may have imagined that you can continually keep painting over your problems with the gloss of a smile. You may well be able to cover up your feelings with a laugh. But, sooner or later, your true emotions will break through because truth always finds the surface. Emotion is always drawn to the light.

I now feel so stupid. I should have been more honest about my extraordinary childhood experiences. And I should have been more open with my emotions.

Please, do not feel stupid. It is better that you feel enlightened. Significantly more people hide away from their life story than you would ever imagine. There are friends close to you whose real life stories would astound you if the truth be known. Everybody has a fascinating story to share. That story is called life.

Never underestimate what is going on under the surface of a seemingly calm pond.

I instantly thought about my father when you said that. He was brilliant at papering over the cracks. Nobody had a clue what was going on under the surface. Now that I'm older, I fully acknowledge that my father's behavior was similar to my own behavior. He, too, was good at disguising his true emotions.

You inherited more than his genes. Many of his characteristics and emotional hang-ups also live on through you, waiting to be healed.

Yes, I'm beginning to acknowledge that. I have the same short fuse, and I also find it difficult switching off from my work. It worries me that my children will inherit my emotional tendencies. I'm concerned that they will suffer the identical fate of *my* erratic behavior. I mean, come on, where does it end? Does the emotional baton keep being passed along the line? Does each generation have to suffer the mistakes of their ancestors? And why must it be this way? Why can't children be given a clean slate when they come into the world? It doesn't seem fair.

I can see that you are angry.

Well, I am. It's not right that our children should have to suffer the karma of *our* mistakes. What should they do to change this around?

Heal the space that they have come into. Fill the gaps that still need to be resolved.

Sorry, I don't understand what you are implying.

I will repeat what I said. Heal the space that they have purposely come into this earth to heal.

I think we are going in circles again.

Life is one continuous circle. You have asked me a question, and I have answered it. If your children want to heal the emotional trauma that has been accumulated by past generations, then they need to heal the space that is around their own lives. They need to break the chain.

I don't get what you mean by "healing the space."

The gaps those previous generations have not healed. Almost every family has accumulated trauma from the past. This denied emotional

111

blockage has been building through generations. It has remained dormant like a volcano waiting to erupt. In the past, these denied emotions could be ignored. They could be covered up, packaged up and therefore not brought to the surface. But that behavior can no longer be sustained.

Why? What is so different about today?

We are now living in changing times. And, as a consequence, our emotions are rising to the surface. As a race, we are truly coming-of-age. You could say that we are now entering the emotional age, a time when we all have the opportunity to heal the misgivings of the past.

The consciousness of planet earth is evolving onto new levels, and as an integral part of that interconnected system, so, too, are human beings.

It was fine for emotions to be repressed and denied in the past. Much of the planet was living unconsciously. People were not aware of their immense creative potential. They were too busy just living and surviving.

But a radical shift is now under way. New levels of consciousness are forming. New ways of thinking are developing. We are slowly but surely beginning to realize that there is infinitely more to the world than we ever imagined. We are awakening to the fundamental truth that the world resonates with us.

This sounds like exciting times, but there is something troubling me. What happens if the emotional difficulties passed down to me aren't healed? What would happen to my children and their children if I were to continue holding back my emotions?

Then your children would simply inherit these issues themselves. And if they ignored them, then it would be passed on down the line.

But wouldn't that make their lives more difficult? Wouldn't *my* ignorance make them suffer more emotional turmoil?

Yes, if that is what you choose.

Well, I don't choose any of it. I would much prefer that they escaped inheriting any of my shortcomings or dysfunctions. I would prefer that any emotional difficulties I had inherited would skip a generation.

But can you not see the process? If your emotional hurdles bypassed your children, and sometimes they do, do you not see that it would then be left to your grandchildren to heal the space left behind? You may not be aware that all denied emotion travels down through the generations, but it does. No emotion just disappears because all emotion is energy. And emotion cannot just dissolve. It has to transform and bring itself out into the light. If you want to deny any of the emotional shortcomings that you've inherited, then fine. But know this: Someone down the line will have to become the healer. A relative of yours will, at some time, be required to resolve any emotional issues.

We are living through changing times. The approaching century offers us the unique opportunity to evolve onto all new levels. But this extraordinary period is also fraught with danger. We presently live in a paradox like no other. On the one hand, these changes could usher in untold opportunities for personal and planetary growth. It is a time when we could become co-creators of infinite possibility, one that is full of imagination and hope. And yet, on the other hand, we are also on the brink of social and environmental catastrophe.

Twenty-Two

I didn't know whether to feel enlightened or threatened by the comment that we could be "on the brink of social and environmental catastrophe." This was pretty scary stuff.

Can you please expand on something for me? What are you referring to by "changing times?"

There are several earth descriptions that best explain this process. Please choose one that resonates with you. Choose one that feels most comfortable.

You can term this transformational period a New Age. The coming age of emotions. The Aquarian age. You may see this changing period as a new evolutionary period, or an evolution of consciousness. The language you choose matters not. What's important is that you fully appreciate that we are now reaching a quantum leap in our evolutionary potential. We have now arrived on the cusp of a new century when humans could rediscover their true creative power. In the next one hundred years, life is about to reveal its most intimate secrets, but only once we all heal our emotional problems from the past. To do this requires that we all bring our emotions out into the light. Only then can the issues from the past be healed.

But how can my children and I reverse this destructive trend? How can we heal the emotional problems that we have not only created ourselves, but also those of past generations?

Heal your emotions in your lifetime, and you will break the cycle. If you want to cut the shackles of a certain emotional difficulty in the family, simply heal it. Break the bond and sever the ties. Then the spell is broken.

Spell? You make it sound like someone or something has cast a spell on us.

In truth, there is no spell. I am using language that will help bring you to absolute clarity. The only issues that you have ever been left with to resolve are those issues that your family members have passed down to you. If you would have taken the time to research your family's background, on both your mother's side and father's side, then many of the truths would have been revealed. The truth is always there waiting to be uncovered. We just have to look.

So a lot of the issues I have been dealing with throughout my life have been handed down to me from my father?

Not just him alone. The mistake, if you could term it that, is to presume that you only inherit your characteristics from your parents. To a degree, that is correct. But it is not painting the full picture. Considerably more of what you would refer to as your character traits or personality flaws have actually been passed onto you at birth. More emotional issues than you realize have been passed down by the lives of those several generations back.

Let me give you some personal examples. Your temperament, as you are already aware, has evolved from your father's side of the family. It's the same for your ability to listen to all sides of the story and be compassionate. These, plus your inability to share your emotions openly with others, have all evolved from several different family members on your father's side.

Now on your mother's side, you have inherited your willingness to overcome adversity. Your inner strength, tenacity, stubbornness and desire to succeed have all trickled down this way.

This is incredible. From what you are telling me, we are born with the seeds of these emotional issues woven into us, and we come into the world with set hurdles already waiting for us

116

to jump. But on the positive side, I could resolve many of the questions I had about certain emotions by simply going back and studying my family tree. By discovering what emotional issues tripped up certain relatives from the past, I could, in fact, find the keys to some of my own locks.

This has always been the case. Ancient cultures understood this principle, which is why they honored their elders as the wise members of society. This is why storytelling was such an important part of life for many. The wisdom gained enabled the younger tribal members to have insight into what characteristics were likely to reappear within them.

Sadly, many people today do not even live close to other family members, let alone talk about their ancestral past. You cannot heal the traumas and emotional hang-ups of the past if you do not afford yourself the time to listen to your family's history.

This is all fascinating. I am already linking several emotional issues of my own with those of other family members I have known about from the past. You are right, it does align. I've never thought about this before.

The indigenous peoples of the past honored and respected their family's history. That is why storytelling was such a profound way of learning about the present. It was a mirror, pre-warning the younger members of a tribe what characteristics they were likely to inherit.

Because certain family members would be mirroring back to their young many of the emotional issues that they would have to resolve.

Precisely. See, you are getting it.

But it all sounds too simple.

Life can be as testing or as simple as you wish to make it. The choice is always there for the taking. Know that you are the one doing the choosing. You are the one deciding what emotional blockages you want to heal. All I am pointing out is that if you wanted to make your life easier, look back because many of the answers about life that you have constantly asked yourself are already buried in the past. In our recent past, the history of our deceased relatives has been, by and large, ignored. But all of that is about to change. The twenty-first century will be different altogether. There will be an explosion of interest in tracing back, what you refer to as, a family tree.

You haven't completely answered all of my questions. How is it fair that some children inherit massive emotional difficulties from their parents and ancestors?

Fairness has nothing to do with it. As I've said previously, it is as it is. Heal the space, and your children will break the chain.
Unless they don't.

What do you mean by "unless they don't?"

Everybody has free will. It is up to each individual whether he or she chooses to heal the emotional problems of his or her past and present. If the responsibility becomes too unbearable, which it often can, then it simply passes on down the line.

So they pass on the baton?

Yes. That is a very good way of depicting it. Families do indeed pass on the baton of unresolved emotional difficulties to those at the end of the chain. Remember this, for it is one of the most insightful and simplistic truths that you will ever bring into your conscious understanding.
All energy of emotion must transform itself into something. This is one of the basic, and yet, sadly, most misunderstood laws of the creative universe. Take this fundamental truth on board, and you will be a step closer to understanding the divine process of creation. Embrace this simple fact, and you will come to realize that no emotion ever disappears. It simply transforms itself into another state.

I've just had a thought. What happens if generation after generation failed to heal their addictions and emotional trauma? What would happen if my trapped, denied emotion just kept piling up?

What do you think?

I think my children, their children and so on would have more issues to deal with, on top of what they need to face on their own. The unfortunate generation at the end of the line would have to suffer my emotional neglect.

That is correct.

If this is true, then I can't believe I have been so irresponsible to my children. What on earth was I thinking?

Fundamentally, that is the problem. You weren't thinking anything. You were unconscious to this truth. Please, do not be so hard on yourself. You did not have the light of consciousness to shine on this issue. Now that you do know, what would it change in your life? How would you live your life differently now that you are aware of this universal truth?

It would change everything. For starters, I would spend considerably less time burying my head in the sand. And I'd stop closing my eyes to those character flaws that haven't served me well.

So you honestly believe that it would change your behavior?

Most definitely. I would want to give my children the best chances in life. I don't want to hinder them with emotional baggage that I have picked up and denied.

I want to believe what you are saying, but a tiny part of me is still skeptical.

Please, do not just believe me. Belief is only one foundation stone in the process of personal change. Instead, experience it for yourself. Experience everything you are taught in life, and only then will the truth become real.

If you delved deep into your own family history, you would clearly see for yourself what is happening here. There is an easy-to-follow process going on. That process is life being passed through you and not to you.

Some of the behaviors that you adopt are learned responses. They are taught to you by your parents and other external sources, including social conditioning. But most are not. The majority of emotions that you demonstrate in later life are actually inherited characteristics from any one of your past relatives.

As I have already informed you, the energy of your emotions only ever changes form. It never disappears. That is why you have inherited some of what you see as unfavorable characteristics from your father. You are now the one holding the baton. You have come into the space to heal the space. The spotlight is now on you, so what do you choose? Who do you wish to be? Will you pass on your denied and trapped emotions to your daughters, or will you be the one who finally brings them to light?

You've suddenly made it seem so clear. Of course, I would want to heal my own emotional issues. Who in his right mind would want to burden his children further? In today's world, there are enough problems to overcome. The last thing my children need is me making their lives all the more difficult.

You are now seeing the whole picture from a higher perspective. That is good. It proves that your level of consciousness is increasing. To become more conscious of your world shows that you are looking at life from alternative angles. There is no better way to align this new consciousness than to be honest and open about your real emotions. Understand and therefore express your emotions fully, and you will do more than just bring more awareness into your presence. You will also discover the magic route to your soul, which is the essence of who you are.

Even if I did change my bad habits straight away and honor all my unexpressed emotion, nothing would change. The genes within my children have already been set. From what you are telling me, some of their inherited behaviors have already been cast.

Not true. Contrary to what is believed in science, your genes are not fixed. The intelligence woven into this blueprint is not a constant. Far from it. Just as your consciousness evolves, and just as you mentally

120

grow throughout life, so your genetics alter. Nothing inside your body, on an energy level, ever remains static. It is all in a constant dance of refining, adapting and altering. On a finite level of creating, your genes and cells in the brain and body are constantly evolving and changing. You are not the same person you were yesterday.

Please do not despair over the fate of your children. The process of energy transference, via emotions, is far more complex than you presently conceive. Just because your denied emotions have been passed to them through their DNA doesn't mean that your changes in behavior cannot influence their lives. Remember, we are talking on a level of energy here, not just on a biological level.

I don't think I follow. If the dye has been cast on their DNA, then surely my emotional "defects," and those of my ancestors, have already been passed on. I have already "infected" my children with my toxic energy.

Here is the miracle I will share with you about this process. Healing your own emotions still has an enormous influence on both their DNA and their emotions. Resolving your emotional problems can still help your children to heal theirs because it is never too late to heal your body at a cellular level.

Know that on an energetic and cellular level, we are all connected. We are all one. Yes, that may sound too holistic and New Age for you. And if it does, I apologize. But it doesn't take away the core truth that all energy in some way or another is deeply connected.

Dying for a Change

Twenty-Three

*T*his conversation was literally blowing my mind away. He had such a brilliant way of describing what could be confusing concepts. Fortunately, he had more to say…

Understanding how the energetic building blocks of the universe fit together can be as simple or as complicated as you wish. Do you wish to perceive life as a set of mysteries never to be told? Or would you much prefer that you were given the golden keys to universal laws? The choice as to what path you choose in life is always yours to make. Enlightenment or confusion? Elation or frustration? In every moment, it is you who decides.

Know that everything in the universe is connected to a field of energy. Know that all energy is entangled. Stick to this absolute truth, and all the laws of the universe will suddenly become more apparent.

That would suggest that whatever we do to others, we do to ourselves, wouldn't it? If we are all linked to an interconnected web of energy, then surely everyone would feel the vibrations of one another, wouldn't they?

Yes, they do. But only those who are consciously aware of this will sense the vibes of others. When you have picked up the vibes of your mother in the past, you are connecting to her by means of this web. That is how you were able to sense her emotions. Your sensory instruments were tuning in to her senses, giving you the impression that her emotions were actually your emotions. When this intricate psychic bonding first occurs, it can be confusing. You can easily become confused as to whose emotions belong to whom.

That is right. To begin with, when it first happened, I didn't know how to interpret these alien emotions filling my body. I struggled to decipher my emotions from the ones my mother emitted. I couldn't understand why I was going to school fraught with worry. After all, I was only eleven years old and barely old enough to be experiencing the type of panic attacks I was having.

But you knew that something peculiar was going on?

Yes, I knew within days of the feelings starting to appear. There were other signs, such as waking up in the middle of night. I knew this was strange because, up until that point, I had slept perfectly well. Those first few occasions, I was paranoid that I was having a heart attack or something. Waking up at two or three in the morning, my heart would feel as if it was about to break out of my pajamas. I would break into a sweat and become all flustered. Then the other feelings would come on. From nowhere, my neck and throat would start burning. My back would ache, and I would feel sick. It was usually at that point that I would get up and see Mum pacing up and down in the living room, smoking a cigarette.

There is something else that has also confused me since I was a child. I don't know why, but every time I trawled up memories about these experiences, the same feelings would return. This has mystified me ever since. I would only have to remember brief glimpses of this period in my life and, bang, all the pain would come rushing back to me. The aches, pains, heart flutters. Everything. How could this be?

We all have the innate ability to bring the past alive inside of us. We are all born knowing that the past is not just some distant point never to be returned to. If you become absolutely conscious of details from a past memory, then it is possible to feel the emotions of the past. In your case, the emotions from nearly twenty-five years ago.

But how is that possible?

Because all emotion is a living energy that is imprinted on your cellular system. Just as your DNA code is woven into your genetic makeup, so are the emotions from your past woven into you. Every emotion that you have ever felt can be revisited if you so wish.

I'm not sure that I would want to keep revisiting old emotions from my past, especially the negative ones.

That is a wise decision. For if you continually kept bringing past feelings alive into your present reality, your ability to function in the world would be severely hampered.

So is this why so many people are emotional wrecks? I have several friends and business clients who could not live without anti-depressants or some form of drugs. They relied on them to calm their nerves. Without this help, their emotions and anxiety levels would be shot to pieces. They would be nervous wrecks living on the edge.

And it is not only sedative drugs that can help to shut out this unwanted emotional static. It's not only anti-depressants that close off the emotional channels that stop the past from being re-enacted inside of us. Alcohol and hard drugs are also deterrents from being in touch with our true selves, as you are fully aware.

I used to feel proud of myself for not relenting and being forced onto anti-depressants. But now I'm realizing that I was no better than anyone else. Taking hard drugs and alcohol was just another way of shutting out my unwanted emotional pain.

It is not a question of trying to be better. Using a chemical substance to obliterate the emotional centers in your body is no different, whether it is a legal or illegal substance. Your motivation was the same. You wanted to block out all manner of unwanted, negative emotions. Unfortunately, what you didn't realize were many of the other consequences.

What other consequences? Are you referring to my health?

No, although that is also a vital consideration. I was referring to the damage that your abuse was steadily having on your ability to properly connect and express your emotions.

What damage?

The damage to your positive emotions such as empathy, compassion, love and caring. What you wouldn't have realized is that the energy channels running through your body feed both your negative and positive emotions. And by cutting off the pain of negative emotions, you were also shutting down your chances to feel positive emotions. All emotions help you to function correctly in the world. They enable you to connect with others on a deep human level. Without them, you are nothing but an empty shell, devoid of feeling.

But my abuse didn't shut down my positive emotions. If anything, it heightened them. Whenever I was high on drugs or alcohol, I would feel more connected to other people. I would feel carefree and more alive than ever.

For how long?

Well, for a few hours. I would feel on top of the world for a few hours, most of the time.

Most of the time? Not all of the time?

No. Regrettably, there were a few occasions when the drugs and drink would heighten my anger, rather than repress it. They'd be times when I just wanted to fight the world and release my anger. It was almost like being possessed.

After a night out, someone would tell me the next morning how I had behaved, and I wouldn't believe them. Some of the stories that came back to me were shocking. It was as if they were talking about another person. I couldn't bear to listen to them. But I was thankful this erratic behavior wasn't common.

And why do you think this sometimes happened?

I'm not sure. I think it was perhaps those times when I'd had a bad day, or everything had got on top of me.

So it had nothing to do with how you were really feeling inside?

Maybe.

Let us clear up something here. First, do not feel shamed by your actions or reactions to the drugs and alcohol. Whatever behavior you demonstrated was simply a manifestation of your innermost feelings rising to the surface. Whatever anger and emotion you were repressing mirrored itself in a physical form. That is the power of unexpressed energy in the form of emotion. It wants to come into the light of your consciousness to be healed, and the only time this was possible was when your guard was down. Plying yourself with chemicals gave your true emotions the perfect chance to escape into the light.

There are many other controlled ways of bringing your true emotions out into the open, be it meditation, therapy, art or any number of other creative channels. But, unfortunately, you denied yourself such opportunities, which therefore left your emotions with no other avenue. And with no release or escape mechanism, it was only a matter of time before something would give.

So are you saying that the drugs and alcohol actually worked in my favor?

I wouldn't put it in those terms, but they definitely enabled an emotional channel to be forced open—a channel that allowed the repressed emotions you were running away from to spill out.

You mentioned that there were other consequences of blocking out my unexpressed emotions with drugs and drink.

There are. And the worst of these is your inability to grow as a human being. Denying your true emotions stunts your spiritual and emotional growth.

In what way?

Let me give you an example. In the past, you have constantly walked away from the opportunities to go into your painful emotions. You have denied listening to your innermost feelings because you were afraid of what they would show you. What I am saying is that this practice has not served you well. It has only served to make the emotion of your inner pain more intense.

Please remember that nothing can be healed if it does not come into the light. And by denying your emotions, you are blocking off any chance you had of developing as a person.

I can see now where I have gone wrong. But, one thing, didn't my behavior at least allow me some time to reassess my situation? Didn't containing my destructive emotions at least allow me to bide my time?

This would only be a correct statement if trapped emotions were not destructive to the body. If all denied emotion was harmless, then you would not have a problem. But, of course, this is far from the case. You may naively imagine that you are controlling your denied emotions with chemicals, but that is not true. What is actually happening under the surface is that your negative, unexpressed emotions are eating into your energy system. They are infecting your whole system with a toxic poison that is substantially more destructive to you and your body than any chemical substance. Just because emotions cannot be seen does not mean that they are not at work. They are, in more ways than you realize. They are slowly altering your DNA, which ultimately leads to breakdowns in your immune system.

Isn't that a bit far-fetched? I mean, come on. Can emotions possibly be that destructive? If that was the case, then why haven't I suffered more physical problems?

You have.

Where?

Where do you think your constant backaches have originated from? Why is it that you are always suffering from nasal problems? How is it that you keep having recurring problems with your stomach, teeth…do you want me to go on?

128

Aren't these symptoms that would be there anyway?

No, not to the degree that you suffer. Do you not yet realize what is going on here? Have you not yet worked out the direct link between mind and body? There is more to the story being played out than you give credit to. Your emotions are affecting the energy throughout your body. Your denied and trapped emotions are having a detrimental effect on your health, mind and body. Everything is interconnected. Both in your inner world and in the outer world.

Then what about some of my symptoms that have been passed down to me by relatives?

As I indicated before, they are illnesses linked to those relatives who have not cleared up their emotional dysfunctions. That is why they have been passed down the line. You are the one at the end of the chain. It is you who is now holding the baton. You are the one who could heal this space.

Phew! I don't know what to say. This is all too much to take in. I never imagined that emotions were playing such a pivotal role in our physical health.

Not only physical, but also psychological, emotional and mental health. Understanding your emotions is essential to ensuring that you live a balanced, integrated and fully creative life.

How do I know that what you are saying is true?

It is not necessary to believe anything I am telling you. I would much prefer that you experience it by living it. Therefore, go out and walk your talk. That way, you will discover a divine truth from the universe for yourself. As I've said many times, you can believe something and have faith in it. You can honor it, and you can know it. But real truth comes alive when you experience it for yourself. For only then will you know it to be true in your heart and in the depth of your being.

Twenty-Four

I now understood the effects of my emotional neglect on myself and my children, but I had a feeling that the repercussions were even more widespread.

What implications will all of this have on society in general? What effect will all this emotional neglect have on how we live?

If emotions are neglected for this next century, just as they have been throughout the twentieth century, then it's catastrophic. It will depend on how the educational systems prioritize the importance of teaching about emotions and energy. All I can say is that the future of our planet relies solely on how we tackle this urgent issue.

You make it sound as if we are facing some kind of Armageddon. Aren't you going over the top on this issue?

Do you think so?

Well, there are several other more pressing issues to address in the future, I'm sure. If anyone was to say that some form of emotional literacy was more important than, say, the climate, the environment, defense or human rights, then they would be carted off in a straight-jacket.

Let us fill in the spaces to this discussion and paint a fuller picture. I want you to get a grasp of the true picture. Now, let's begin with all the

131

*murders and suicides that are committed around the world every year.
Why do you think there are so many?*

Mental health reasons for the majority of suicides. Add to that depression, fear of the future, debt, loss of job and any number of other causes.

And what do you imagine are the root causes of these mental illnesses across the board?

I'm not certain. It could be any one of several different factors. Don't tell me, you are about to say…

Emotion.
How did you guess? Emotion is attributable to the majority of cases. In most situations, suicide has been committed because there is an imbalance in someone's emotional nervous system. Their emotions may have been denied, neglected, masked over or unexpressed.
And what about murders? What are the reasons for the majority of murders carried out?

Jealousy. Hatred. Revenge. Rage. Anger. Not to mention mental health problems again.

So you agree that it is emotionally linked again. Jealousy, hatred, revenge, rage and anger are all forms of negative and destructive emotions—emotions that, if not contained, will often spill over into sudden and shocking violence.

I'm beginning to see your point.

But there is more. What if I told you that the majority of murders were mistakes? What if you discovered that most murders involved someone losing control of their emotions?

Really?

A significant number of murders around the world are not committed by people who meticulously plan to maim and kill. They are carried out by people who briefly and destructively lose self-control. You could say that most murders, outside of terrorism, occur because someone has lost control of his or her senses. And by this, I mean emotions.

So, a sudden head rush is directly attributable to most murders that are committed?

By people who would never see themselves as murderers.

And all because of out-of-control emotion. It's hard to believe until I remember back to that time my father absolutely lost it. When he threatened to torch the house with us in it, it completely altered my opinion about how power, anger and repressed emotions can affect a person. My dad is one of the kindest, most sincere people that anyone knows. But push him too far after he had a drink, and he was totally unpredictable. It makes me shudder when I think about what could have happened. If he hadn't suddenly come to his senses, then none of my family would be here.

And there have been plenty of murders when someone hasn't managed to take a grip of their emotions. Times when they have tipped over the brink, causing devastating consequences.

I remember many years ago when the Scottish village of Dunblane was ripped apart by a gunman who went on a rampage. He burst into a primary school and slaughtered more than a dozen five- and six-year-olds before turning the gun on himself. The whole country went into mourning for weeks afterward. It was heart-wrenching. I remember the reports in the papers. They implied the gunman was emotionally unstable. Speculation and rumor were rife that the killer, Thomas Hamilton, had been ridiculed and embarrassed by several events involving local villagers and a scout group. Some of the papers reported that, prior to the event, Hamilton was sick and tired of not having his opinions heard. They said that he was angry and bitter that his feelings were not listened to. Committing that atrocity was his twisted way of getting revenge.

That was a devastating tragedy, but unfortunately, not the first and certainly not the last. That was a horrendous example showing the effects of emotions out of control.

It makes me think about several times when I have completely lost it. The times when my emotions have almost taken me over. I wouldn't even want to think about what would happen if more people carried firearms in this country. Owning a lethal weapon at a time when my emotions have overwhelmed me doesn't even bear thinking about.

And all it takes is one moment of madness. A split second when emotions can explode with catastrophic consequences.

But why are we seeing an ever-increasing demonstration of rage and anger? Why are we witnessing these sudden and shocking examples of violence and hatred?

The whole dynamic is complex, but a large number can be directly attributed to unbalanced emotions. Read the report to every homicide, and the cause of death will inevitably be the same.

So where will it all end?

It won't. So long as emotions are ignored by social researchers, scientists and educators, nothing will ever change, which is why a whole new approach is required. If society continues to ignore the important role that emotions play, then we will witness increasing levels of emotional distress and imbalance.

Emotions *are* a fundamental key to resolving society's ills, aren't they?

They are essential if modern society is to understand why so many sudden demonstrations of violence occur. You could say that if a person's emotional distress is not healed, then nothing else can follow. Only a person who is emotionally balanced will truly care about both their kin and the environment around them.

Everything begins at a core level. If people are emotionally stable, they are more likely to be empathic, loving, caring and compassionate to both their fellow kin and the state of the world. All stability evolves from the emotional stability of all.

I'm really getting to understand that emotions are one of the most urgent issues we all face.

On a global, regional and local scale. If emotions could be expressed openly, honestly, and at the time they arise, the human race would take several steps toward a new evolution. Deny that emotion plays a pivotal fulcrum in the process of peace, and society will pay the ultimate price.

I don't like the sound of that.

Then be a living example of this new, awakened consciousness. Express your emotions openly and truthfully at every single opportunity. It is possible to honor a person's dignity by telling him exactly as it is. You simply have to tell the absolute truth, not some of the time, but all of the time. Then you will become a living, walking and talking example of this higher truth that so many now cry out for. You will become someone who not only honors the true emotions within himself, but also the emotional truth in all others. Emotion is all about bringing your truth to the surface, regardless of whether it contradicts an established truth or ruffles a few feathers.

But there are many people like me who have spent their lives locking away their true emotions. They have spent and wasted ridiculous amounts of energy trying to hide their true emotions. These people, who are probably mostly men, aren't going to change their habits overnight.

But they just may if they knew their health, life and well-being depended on it. Then they would sit up and take notice.

Is that honestly going to happen? Will those who are stuck in their old habits, acting out destructive mannerisms, actually come to alter the way they think about dealing with their emotions?

Yes, I believe so. If you were told that you could put twenty extra years on your life by simply changing one part of your life, wouldn't you at least give it a go?

I'd grab it with both hands and say "thank you very much."

Well, this is precisely the case if you were to begin by honoring your emotions openly and fully. If you brought every trapped and denied emotion out into the light, then I could guarantee you that, within twelve months, your health would improve. After that, your self-belief would rocket, and your esteem would go through the roof. Then, you will reach a point when every relationship that you have would take off.

What do you mean by that?

Every relationship you have with your friends, foes, the environment and the planet would all improve. You would begin to connect with others on a deeper, more profound level of love and understanding.

You make it sound so simple. I wish that it were that easy.

It is as simple or as arduous as you choose to make it. The choice is always there for you to make. If you say that you are sick and tired of the way life is presently, then change it. The best way to do that is to change your self. Nothing in the world can alter until you make the conscious effort to shift your understanding. Nothing will shift in the outside world unless you cause a shift in your inner world. It all begins with inner transformation. Then outer transformation will follow.

The mistake, if you could view it that way, is that you have held onto the belief that change will come from others. You have believed that once others change their ways, then you and the world will follow. But do you not realize that your holding back is actually holding back the evolution of the world? Not to mention that of the universe. Can you not see that everyone is waiting for someone else to be the inspirer and change-maker?

I suppose I am looking around for inspiration and guidance. I am waiting for someone to be the example I can follow.

You are the guidance and the inspiration. You all are. The trouble is that most people don't believe in themselves enough. Most haven't the confidence or self-belief to see that they are the ones who they have been waiting for. My friend, please do not only look outside yourself for inspiration. True wealth comes from within. Do not hold onto the false belief that other people out there are driving the much-needed change.
For you are that other person.

Twenty-Five

*S*o, it was up to me to be the "change-maker." But where should I begin? I wasn't sure that I was the man for such a monumental task.

But what should we do to help change others? How can we make people see sense?

Let me be very specific here. You don't need to change anyone. And you cannot make people see sense. If you try, then you meet nothing but resistance. Have you ever tried to change people who weren't ready?

Yes.

And what was their reaction?

They resisted.

That is because you cannot do other people's soul work for them, for if you try, they will resist.

What do you exactly mean by "soul work"?

The life they have incarnated into, to experience who they are. Soul work is the life journey that people have to sign up to. It is the hurdles they need to jump over. It is the challenges they need to face. The issues they need to deal with. If you interfere with that, then on a subliminal level, they will sense it. On a deep spiritual level, they will feel that you are interfering with their life.

And that is why they resist?

Yes. That's the reason why people will fight change until the last if you are the one trying to instigate that change. People need to come at personal change when they are prepared and ready. Try forcing people to change, and they will rebel, often with devastating consequences to their own growth. Therefore, do not waste your time and energy attempting to change others. You will expend valuable life energy that could be used far more productively. Instead, be an example of the highest truth—the truth of who and what you really are. And then you will inspire people to change. The most appropriate way to show this is to live your truth in every single moment. Be an example of your truth by demonstrating it. And how is this achieved? By expressing every one of your many emotions. And by bringing all your emotions to the surface.

Each and every one of us is growing at different speeds. We are all evolving at our perfect pace—the pace that suits us, and no one else. If you try to fast-track this process, then you will experience nothing but strong resistance.

I understand what you are saying because I have experienced it for myself. There have been many occasions when I have tried to force the issue in someone's personal development. As an employer, I have sometimes grown frustrated by a person's inability to become conscious of certain issues. And when the person hasn't grown quickly enough, I have occasionally become annoyed. I'm not so much annoyed with the person, but I'm angry with myself. I see another's failings as my own inadequacy at teaching.

Do not be annoyed with yourself for another not waking up. That is not your concern. You can only show others signposts of where to go. You cannot go on the journey for them. You can only show others mirrors of themselves. You cannot be that person.

If you only made your life an example to them, then you will be giving them the greatest gift possible. You will be allowing them to stir up the emotions and drive within themselves.

Remember, you cannot change anyone, but you can inspire them, for it is not the change itself that many fear most. Their greatest fear is that another will force them to try to change.

It is pointless making people face up to their emotional difficulties before they are ready. All negative emotions require the healing light of love to heal them. So, whenever a friend or colleague is in need of help, don't just tell him what to do. With all the heart and compassion you can muster, show him. Show him by your lived example.

Can I now ask you something about emotions? Aren't some negative emotions best left alone? Shouldn't we keep the nastiest and more destructive emotions locked away where they cannot do harm?

But do you not see that any emotion unexpressed will become destructive? If you deny an emotion because you are fearful that it will show you in a bad light, then you have not grasped what I am telling you. Leave a negative emotion hidden, and it is bound to resurface anyway. And when it does, you may not be able to control it. However, if you deal with negative emotions as they arise, you are more than likely attacking them before they develop into an uncontrollable monster. Look at what happened with your father. Were he to have brought his angry and denied emotions out earlier, then those events wouldn't have occurred.

You have mostly talked about negative emotions and feelings. What about those positive and joyful emotions that many people keep locked away? Fearful of making a spectacle of themselves, some prefer to squirrel their feelings of elation away.

It is not uncommon for some to ignore their positive emotions and take them completely for granted. For others, they will not demonstrate their true emotions such as gratitude, compassion, empathy and love, for fear that they will expose themselves. There are many people who are not comfortable sharing their inner world. They are perhaps afraid that others will see this as a weakness and try to manipulate them. But let me tell you, you will endear people to you if you expose your emotions in full. Others will magnetize toward you when you're open with your emotion because truth is a powerful healer. The truth of our emotions emits a positive charge, one that can become inspirational and contagious to others.

Not only does our health improve, but we also attract other like-minded people toward us.

Yes, that is the great miracle that happens when one person chooses to share and express his or her true emotions openly. It gives the other permission to also bring true feelings to the surface. Share a truth to another, and he or she inevitably shares one back. Those who have strong relationships know this fact. It is something that makes us all feel more connected and human.

I definitely know this to be true. There have been countless times when I have experienced this for myself. When I have taken my clients on trips abroad, I have been the one who, after a drink, starts to open up. It's usually me who normally begins spilling my inner world of how I really feel about work, my relationships and the state of the world. I'm forever amazed that this honesty seems to open the floodgates. And, within no time, everyone is doing the same, revealing secrets and emotions that have never been shared before.

And how do your clients feel after your trips?

Most of them have said that they enjoy their trips away. It gives them a perfect opportunity to wheel out their true feelings about their business dealings, their financial dealings and much more. A few of them have even intimated that our trips away are akin to some form of therapy. Opening up their world seems to do them all the power of good.

And all because they have the chance to express their true feelings?

Yes, it's incredible, isn't it?

When you come to understand the basic universal laws of life, you will discover that all of life is a perfect mirror. What we give out to the world, we get back in return.

What goes around comes around, as my mother always says. Is that what you mean by karma?

Be careful, because there are several interpretations of the word "karma." If you are referring to it only in the context that bad things bounce back to you, then be careful, for that is not truly correct. A closer meaning of the word "karma" could best be described with the expression, "As within, so without."

Or what's within us reflects outside of us?

And that includes everything, not just the so-called bad life situations that show up. It includes what you would perceive as good ones, too. In reality, there are no bad life situations being mirrored back to you. Even those events that you would view as bad are actually leading you back home to the truth. They are helping to mirror back to you situations that contain vital life lessons—lessons that enable you to find out who you are and what you want.

Try to think about those seemingly desperate situations from the past that have appeared from nowhere into your life. Try to remember how you initially felt about them when they showed up. You were apprehensive and anxious. You may have been fraught with worry and stress. Then think ahead. Try to recapture what every situation actually ended up teaching you about yourself. You will be shocked to discover that every single one brought with it the gift of a lesson—a valuable life lesson about the path that you say you want to go on.

So every life situation turning up, regardless of whether we initially think of it as bad, is a direct reflection of something that *we* have called forward?

That's it. Look at every life situation that shows up, and you will come to the divine truth that what we put out there boomerangs back to us. This is because life is a perfect reflection of our innermost thoughts. What we experience is often a mirror of how our mind sees the world. You may think that random events are just showing up in your life by chance, but they are not. They have been magnetized to you, by you. Everything you feel and witness is being drawn to you by your level of consciousness. When you come to live this level of understanding,

*you will have made one of the most profound jumps in your conscious
awareness. You will come to realize that everything you experience in
life, and every person you stumble across, is there for a reason.*

So every single person that ever shows up in our lives is there
for a purpose. He or she has shown up at the right time and the
right place. I find that hard to believe.

*Once you reach this level of awareness, you will come to not only
understand this as a concept, but you will live it as an example. Don't
take my word for it. Feel this truth in your heart first. Feel it in every cell
and bone of your body, and then you will experience it for yourself.*

*All the people who have shown up at every crossroad of our lives
have shown up to serve our intentions. They have appeared to us
because, on one conscious level or another, we have magnetized them
toward us. And that is because the relationship they bring into our life
space offers numerous lessons for where our thoughts and emotions
say they wish to take us.*

*Every emotion that we project out into the world is reflected back
to us by a life example. On a deeper level, you will already be aware
of this fact. If you continuously project out hate, anger and bitterness,
then you will simply manifest more of the same back to you. The same
is true of compassion, love and integrity. Push out these energies into
the world, and similar energies will bounce back to you. This universal
law is exact.*

*I feel that you are not convinced. What is troubling you about this
understanding?*

I just had a thought. What about those occasions when a deeply
loving, compassionate human being attracts bad life events toward
himself? What about the countless times when someone loses
a loving and deeply caring person who they knew would never
harm a fly? If your reflection theory is true, then why are these
compassionate people experiencing hardship and desperation?
They certainly wouldn't be drawing negative, life-threatening
situations toward them, would they?

*First, please refrain from seeing any life event that shows up as bad.
There are no bad life situations except those that you define as such.*

144

You are confusing the intention that someone puts out there with the actual life events that serve his or her wishes. Let me try and make this easier by explaining it further.

Say, for example, you are single and desperately lonely. All your relations and friends have either passed on or moved away. Now let's imagine for a moment that you craved more compassion and love from other people in your life. Let's say that you are dying for it so much that it almost becomes an unhealthy addiction to your thinking. It has become a compulsion that you are passionate about above all else.

An obsession almost.

Fine. Now, what life situation would you magnetize toward you to serve these wishes?

Going on what you have implied, I would try drawing toward me life situations that answered my calling for more compassion and love. I'd probably attract people who were going to help fulfill my desperate craving.

Good. Now have you thought about what type of situations would best serve your intentions and requests?

No, not really. I was hoping that the mystery of life could manifest one for me.

So, it wouldn't matter what life situation shows up, just as long as you can have your needs met for more love and compassion?

You have it.

What if I told you that what, in fact, you ended up manifesting was some form of cancer or terminal illness? What would you say to that?

But I didn't draw that to me. Attracting a life-threatening disease wasn't what I had in mind.

You are dead right. You didn't have anything on your mind regarding this. But you did have on your mind that you wanted more care and attention, loving and compassion. And that, my friend, is precisely what you attracted. You drew toward you the perfect life situation that would honor both your thoughts and feelings. You magnetized a perfect scenario where lots of people could shower you with attention, love, compassion and caring.

But I'll state again. I didn't request a life-threatening scenario.

Nor did you not request it. But it needed to show up in your life as the vehicle to carry forth your intentions. Your life-threatening situation had to come into being as the springboard of your prime intent, which was the request that both your heart and mind craved above all else. Even above your life.

You are correct in that you did not consciously order up terminal cancer, but because you put your intentions above everything else in life, the universe gave you exactly what you wished for.

More compassion and love from others.

That's it. And the illness was the fastest vehicle to deliver that order.

From what you are saying then, the universe delivers exactly what I order. So what is going on with the terminal illness? Why did that show up when I hadn't ordered it?

Try to imagine the universe as a giant copier machine that is constantly churning out not only your requests, but every other request from every other human being. Now try to grasp hold of what I am about to say. For if you master this understanding, you will inherit many of the keys to creation in this universe.

Twenty-Six

*M*anifesting. Creating. Magnetizing. I'd had no idea that we were such powerful beings. I could hardly contain my enthusiasm.

This sounds exciting!

My good friend, beyond the wildest of your wildest dreams. Now think back to a time when you have craved something above all else. What were your feelings and thoughts at that time? And what were your intentions?

One comes to mind straight away. Since about age fifteen or sixteen, I dreamed about marrying, moving away and having three daughters. Don't ask me why, but it was almost a compulsion. I was young, and at that time, I was just beginning to get into drugs and alcohol in a big way. Even though I was enjoying growing up, I still longed for a time when I could escape from everything. Find the right person to marry and settle down with three daughters. These thoughts, above all else, eclipsed all other feelings I had. They practically possessed me night and day.

Any other periods in your life when your desire became an "almost obsession"?

Yes, when I first joined the company I am presently with. I had been recruited by a headhunter. The package was considerably better than I had at my previous company, so I risked a change

147

and jumped ship. But within weeks of joining the new company, I discovered the truth of why I had been approached: the company was in big trouble and leaking money like a sieve. I was devastated. I had left a good, secure job and a lot of close friends, and I had dived into a regional office that wasn't even assured of its future. I felt like crying.

So how did you react?

Initially, I was in shock. Then I thought, "Right, I need to start turning this around." I started going into the office on weekends and working late in an attempt to cut out the deadwood. I started doing what all salesmen do best, which is knocking on doors of potential clients I'd never met before.

And what happened?

Slowly but surely, things began to turn around. They had to. I had my neck on the line and a young family to support. A year into my contract, the existing manager left, and I was promoted to the top job. It was great because it allowed me to implement all the changes that I was desperate to introduce. With good backing from the directors, I poached a seasoned and respected salesman from another competitor. That was probably the big turning point for the office. After that, we managed to attract very good sales support, and then we were on our way.

With a positive attitude all round and dedicated staff to back us up, we soon began to fly. Business started booming, and the orders began flooding in. Five years in, which was last year, we hit the top spot. We were the most profitable and yet also the most lean company in the whole of the UK operations group.

That was some turnaround.

Yes, but it's also involved considerable sacrifices. I'm not certain I would do it all over again. Fine, we've built up one of the strongest regions in the UK, but at what cost to my sanity, my health and my family? We've become one of the most profitable offices, but I've hardly seen my children grow up. I've missed out on those special events like their school plays and Christmas shows. Worse still, I practically see nothing of Alison. We are like ships passing in the night. Calling it a relationship would be stretching the truth. It's impossible to try to maintain a loving and compassionate relationship when neither party is ever present. Alison has her business to run, and I have mine. We have everything we've ever dreamed of having, and yet I still feel like I have nothing.

I hate the hollow and meaningless life I have created. I know it's my fault. There is nobody else to blame but myself. I've made a right mess of my life. This is not where I wanted to be.

So why did you choose the life you are living? If this is not the place where you wanted to end up, how did you get here?

I didn't choose it. It chose me. I simply pointed the compass, and off I went. When I first discovered that the office I had committed to was on its knees, I mustered every last piece of energy I could find. With my back against the wall, I poured every hour and every last ounce of effort into building up that business. I was determined not to go down with a sinking ship.

So your intentions and desires were fixed?

Fixed! They were an obsession. Every thought was channeled into the effort. My intention, as it has always been, is to do the best I can in whatever I do. The huge, overwhelming challenge presented to me was no different. I was more determined than ever before to succeed. And once things began turning around, my intention was to keep building on it.

And there wasn't a single doubt in your mind that you would fail? You had no fear whatsoever that everything would collapse, leaving your dreams shattered, and you out of a job?

No way. Not a single thought or feeling was allowed to pass through me. I was determined that I would keep positive. Our office would reach the top. Whatever the circumstances. Whatever pain it inflicted.

Very interesting use of language. You were clearly prepared to sacrifice everything to ensure that success came your way.

Yes.

Even the love of your family?

Phew! That was one in the groin.

I'm sorry. I am trying to get you to fully express where your energies were in relation to how you manifested your wishes. From what you have described, you were prepared to move heaven and earth to realize your dreams. You were clearly determined and passionate about making a resounding success of the business. But you took one aspect for granted: your family.

I didn't once take them for granted. That is grossly unfair. They were always at the back of my mind.

You have just answered your own statement. They were at the back of your mind. Whereas the company you worked for was at the front of your mind.

I see what you mean. I've really messed up, haven't I?

My beloved friend, please do not think for a moment that I am in any way condemning your behavior. I am most certainly not. I never have done and never will. I wanted you to empty out the truth of your situation so we can pick over the bones together. Now let's begin by going back a few steps.
First, do not be harsh on your life decisions. You did what you imagined to be right at the time. Your actions were built on the solid belief that protecting the security of your family is paramount. That is commendable. There is nothing wrong with that. But in honoring your

150

intentions to give your family and your company everything, you forgot one thing: You neglected to give anything back to yourself.

You forgot that you also have needs in this cosmic equation. Needs that have to be fulfilled if you are to enjoy an abundant, creative and inspiring life. It is not good enough to imagine that your needs don't have to be fulfilled. They do, which is why you should have focused a bigger share of your intentions on what you wanted from your family life.

Life is a perfect mirror to our inner thoughts, feelings and intentions, which is exactly why you have manifested the life you now see all around you. Yes, you did create what you were constantly holding onto in your mind. Life did reflect back to you the passion and belief that you felt in your heart. So, in that respect, you created your outer world in perfect alignment with your inner world. But there was one aspect you failed to be grateful for.

My family.

Yes.

I forgot to be grateful for all the love I already had around me. I stupidly took for granted something that I should have been grateful for every day.

You are not alone in this. You could say that this is an epidemic of global proportions. So many others expend all their life energies on what they want and not on what they already have. There is so often an abundance of love and caring around us, and yet most of us look straight through it.

And rarely give it a thought.

That is a very good point. You are correct. You didn't give it a thought.
It is good to set intentions. It is life-expanding to desire more and want more of yourself. That's exactly what will show up in your presence, if you appreciate it. More of the same. However, if you fail to be grateful and stop thinking about all the beauty and wonder visible around you, it falls away.

151

That which you give attention to blossoms and grows. That which you neglect withers and dies.

The universe cannot reflect back to you that which you are not looking at in the mirror. For if you pour no energy into the machine, you cannot expect to get anything out.

Are you implying that the universe is a machine?

You can describe it in the most appropriate manner that you wish. A mirror, a quantum soup, a field of energy, a copier. Use whatever imagery best fits into your present conception.

A copier! You used that analogy before. Isn't that making the universe appear sterile and dead?

Do not become overly attached to the words. They are only signs to help you understand more about the miraculous process of life that is evolving. I am attempting, with the most basic language available, to convey to you the fundamental laws of our universe. Whatever terminology you use, know this: The universe delivers what you request.

Sorry to spoil the party, but this still doesn't feel right. If it was that easy, then we'd all be manifesting our wants and desires, wouldn't we?

Who said anything about wants and desires? I am referring to what we all need to survive and thrive. What we need to help us on our path of self-realization, those needs that we must fulfill if we are to truly discover who we are.

Wants and needs are poles apart, as I have already intimated. Let us take your life example. You craved success more than anything, and that is exactly what you produced. Success beyond all measure. Your state of mind manifested for you an abundant wealth that you could only have dreamed of several years ago. But did any of this success fulfil your needs? From what you have described to me, I will guess not.

I suppose I've never slowed down to assess what my real needs are. I have been so busy sprinting through life that I've not allowed myself the luxury of stopping, thinking and, more importantly, reflecting.

Does the language you are using not tell you something? You view any time spent on looking into your vital life needs as a luxury. I will say that this is a necessity, especially if you wish to live a life that is free from stress, heartache and anxiety. Instead, work out what you need to be happy, healthy and fulfilled, and everything else will follow.

So you are saying that all my life priorities were the wrong way around?

I am not telling you anything. As with all truth, you must see it for yourself. You must see it and live it. Only then can your new wisdom be used to improve your life.

If focusing on success was your prime goal in life, then fine, you have scored a hat-trick of goals. You have won that game without question. If showing off to the world was your core intention, then great, you have achieved your aims. What I am asking you to assess is this: at what cost to yourself? What has chasing outer material success taken away from the needs of your inner world?

Inner world?

Your spiritual needs. The needs that we all have to make us complete human beings. The needs that are essential if we are to find true inner peace and contentment.

Again, I am now feeling more confused than enlightened. I understand much of what you are saying, but I'm still struggling to find out where I went drastically off course.

Life is a walk, not a sprint. Do not chastise yourself, as you have done many times before, when the answers to life first elude you. Your life is a journey, not a fixed destination. Therefore, allow the truth you are constantly searching for to slowly bubble to the surface. If you would have taken more time with the important issues in your life, then many of your answers would have been revealed. Only when you slow down can the truth to your life be uncovered.

In your insane drive to be someone in life, you unfortunately looked past the very essence of what is important. You took for granted those things of beauty that you should have cherished close to your heart.

Just ponder for a moment. You enjoyed great health. You had a secure, loving family. Yet this was all taken for granted. You wanted more, and yet, sadly, you did not realize that life's treasures were already in your possession.

I can now see that.

But can you feel it? Can you feel this loving truth in the depth of your heart and soul?

Yes, I can, and it hurts. I'm coming to realize where I had crashed off the road.

That is good wisdom. You are gaining wisdom as you go along by fully opening up your heart. Now, can you begin to see the power that our thoughts and feelings have over the life we create? Are you coming home to the truth that where attention goes, energy flows?

I heard that expression today on the radio while I was out in the car! "Where attention goes, energy flows." The writer who was being interviewed used it. I didn't grasp its meaning at first, but now I do. It all makes sense to me.

See, you are growing in ways that are opening your consciousness up to a new world. That is the power of change. It enables us to take the same life situations and make more sense out of them.
When we focus every part of our attention onto something, the energy of life force flows.
When we train our mind on an intention, we kickstart the process of creation.

I really like that. "What flows must grow."

And there is more. Reverse that profound statement, and it reads, "Where energy flows, attention goes." Put all your energies into anything, and the creative energy of the universe will follow. Pay attention to anything in your life, and the universe will also attend to it.

Does this apply to everything?

Everything and more, my friend. This is a universal law that cannot be contradicted. The love and attention that you shower onto any part of your life is directly proportional to what you receive back in return.

Because the world reflects back to us what is inside of us.

See, there you have it.

So I really was creating everything that showed up in my life?

Now you are beginning to open up to the truth of how your life has been formed. Are you now beginning to see how powerful your thoughts and feelings are?

Yes, it feels like a dam of understanding has burst open within me. My thoughts, and the energy behind them, have all conspired to create the life I am living. It's all making sense.

In the example you used before about manifesting cancer, I can see now where I had tripped up. I forgot to be more specific with my requests to the universe.

How do you mean? Can you explain it more explicitly?

I desired compassion and love more than anything. I craved nonstop that I would be comforted and cared for. But, and here's where I think I went wrong, I didn't fill in the gaps. I never set any other intentions. And so the universe manifested for me a random event, one that would fulfill my needs.

The first part of your assessment was exact. Yes, you did create your own life by means of pouring all of your energies into what you craved. Your thoughts and emotions aligned, which created a huge energy force.

How?

Bringing the two together moves the creative force of the universe into alignment. Know that thought is only one level of power and creation. But add the strong feelings of emotion into the pot, and the combined sum is greater than the two parts.

So emotion is vitally important to the whole process of creation?

Immensely so. It is the fuel that drives the process forward with great power and velocity. Emotion is the energy that feeds our thoughts. You can carry thoughts and dreams around in your mind for the rest of your life, but until you light them with emotion, they will crawl along at a snail's pace.

Twenty-Seven

I still had some unanswered questions—some gaps in my understanding—about manifesting.

So many life situations have turned up that I categorically know I have *not* created. If so, then why have they shown up?

You have created everything in your life on one level or another. Fact. Make no mistake about that. What you may not always be aware of is that you are also creating unconsciously. Just because you may not be aware of it does not mean that what shows up cannot be traced back to your initial thoughts. Let me clear this up because you have asked an important question.

When you create something consciously in your life, it is easy to trace back your initial requests. I will give you the example of your success in the business. You knew where you were heading and what you wanted to achieve. Your goals were fixed. Your intentions were certain. There was no confusion whatsoever in your thinking or emotions.

Hence I created exactly what I asked for.

Yes. Now let's break down the smaller components that underpin that huge request to the universe. Can you remember any other intentions besides the success of the business?

No, that was my sole intention.

Fine, so were you focused one hundred percent?

157

Absolutely.

Now what about some of the insurmountable hurdles that you had to overcome? Did you ever wonder at any time whether you were heading off course?

Yes, especially those times when everything seemed to be going against me. There were occasions when I wondered whether the world wanted me to fail. Huge barriers seemed to be constructed that prevented me from going where I needed.

And what did you do?

I got my head down, worked at it and found another route through. The strange thing was that no matter how bad a hurdle first appeared, I always climbed over it somehow in the end. There were several times when I seemed to be weaving completely off my intended pathway. But then, suddenly, everything would be made clear. Once some water had passed under the bridge, it always became clear to me. It appeared that everything was happening for a reason. Even those events that tripped me up and slowed me down later turned out to be useful delaying tactics. They were events that turned out to be the best for the business in the end.

That is the point I wanted you to arrive at. So, in your opinion, all obstacles showed up to help you, rather than hinder you?

Yes, that's fair to say. Although, at the time, I rarely saw it as a help. It wasn't until much later, with the gift of hindsight, that I could appreciate why certain hurdles showed up.

The insight you have shown here has clearly been an important factor in the success of your business.

It's a pity that I didn't use that same insight with regard to my family. Perhaps if I had, I would have been a more able and useful father and husband.

You were once lost in the world, but now you are found. Count your blessings that you have finally arrived home at this truth. Many others could live for several lifetimes and still not discover this gem.

Knowing that certain difficulties show up in your life for a reason gifts you with a wisdom that is priceless. For when you fully understand the process of creation, you will see with blinding insight that everything turning up has originated from you. Everything has been drawn to you, by you, so that the lessons you need to learn turn up in the correct order. Nothing is happening out of chance. No one person that appears in your life shows up without a reason.

One of my friends, Paul, has always carried a similar mantra. He says that, "Everybody coming into our lives shows up for a reason, a season or for life."

That is very good wisdom. Apply that mantra to every human being entering your space, and you will eventually come to acknowledge that all relationships are divinely unique. And then you will realize the precious and beautiful gift that every person brings into your life.

All relationships bring to you a mirror that helps you to see those parts of yourself that you may not have yet recognized.

You surely don't mean those relationships that bring us nothing but heartache and trouble?

The people with whom we are most uncomfortable often gift us with the biggest potential for growth. The most intensely painful and challenging relationships always offer us the largest life lessons. They bring us the most unique forms of inner healing possible. And they enable us to see the world through all-new eyes.

I feel deeply ashamed after what you have said here. There have been plenty of challenging relationships in my life. I have experienced numerous occasions when I've backed away from someone because of my fear of confrontation. From what you are saying, I have denied myself countless chances to grow and evolve.

And not only that. All relationships offer us the unique ability to see and feel the world from another's perspective. That is the gift that you deny yourself when you run away from what may initially appear to be challenging people. When you truly get under the surface of another's life, you inevitably begin to see why they behave in a certain manner.

But I haven't even given most people a chance. I'm often way too quick to condemn someone for his or her actions, before I've even scratched below the surface.

Then you have denied yourself the experience of feeling true compassion. You have walked away from the unique emotional experience that bonds us all together. Empathy.

When you fail to see the truth underneath another's life, you fail to understand that which brings us all together on the web of the universe. Empathy is the channel that enables you to feel the emotions of another as if they were your own. If everyone was empathic of their fellow kin, then there would never be another war. If the channel of empathy were fully open in all, there would be no more destruction of the environment either.

But isn't it bad to be overly empathic? I once worked with a woman who was almost a nervous wreck. She was so sensitive that it hindered her ability to function properly in society. She felt the pain of everyone and everything, and always took every person's side in an argument. If a critical environmental issue appeared on the news, then she would practically become hysterical the next day at work. And if there was an article in the papers about the abuse of human rights, or the abuse of corporations on those too poor to fight, she would go berserk. I liked the fact that she was deeply passionate about important issues, but the poor woman constantly lived on her nerves.

In empathy, you have observed a very good point that will be played out in the next century ahead. When you come to understand how and why the vibration of the planet is fast-altering, you will discover why empathy is set to become such an important issue in the future.

In what kind of way?

160

Empathy has the potential to both save our civilization and destroy it. It can either bring us to a place where we will honor the uniqueness of our diverse cultures, religions and creeds, or it will send us down a track where nothing is guaranteed.

This sounds scary.

I don't mean to alarm you, but if we carry on the same path where we are heading, then we will not be around to discover the full effect of the choices we are making.

By "we," do you mean all life on planet earth?

No, I was specifically referring to human beings. Life throughout the planet will always survive many of the changing conditions. It can adapt to the harshest and most adverse conditions imaginable. Unfortunately, human beings are more sensitive to change. They require a substantial amount of heat, fuel and water to survive, let alone thrive. And because humanity has placed itself at the top of a self-appointed pyramid, it will be the first race to suffer when the environment kicks back.

I don't like the sound of that. What do you mean by "kick back?"

The ecosystem that helps us to maintain life here on planet earth is one of the most refined systems in the universe. Every intricate fluctuation ripples through the whole organism. If we continue to manipulate and destroy the very organism that sustains us, then it will kick back. It will do whatever it is required to do to ensure that it survives.

Hang on. Why are you saying that the world is an organism? I haven't ever heard it expressed through that term before. An organism would imply that the world is acting as a living, breathing system, with us as part of that system. I think science would have a lot to say about that, what with its beliefs in reductionism and separation.

Do you honestly hold a belief that the world is nothing more than a dead piece of matter floating aimlessly through space? And do you honestly believe that human beings are separate and detached from this perfectly arranged organism?

My dear friend, the world and every part of life contained within it are connected in ways that even the brightest scientific minds haven't yet come anywhere close to understanding. For now, know that we are all one with each, and with one another. We are all joined by a universal thread that vibrates out into the extremities of the universe. In the coming decades, some of the greatest minds to have walked this earth will reveal this core truth. And when this shift occurs, life as we know it will move into a new gear. I cannot explain to you the treasures that await the human race in this century ahead. We have the potential to move into an age when the unbelievable becomes believable. We are entering a time when the extraordinary will become the ordinary.

Didn't you just say that we are entering a period when we could wipe ourselves out as a race? How can we be doing both?

Both are possible in these changing times. A paradox exists unlike any other time in this planet's history. We have the potential to create our wildest dreams or our deepest fears. The possibilities exist for us to create a new future or no future at all. Both exist at this critical time in history.

I have a strong feeling from what you are telling me that empathy will play an increasingly important role in this.

And you are correct. Empathy will be pivotal to the survival of our race because empathy is a human response, built into our genetic makeup. It is an instinct. Just as the planet has its own immune system to sustain balance and life, so, too, do all humans. The question is not whether the ability to empathize exists inside of us, but will we wake up in time to ignite it? When you come to know why more empathy is required among humans, you will see how the matrix fits together.

Twenty-Eight

*E*mpathy—or the lack of it—clearly could have a major impact on the future of our civilization. I knew it was important to fully understand this concept better.

Can you tell me more about empathy's role?

Let me begin by opening up a question. It may help lead us to better clarity. I need you to be absolutely conscious of what I am trying to piece together here, for when you truly grasp the important role of empathy, you will see where humanity is evolving.

This is exciting.

My beloved friend, you have no idea how exciting. If you could envision where humanity can head in the future, you would be both astounded and amazed. The planet's consciousness is rising to levels that can match all previous attempts at evolution.
Now think of a time when Alison and you have been in tune with one another, a time before this hectic time in your life, when you were both closer than ever.

That is easy. It was two years after we were married, when Jenna was first born. I would say that it was easily the happiest time of my life so far. We were living in a cramped, two-bedroom house, which was our first home. And even though it was tiny, we loved it. Those early months after we'd first brought Jenna home were magical. Every day seemed special. I often look back at the pictures and wonder how we coped at the time. We were so young and barely adults ourselves. The prospect of bringing up another tiny human being was both frightening and exhilarating. But I enjoyed every experience. Alison and I seemed to have more time to spend together. There didn't seem to be all the distractions we have now, and we were so content with what we had. Admittedly, we did still like nice things, but back then, we weren't obsessed with attaining more. We were happy with our little world.

And with reference to your relationship, how did you get on?

As well as ever. Without the million and one distractions of me being away and Alison's business, we always seemed to have plenty of time to be together. And it was the abundance of time, I suppose, that enabled us to be close and intimate. There were always opportunities to talk about the day, work through our issues or catch up on the world. And even though Jenna wasn't an easy baby, our life was good. We still had the occasional money worries, like all newlyweds with young children, but it never seemed to pull us down. We still lived life to the full. Even though we were short of money back then, I often crave that wonderful time. I know I was much happier. Life was far less stressful.

And anything else about the closeness of your relationship?

Only that Alison and I seemed to be on the same wavelength most of the time. Neither one of us had many outside influences pulling us in different directions, so our connection was stronger than it had ever been. We'd often remark how strange it was that one of us would say something just as the other was about to speak. After a while, we became used to it, but I remember it freaking us both out at the time. It was as if we were tuned into an identical frequency.

Good. That is the point I wanted you to arrive at. So you took these unusual phenomena for granted after a period?

Yes, we never thought much about it after a while. It all seemed like normal behavior.

Normal behavior to read one another's thoughts?

Yes. I suppose I have never really thought about it that deeply. But there was another thing, too. It wasn't just our thoughts that fell into line when we were close. Our feelings also seemed to align. When our relationship was at its most intense and emotional, our feelings also correlated. I can give you a good example.

Shortly before Jenna was born, Alison would get severe panic attacks. She would begin to worry about all manner of things: how the birth would go, whether the midwife would be good, whether we would make suitable parents. The strange thing was that I would be out on the road selling during the day when these overwhelming feelings of dread and anxiety would sweep over me.

At first, I didn't know what to make of these unusual feelings of dread. To begin with, I imagined that I, too, was beginning to worry about the birth. But it perplexed me because I was always pretty much laid back about whatever was coming up in my life. It wasn't until the evenings, when we were chatting over dinner, that I realized what was going on. I was picking up on Alison's fear, just like I'd done with my mother all those years ago.

I told Alison about everything I was feeling. I explained to her what I'd experienced and what time of the day it had happened. The coincidences were startling. I couldn't believe how many times I was spot on. It was as if I was tuned into her emotions.

Alison would often laugh it off. She'd joke about it and always say that I was coming out in sympathy. But I knew in my heart that something deeper and more profound was going on. I absolutely knew that I was tuning in.

That is a good story and perfectly depicts what I want to say. You were right not to just pass it off as coincidence. Nothing in this world happens by just coincidence. All of life is happening for a reason. It is all happening in a divine order to mirror back the feelings, thoughts and intentions of us all.

So what was happening? Was it an identical situation to the one I experienced with my mother when I was a child?

Similar, but not identical. The type of love that became the bridge for you to pick up the emotional resonance of Alison and your mother was different, but the process was the same. When we are emotionally attuned to someone we love, a higher frequency of communication, or empathy, is established. And when we share the same thoughts and desires as another, we come into alignment with the energy of that person. We literally feel their emotions as if they were our own. That is empathy. It's the ability to be emotionally intuitive, or in tune, with something or someone who means a lot to you.

So, presumably, this is possible for everyone? Our partners and relatives all tune into us on deeper levels of understanding? We all pick up the energy of emotions of those closest to us?

No, not exactly. It is a fact that we all have this intuitive ability, for it is woven into our genes at birth, and it is embedded into our energy system. But, unfortunately, few people believe this is possible or try this principle out for themselves. A couple could be married for sixty years, but this means nothing if the love that they share is not unconditional. Only unconditional love between two parties allows the true relationship bridge of empathy to be fully used and engaged. Only then can two people connect on a deeper, more loving, soul level of understanding.

Are you referring to soul mates?

Not necessarily. What you may term a soul mate has been grossly misinterpreted. For many people, their life-long dream is to find their soul mate, a person who they naively imagine will fulfill all of their emotional, romantic and spiritual needs. Many hold the notion that there is only one person out there, a soul mate, who is waiting to come along and make their lives more loving and abundant. I don't want to shatter this myth, but soul mates come in many different guises and relationships. A soul mate is any person who plays a key role in one or more of the important relationships throughout your life. You will, therefore, have several soul mates in your lifetime, not just one.

166

So a soul mate is not just a romantic partner? It is not restricted to only one person?

Goodness, no. Most definitely not. Although this is often the most common misconception among many people, it is not true. And, anyway, what would you possibly learn from the miracle of life and other people if this were true? What growth could your soul attain if you were to restrict your deepest intimacy to only one person? Soul mates are those close friends, and often loving partners, who help you to discover deep parts about yourself that perhaps even you had not noticed before. They are people who gift you with open and loving relationships that show up just at the appropriate time in your life.

But how do we know when a soul mate first shows up?

Believe me, you just know. From the very first moment that you meet with a soul mate, every cell in your being will tingle if you are sensitive to your own energy field. And if you are intuitively tuned into their wavelength, they will also pick up on this and feel it on an energetic level. Have you not felt the spark of this sensation before? Have you not met a stranger and immediately felt as if you have known that person all of your life?

Yes, I have. On several occasions.

A few years back, a new company rep made an appointment to come and see me. He was new to the industry and was prospecting for business. The manager I was working for back then told me to ignore this new rep and show him the door. He said that we already had adequate suppliers and hinted that I should not waste even five minutes on this guy. But a strange thing happened. Initially, I obeyed my manager and cancelled the appointment. But then, when he'd left the room, I rang the rep back up and reinstated our meeting.

I'm glad I did. When the rep turned up, we sat and chatted for nearly two hours. I felt like I'd known the guy all my life. We got on brilliantly. There was a weird, intuitive hit in my body. Don't ask me why, but I had a strong feeling that this new rep would play a fundamental part in my life. I didn't know what that would be, but somehow I just knew it to be true.

And what happened?

My gut reaction was on the nail. The guy, Simon, turned out to be someone I hit it off with. Even though my manager clearly detested him, I got on fine with Simon. And now, several years later, we are the best of friends. We've been everywhere together. He is just like a brother to me. What's been even more important is that Simon and I have the most intense and deeply profound chats imaginable. I share intimate details with him that I wouldn't dare share with my wife or other male friends. I sometimes feel guilty about this, though. I occasionally think that I am being dishonest, telling Simon about parts of my life that even my own wife doesn't know about.

I'm glad you have mentioned that. That perfectly describes what I wish to tell you about soul mates.

Please do not feel guilty that you bring out parts of your inner world to others that you do not share with your wife. That is what soul mates, if you want to use that expression, are for. Different soul mates are there to give you the perfect platform for the relationships that your soul requires for you to grow and evolve. And they breeze into your life to help you connect with your soul's essence, the deeper part that is the truth of what and who you are.

It is unfair to put all the pressure on one partner alone. If you were to burden only Alison with every single question you have about your life's journey, then it would not only pile onto her an unfair amount of emotional tension, it would also literally suck all of the loving energy out of your special relationship.

So we shouldn't empty our inner world out onto only our partner?

I am not intimating whether you should or shouldn't. What I am saying is that every one of your special relationships brings something different to your table. They all, in their uniquely special ways, gift you with different opportunities of expressing yourself.

Do not get caught up in the illusion that one person alone can service all of your many needs. For if you make this assertion, you will not only spend your life unfulfilled, but you will also suffocate that one special relationship with your partner.

I'm not sure why or how I know this, but I've always had a strong feeling that what you are saying is true. I know I have sometimes felt guilty about this, but on another level, I knew it was fine. So it is okay to be intimate with another person outside of our own special relationships?

All of your friendships are special. Every one of your close bonds is divinely unique. There is not a single one of your present relationships that isn't serving you in some way, even the ones that you may critically judge to be negative and harmful.

Of course, your question depends on what you personally mean by the term "intimate." If you mean your deepest, innermost experience, then yes, sharing your intimacy with a number of your soul mates will definitely help you with your personal development. Those who are mentally and emotionally stable enough already know this to be true. They know that the key to good mental and emotional health is being able to express the inner world of their true feelings with a variety of sources, not just their partners.

And what about sharing our life experiences and feelings with complete strangers? Is it okay to open up our true emotions to someone we've only just met? Even if he or she does feel like a soul mate?

I am not the one to judge you on this. It is up to you to decide whether a stranger will be able to throw better light onto one of your life situations. It is up to you to decipher whether a relationship has lessons for you to learn. What I will say, however, is this: Do not ever close off the avenue that sudden, brief encounters can bring to your presence. Don't disregard the beauty that a new relationship can bring into your life because you may just be turning down the chance to meet a new soul mate. If you approach every relationship with an open mind and a willing heart, you will not go far wrong.

But hang on. What about the times when I have literally felt toxic and angry emotions emitting from a stranger? Are you saying that I should be open-minded to *all* people, regardless of whether I feel a bad vibe coming from them or not?

I've experienced several occasions when I have sensed and picked up very angry and bitter emotions from people I have only just met. The energy I felt inside my body was practically poisonous. What do I do in this situation? Ignore them? Move away from them?

You are the one doing the choosing. You may either move closer or walk away. The choice is always yours depending on what you wish to learn from a relationship. You should not entertain any bad vibes or energy that you don't feel comfortable with. Remember, you are the one who allows people into your space. You are in control of your own destiny. What I am saying, however, is this: At least give yourself and the other person a chance for the relationship to blossom. Do not only watch for your initial gut reaction, for it is not the only reliable source.

But haven't you said before that our first impression, gut instinct and intuition, are all valuable pointers that we should initially watch out for?

They are, but here is the rub: Remember that you are only picking up and sensing vibes that the stranger is vibrating out into the world. If the person is afraid of you or not open with you, then you will not be feeling the whole picture of who that person really is. You will only be sensing the emotions that sit on the surface.

So that is not the truth of who they really are?

No, of course it is not. It is only a part. Why? Did you think it was?

Yes, actually I did. I thought that if I was sensitive and intuitive enough, then I could pick up the feelings from another person, just as I was always able to do with my mother.

When you sense a stranger's thoughts and underlying emotions, you are not making a true connection to him or her. For that to occur, both parties have to be conscious and open to one another. They have to express unconditional love to each other.

Even strangers?

Yes, even if they are strangers to you. Only then can true empathy be experienced. Only at that point can you feel that special moment when you briefly touch something deeper and more profound than yourself.

This is the gift of kinship on a soul level. You and the other become one. In some cases, it may only be fleeting, but when you experience this kinship, you will then know what it feels to be truly alive.

So do we have different levels of intuition, depending on how emotionally linked we are to a person?

You are correct. You have observed well. That is a very good way of phrasing it. When you are unconditional with your love and tenderness toward another, you reach a higher level of love and compassion that goes beyond words. When this occurs, you could sit next to someone and stare all day into that person's eyes without uttering a word. It will not matter, for you will both share something deeper and stronger than any one word could hope to convey. That is because a bridge has been created. You have both built a bridge where every part of your energy flows freely to the other. When this occurs, you both know it.

But how do we know? Is there an obvious sign or something?

You just know. Every cell in your body will shout to you in celebration. And if you are both open and sensitive enough, you will both feel this at exactly the same time.

Unfortunately, when you first come close to a stranger, there is no bridge of love to connect two people. There is no deep connection and high level of compassion. This is because you are only reading the stranger's energy field on a shallow, superficial level. When you meet someone for the first time, you are only feeling what is on the surface of his or her core emotions.

But putting that aside, we still shouldn't judge a book by its cover? We shouldn't pass up this opportunity to at least try to connect with a stranger?

Yes, you are correct. There is a depth to every human being that cries out to be revealed and uncovered. When you first meet a stranger, you are not seeing, or rather feeling, the entire picture. Therefore, before you run a mile and throw away the chance to develop a new relationship, at least allow the person a fair opportunity to show you his or her best side. Always try to give people the benefit of the doubt by allowing them time to open up, and therefore close down, their fear of meeting strangers. Who knows, once the ice is broken, you just may find a soul mate waiting to be revealed under that tough-looking veneer.

Always use unconditional love when you first approach strangers because on a level of life energy, they will feel your intent deep within them. If they are highly sensitive and intuitive, they will pick up on your true intentions. Before you even utter a word, they may well feel your emotions in their body. They will possibly sense your thoughts, too.

Boy, that would certainly change everything in the world, wouldn't it?

Twenty-Nine

*C*learly, we are all more connected to each other than I had ever realized! Another repercussion of this concept occurred to me.

If we all knew that another person could tap into our thoughts, then we'd certainly watch out for everything that arose in our minds. We would certainly be wary of what we discussed behind people's backs, too.

Don't forget that emotions are significantly more intense than thoughts. Emotions carry a much stronger charge of vibration in the body than any of your thoughts. That is why you are more than likely to pick up the emotions rather than the thoughts of a stranger.

And we can do this with anyone at all?

Yes, anyone. But please remember that it is not only the energy of one person that you can tune into. You can also sense the collective energy of crowds and places. It's also possible for you to pick up the joy or fear of a collective group.
If you are struggling to hold this truth in your mind, use visualizations to remember a time when this has happened to you.

I am not certain of what you mean by "visualizations." Do you mean images and memories from the past?

No, not exactly. By visualizations, I am referring to both your images from your past and the emotional responses that overlaid your

experiences at the time. You may well be able to remember many of
your memories from the past, but only once these are injected with the
energy of emotion do they really come alive inside of you.

Now, try to think back to a period when you were absolutely petrified,
a time when you feared for your life.

That is an easy one.

Well, then, when was it?

I was only a teenager at the time, and I remember it vividly. It
was when New Wave music was all the rage in the late '70s. The
revival movement I belonged to was called The Mods, a group of
teenagers who met up every national holiday, usually close to a
seaside resort. We used to all dress up smartly in sharply cut suits,
shirts and ties, and most of us had our own motor scooters.

On one particular August holiday, a huge fleet of rockers on
motorbikes rolled into town. They spent hours riding menacingly
up and down the seafront, throwing things at us. They were
clearly spoiling for a fight. There were hundreds of police officers
around, so naively we thought that we were safe, but we weren't.
Suddenly, the bikers stopped, dismounted from their bikes and
charged at us. I have never been so scared in my entire life. The
bikers charged through the police cordon and went for us with
knives, knuckle-dusters and baseball bats. It was anarchy. Fights
broke out everywhere. Scooters were picked up and thrown into the
sea. Beach huts were smashed to pieces. It was a living nightmare.
Hundreds of girls were shouting, screaming and crying. And even
families got caught up in the fracas.

Before we realized it, hundreds of bikers had trapped us at the
end of the pier. We were cornered like rats. There was nowhere to
go. Some of my friends jumped the railings into the sea. Others
tried to stay and fight, but it was useless. It was men against boys.
Because I was a fast runner, I somehow managed to sprint clear
and head for the entrance. I still don't know how I escaped with
only a few cuts. A lot of the others ended up with slashed faces,
ripped clothes or deep knife wounds. Fortunately, no one was

killed that day, but it frightened the hell out of me. A few of us never went on bike rallies again.

And are you still able to recapture how you were feeling at the time?

Recapture it…I'm practically feeling it inside of me right now. I can still go straight back into that very same moment and feel my heart racing. It's as if I am back there again.

You are back there again, my friend. You are back there reliving it another time. That is the power that emotions have over you. If you allow them, they can reappear at any time you choose. This is what I have wanted to describe to you by using the word "visualization." If you imagine an event from your past, and then inject it with emotion, you will literally bring alive again those same, identical feelings.

How can I purposely inject a memory with an emotion? My mind just brings these thoughts up to the surface when it wants to, doesn't it?

Your mind does not control you. It is the other way around. Do not for a moment believe that you are the servant to your mind. The reverse is true. When you become fully conscious of this truth, you will have gained much wisdom.

You asked how to inject emotion into the images of your memory. Well, you simply concentrate every bit of your conscious attention on the moment you wish to reconnect with. To do this entails that you clear your mind of all other thoughts. You become aware and present. You also clear your body of every single emotion, and then you will open up to your past. Do this often, and you will be shocked by how vivid and real your memories can become. In some cases, it will be even more authentic and real than the original experience itself.

How can that possibly be?

When you return to an original moment that has been experienced in the past, you are often more conscious the second time around. Your attention, awareness and level of consciousness are often more attuned to what your senses and emotions were showing you at the time.

175

I know that this is happening to me time and again, but I still find this whole thing fascinating. It's almost as if we are able to time travel through the emotions and feelings of our own bodies. We are able to re-enact and recreate our past in the present.

I like that interpretation. What you are saying is very close to the core truth of what is happening throughout our lives. Know that the past continues to live on inside of us through the power and energy of our emotions. And the best way to connect with that past is to get in touch with your emotions, for they are your signposts.

Signposts?

Signposts that can point you exactly to what is going on within your own mind. In a harsh sense, your emotions are nothing more than combined reflections of your thoughts in a physical form.

Can you answer a question? Why is it that we remember certain memories more vividly than others? I have memories from my childhood, twenty-five years ago, that I now remember more distinctly than something that happened yesterday.

It all has to do with how emotionally conscious you were of your sensory data at the time of input. Put another way, the more aware you were of your emotions, the greater the chance of retaining that memory. This is because the energy of emotion enables us to be highly conscious of the world around us. But if you are shut off from your emotions and locked in fear, then you will not lay down a strong memory. And here is something that you should also be aware of: If you allow the mind chatter to rule over you, you will look right past many of those special moments in your life.

I want to get this point right. What you are saying is that the more aware we are of our emotions, the more conscious we become of the world around us. And the more consciously aware we become, the more likely it is that we will retain a memory.

See, you are now beginning to gain great insight into the miracle of life. But there is something else you should know. Your past can also create a much deeper impression in your memory when your emotions are tuning into the emotions of many other people.

Do you mean situations where I have shared my emotions with a group?

Yes. Never underestimate the power that a group-consciousness can have over how you act. If you have been part of a very large celebration shared with thousands of other people, then you will already know what I am talking about. It is no coincidence that the most vivid and memorable experiences that we possess are also associated with those times when we were part of a large crowd or group.

Just as I was with that crowd on the pier, when we were being hounded by the bikers.

Correct. The combined energy and emotion of that crowd imprinted into the memory of your cellular system. These are powerful emotional triggers that will stay with you for your entire life. Have you not ever wondered why fighting now disgusts you? Have you not thought why all forms of violence immediately trigger great fear within you? What happened to you that day on the pier left a deep emotional impression on you. It would be something that would remain in your head to this very day.

Something has just made sense to me. This is the same for all emotional memories, isn't it? Be they good *or* bad ones. That's why some of the fondest memories I have are all those times when I was most conscious and highly emotional.

But hang on. What about those bad memories that do not serve us any longer? What about the terrifying memories and fears that chain us to the past? How can I ever shift those emotions if I no longer want them to be part of me?

Old emotional memories will always be a part of us. They cannot be separated from us because they are imprinted and woven into our cellular system.

Does that mean, therefore, that we all have to suffer the old emotional traumas forever? Are you telling me that our negative past emotions will always sabotage our present?

If that were the case, then we would all be walking around as emotional, nervous wrecks. Were that to be true, then we would not be able to function properly as human beings. We are thankful this is not the case. Emotions that no longer serve us can be healed, and emotions that sabotage our lives do not need to constantly be present in the body.

So how can we heal them? You have already stated that all energy never disappears; it just transforms. So how can we rid ourselves of these emotional chains that hold us back and make us hide away? What must we do to ensure that these emotional traces don't ruin the rest of our lives?

Are you touching on the edge of your own personal experiences?

Yes, as a matter of fact, I am. I was remembering my English teacher back when I was eleven years old. Some of the painful memories still live on within me. I am positive that many of my fears about standing up to speak in public are attributable to those awful memories.

And you have observed very well. That is precisely the emotional memory that ignites your fears.

Then what can I do about it? Every time I get up to make a presentation to clients, I always remember back to that time in the classroom. I begin sweating. I feel nervous and flushed, and there are times when I start stuttering and stumbling. It is so embarrassing. I hate it that some past event is holding me back this way. I've moved on from that. I've developed and grown in so many other ways. So why does this fear from the past constantly keep hijacking me?

Because the emotional channels that you have formed have become deeply imbedded in your psyche. A deep groove has been formed into which you keep falling. What you are doing every time you get up to speak is reigniting old trapped emotions from the past.

Must it always be this way?

No. Most definitely not. Do not imagine for a second that your emotions fix your behavior forever. You can heal the energy that is trapped within your emotion by transforming it.

To what?

By transmuting it into a positive emotion. When you release the life-force energy from what you would term a negative emotion, you can then convert that same energy into a positive emotion.

How?

There are two simple processes. The first involves cutting off the energy force that has been feeding these negative emotions in the past.

What energy?

The energy of your thoughts. Your negative and self-critical thoughts have been feeding and igniting the emotion of fear in your body. Try to recapture a memory of this process, and I will show you how. Can you now bring this type of feeling into your consciousness right now?

Yes, I can. I don't believe it, you are right. I'm now imagining standing up in front of a crowd. My heart is racing, and my breathing is labored. I feel sick with worry.

And what are you remembering?

I'm recalling that moment in the classroom when I was ridiculed by the teacher for messing up my lines.

So you are reliving the past in a present moment?

Yes. All those same feelings are returning: the apprehension, embarrassment and fear. So what is going on, and how can I stop it?

The secret is to realize that you are not your past. You are your present. What you are doing is letting the emotions and thoughts of more than twenty years ago bully you in your present reality. You are letting them sabotage every experience that is related to speaking to a group of people. Stopping it is simpler than you think, and I mean that literally. If you want this behavior to end, simply stop thinking back to that time. Cut off the power supply of your emotions, which is the energy charge of your thoughts.

This sounds so simple that a child could understand it.

It is simple when you know how. The process is one of the easiest laws to master, and yet some people go their entire lives trapped in this loop. Master this simple process, and you will become both the creator and director of your emotions. You will then come to acknowledge that controlling our emotions is one of the fundamental aspects of living a full and abundant life. This truth is so simple that it should be taught to every single child in the world. If it were, then much of the shocking violence you presently witness would dissolve.

You mentioned that there were two key principles to transforming negative emotion into positive emotion. What is the other one?

You are now aware that the energy of your thoughts feeds the life force that constitutes an emotion. The second way you can alleviate negative emotion in the body is by transforming it into a creative and positive force. Let me give an example that is relative to your life situation.

When your English teacher scolded you for your inability to read properly from a book, it imprinted onto you the negative emotion of fear and indecision. His condemning behavior and complete lack of compassion literally set the tone for your unstable emotional patterns.

You could say that certain emotions have made you a prisoner of your own life. They have formed a deep emotional pattern that is hard to break out of. Now, let me ask a question. How did this whole event leave you feeling?

Helpless. Stupid. Angry. Annoyed. Victimized. I could go on.

Right, I get the picture. A lot of repressed anger is still alive inside of you, and a lot of stored, unexpressed emotion is waiting to climb out and find the surface. Now, what do you imagine will happen to these emotions if you just carry on, not attending to them? What do you think will happen to your energy levels, not to mention the state of your mind, if nothing alters?

From what you have said before, these repressed emotions will begin to eat away at me on an energetic level. My trapped and denied anger will begin to manifest itself in the form of pains in my body. It will also, I suspect, drain me, leaving me tired and exhausted. There could be any number of other physical symptoms.

Good. So what if I now told you that these same negative emotions could also inspire and energize you? What if I said that all the poisonous and toxic emotion that you have built up over the years could all be transformed into an energy that will engage and enrich you? Could you believe that this is possible?

I'd like to believe that, yes. It seems like a win-win situation to me. Who in his right mind wouldn't want to be healed of those negative emotions from the past that hold us all back?

You'd be shocked if you knew the true number of people who are letting their trapped emotions dominate and bully them. And that is only the conscious ones. What many don't realize is that their negative and denied emotions are affecting their lives anyway, whether they choose to bring them out into the light or not, regardless of whether they are consciously aware of it or not. Try to remember those occasions when you have suddenly lost your temper over something mundane and trivial. You weren't blowing your top at the seemingly insignificant matter. You were letting your emotions explode because of the combined, undealt-with emotional difficulties from the past.

This is astonishing and yet so true. That is exactly what happened with my father. He kept his true feelings bottled up, and then he would explode into a rage because of something trivial and ridiculous. And I can relate many of my own behaviors to this pattern, too. I remember occasions when I would flip because of the most ridiculous matter.

Do you remember what I told you earlier? Many murders are committed in this manner. It is very rare for a person to meticulously plan a murder. Most murders happen on the spur of the moment. They happen because a person suddenly loses control of the emotions inside his or her body. Most demonstrated rage is an instinctual and sudden response that barely lasts more than a few moments.

There is something deeply sad and yet so true about what you are saying. It is so easy to have a head-rush of emotion that can ultimately lead to shocking consequences. But it shouldn't have to be this way, should it? We should have lessons about how to control emotion as a child. And it should continue well into adulthood, I think.

I was taught so many subjects at school that I just knew would have no practical use to me in the outside world. And yet I don't think that emotion as a subject came up even once in all the time I was in education.

Do not make the mistake of just blaming the education system. Around the time when you left school, the topic of emotion wasn't even on the radar. Society was in a different place. And so, too, was the collective consciousness of the planet. But the times we are now living in are fast-changing. What worked then will not work today. The world has shifted, and so have we. What we now require in the twenty-first century is an education based on community, connection and empathy. We need a system where children's education centers on, and around, the environment that supports us. We need a system of training and reverence that honors the planet that sustains us, not a system that is hell-bent on conquering, manipulating and destroying nature.

But this will never happen in my lifetime.

It will happen because it is imperative. It has to happen. For without these changes to our education and thinking, we will cease to exist as a human race. Our very survival rests on society altering its perception of how the world comes together. It is therefore vital to our evolution as a species that these changes in thinking are implemented, for if we don't break through as a race, then we will break down.

From what you have been vividly describing to me so far, I'm not sure if I am more shocked and horrified by revelations of an approaching Armageddon, or the fact that emotions and empathy are about to play such a key role in our very survival. I find this ironic, especially when science won't even take the role of the emotions, or the subjective, seriously.

That may have been true at the end of the twentieth century, but it will not be the case throughout much of the next. And please let me make an important point here: Do not ever become discouraged or depressed by images of what could possibly be created in our future. As with all truth, we have to first sometimes stare into the abyss before we can move away from it. What I am portraying should motivate and inspire you, not frighten and alarm you. I am merely pointing out scenarios that will occur if we don't change our direction and wake up in time. My words on this matter are not a certainty. The only certainty I can assure you of is this: We still hold the future in our hands.

Thirty

I was frightened by the thought that our future is at risk. It appeared that we needed to make some difficult changes as a race if we are to ensure our survival.

This entails that we take more responsibility for our own actions and emotions…

Responsibility is a great word, probably the best word that perfectly describes the critical work that lies ahead of us. We must take on more ownership of what we are creating, be it inner peace, joy and love, or the death and destruction in the world. The choice is ours. It always has been throughout all of time. The only difference today is that we are only just beginning to become conscious of this undeniable truth. We are only now waking up to realize that we hold the golden key to creation. We are not only the genie in the bottle here. We are also the Aladdin making the wishes.

Wouldn't this new attitude require a major overhaul of the way we view the world and how it all connects? Wouldn't this mean that the very laws that underpin scientific inquiry are rewritten?

The laws that govern the nature of reality have been constantly changed and altered over time. Science has readapted its principles and reassessed its theories. Since splitting from religion in the Age of Enlightenment, science has constantly rewritten how it views the nature of reality.

So the scientific laws are a work in progress? They're not complete by any stretch of the imagination.

Heavens, no. Science is by no means complete. Like us all, it is in a constant process of evolution that is forever altering and expanding. What was yesterday's scientific truth is not necessarily the truth for today. The only fixed certainty about science of the future is that it will be consistently changing and evolving to new forms of understanding.

But this evolution in the scientific protocol is clearly not coming quickly enough, is it? Don't we now need a more complete science to break through? Aren't many of us now crying out for a new science that integrates the mystical and unusual, the profound and the extraordinary? I think we are screaming out for a new science that entertains both the supernatural *and* reason.

Do not fall into the habit of condemning the scientific reason that has served humanity well. It has given us phenomenal breakthroughs in health care and medicine, and it has prolonged life and eradicated many of the lethal diseases that have wreaked havoc around the world. But you are right in your observation. Science in its present form is not close to discovering all the answers. Nor will it. Not if Newtonian science continues to remain distant and detached from the universal laws of spirit and energy. Only when life energy comes into the equation will science begin to come close to finding its much awaited "Theory of Everything."

The current scientific paradigm definitely isn't coming up with all the answers that so many of us are desperate to discover. I want to know why many experiences, similar to those I have felt, remain unreported and kept out of mainstream understanding. More than anything else, I want to know about the link between mind and body. I'm positive that as human beings, we don't yet have a fraction of the full picture yet.

You are right to question the existing paradigm that has served us for several hundred years.

Served us? Really! You've got to be kidding me. I agree that reason had to replace superstition. Then the society of several hundred years ago could be introduced to a more grounded and proven understanding of the laws of nature. But, come on, hasn't it now tipped too far the other way? Hasn't science now tried to dominate matters of the spirit?

Please do not misinterpret my message here, but what I have to say on this matter is highly important. Everything in the evolution of consciousness has moved along in perfect order. All the discoveries, breakthroughs and paradigm shifts were all in perfect alignment. Stringent scientific laws needed to be in place to help humanity gain a better and more complex understanding of reality. It needed to construct a solid base from which to build.

Are you about to defend science here?

I am not about to do anything of the sort except point out to you some unquestionable facts. The process of science throughout history has forged ahead in helping to interpret how we see the universe. What I am now saying is that science is about to undertake radical changes of direction in how it measures, gauges and interprets the world in which we live. Whole new disciplines are forming that will very soon point the spotlight of inquiry onto all new fields. And this much is certain. The science of the twenty-first century will be unrecognizable from that of the twentieth century.

How?

In numerable ways. To begin with, new insights into what we perceive to be real will open up. Whole new theories will develop around fields that science would not have been interested in several hundred years ago. This much is certain. What we once believed to be the core tenets holding science together will begin to fracture and fall away. Replacing them will be a whole new evolution of human capabilities that will flower and, therefore, demand that science take a closer look at what reality is and how creation works. The most exciting developments will be focused around studies into consciousness.

What many will see in this lifetime is the coming of a scientific revolution so deep and so profound that it will completely shatter our wisdom of the past. An entirely new paradigm is opening up before our very eyes. Human beings are about to discover that they have not only the capability to heal themselves of most diseases, but they can also create many of the events that happen in their world if they are conscious and present enough.

I knew that we had the capacity to heal much of our own pain. It's something I have been very aware of since I was younger. There have been numerous occasions throughout my life when I have used this rock-solid belief of mine. We *can* heal ourselves because I have experienced it.

Several months after I was knocked down by a car, I started to become acutely aware that my thoughts determined the state of my health. I'm not certain *how* I knew this, but I did. It was something that just came to me one night in bed. Whenever I contracted a cold or flu from a friend, it would immediately kickstart a game in my head. I would imagine that I was in control of my own thoughts, and if I didn't want any illnesses inside of me, I simply zapped any negative thoughts away. For me, any negative thoughts in my head were destructive, whereas all the positive thoughts carried with them huge opportunities for growth and good health.

So what was the outcome? Did it work?

Always. I was rarely off sick from school. In the end, this whole process became a game to me. The moment any illness showed up, I zapped it before it ever had a chance to take root. I simply bombarded my mind with only positive thoughts.

And did you ever share this process with any of your friends?

Not likely. They probably would have thought I was bonkers. After all, who would believe that my positive thoughts could heal most of my physical diseases?

You should have shared your incredible secret. Discussing how the process of belief can alter the cells in your body is a wisdom that will become more openly accepted in the decades ahead.

How will it become accepted? How is anything going to change if so many people are entrenched in their unmoveable belief systems? If so many believe that a particular theory will not work for them, then surely nothing will change. You have to believe in something to see it and feel it.

My answer on this will always be the same. Always go out and turn a theory into experience. It is then that you will begin to piece together how incredibly powerful and creative each human being is. Do not ever be told what you cannot do, just because science or medicine says so. The secret is to always challenge the same record you have had in your head for all these years. If you do believe that something is possible, or you don't believe it, either way you are correct.

Because we are creating a self-fulfilling prophecy here, aren't we?

You're right. That is a very good way of seeing it. You do create a self-fulfilling prophecy with the beliefs and thoughts that you create. What we think, we create. What we deny falls away. You are beginning to touch the core essence of what makes us all uniquely different co-creators in this universe. By piecing together the fundamental principles of creation, you are touching a truth that had laid dormant for way too long. Your thoughts, feelings and actions do create the life you lead. And how you perceive the world from inside of you does project a carbon copy onto the reality of your outside world.

For way too long, my friend, you have not always believed in your own unique ability to create the life you want. You were content to just gamble and let fate play its hand. But here is one of the great revelations for your life: There is no fate, except for the one that you and your mind construct for you. Everything that is showing up has in some way been magnetized toward you, by you. It all happens for a reason.

I have now given you this insight and understanding in several different ways, but what will you do with this wisdom? How will you use it to create what you wish in life?

189

I would hope to share this knowledge with as many people as were prepared to listen. I would shout it from the rooftops and scream it out loud.

But, please, you would not need to evangelize these core truths. For to preach to others makes them nervous. Better still, live your truth out in the open. Be an example for others to follow. Then your truth will generate real power.

I'd like to know something. Will the blinkers ever be taken off science so that we can all begin to live in healthier and more sustainable ways?

Do not worry, for this is already happening. You may not be overly aware of the changes now happening, but believe me, a new and more enlightened paradigm is evolving. It may not be as fast as many would like, but make no mistake, the world is shifting. Science does need to move onto a new, more connected way of interpreting nature, just as the right and the left side of your brain need to work in unison. And just as the feminine and the masculine energy within you needs to become one, so too does the rational and the irrational. For if science remains isolated from the work of spirit, and if it ignores the power of the mind, then it will forever remain wanting and incomplete. However, bring in the subjective emphasis of emotion, experience and empathy, and science will become an integrated and whole discipline.

The study and emphasis on reason, testing and measuring may have served the scientific fraternity of yesteryear. It may have enabled enormous breakthroughs, but that is in the past. What is now urgently required is an integrated way of looking at the world. We need a measure that can bring a gentler, more holistic approach to the field of science and spirit.

This is so inspiring and encouraging, and yet what we are desperately crying out for is something that makes us all feel fully human again. We need a science base that makes us feel connected, alive and whole, not detached, depressed and uninspired.

There you have it. I couldn't have put it better myself.

And we need a platform where those of us who have encountered mystical experiences aren't made to feel as if we are freaks. Just because modern science says that something is not possible doesn't mean that I haven't experienced it.

My good friend, we are all experiencing the miracle of extraordinary mystical encounters. It is not a question of whether they are happening within our lives, but whether we are open-minded and conscious enough to appreciate them. A definitive key to becoming conscious of this process is to be in tune with our own emotions. We must observe our emotions because only then can we work out where we are in relationship to all others.

Can you expand on what you mean by "others?"

By others, I am referring to every other living entity on this earth that also broadcasts on an energetic and emotional frequency.

Do all animals really have emotions like some scientists say they do?

Please. Have you not ever looked into the eyes of your pet dog and not felt deep emotions of love and friendship? Have you not stared into the eyes of a horse and felt something substantially deeper and more profound? Of course, animals have emotions. Many are more emotionally attuned than their human counterparts. That is because animals live on their natural instincts. They live by their truth.

If I am not mistaken, you have implied that emotion lives on in all living matter. I'm confused. How can a tree in my back garden be full of emotion?

If you stay rooted to your old ways of viewing the world, then yes, this does sound almost preposterous, doesn't it? If you continue to restrain your beliefs, then I can understand why this concept would sound so alien to you. But let me assure you, it is most certainly not. Scientists are only recently beginning to discover that the very same matter that constitutes a tree is also the very same matter that is evident in human beings. We are made up of the same stuff, only in a wildly different combination. *Have I not said before that all living matter contains the energy of life force? And have I not intimated that this energy is constantly dancing in and out of all life?*

Yes, you have.

Well, isn't emotion simply energy and sub-atomic particles weaving and flowing around in one body at great speeds?

Yes.

Then I rest my case.

You sound like you are a judge passing sentence in a court.

My friend, it is humanity and its present, narrow mindset that is in court by appointing itself as the judge, jury and the witness. The saddest fact is that those up on the stand aren't being afforded a fair and reasonable trial.

You're referring to nature and the environment, aren't you?

I am referring to every other living system and organism on this planet that we use, abuse and destroy for our own material needs. As humans, we use and abuse our life-sustaining ecosystem as if it is our own personal servant. Worse than that, we judge everything else outside of human beings to be a threat to humanity when, in fact, the opposite is true. Nature and the wonder of its miraculous ecosystems are the processes that keep us alive. It is the trillions of minute particles, cells and organisms that prevent us from being eaten alive, and it is the proteins and bacteria that prevent our bodies from decaying. The saddest part of our human story is that we just cannot see this wonderful miracle taking place. In our insanity to dominate and control Mother Nature, we have become lazy and complacent. We have looked past the most important part of the equation, which is this: The environment sustains and protects us. It feeds and clothes us.

I feel deeply ashamed of myself here. I have carelessly neglected everything in the world around me. I'm guilty of turning away and burying my head in the sand, of sitting on my hands and doing nothing.

So, why do you think that is? Why have you not done anything about the state of the world?

That is the million-dollar question. I suppose, deep down, I was secretly hoping that someone else would take care of all these problems in the world. I have been trying so frantically to make something of my life and become successful that I neglected to see past my own self-constructed illusions. I have been trapped inside my ego and living out a false life. This may sound pathetic, but I'll say it all the same. I stupidly believed that someone else would be taking care of the planet's ecological needs. I naively imagined that the conservationists and environmentalists would take care of the earth. I believed that somebody else would look out for the planet and rescue us.

But do you not realize that we are that someone else? There's nobody else out there to save us. We are all custodians of this earth. We are all environmentalists who are an essential part of a living, breathing and ever-evolving ecosystem.

I now know that, and it hurts me to finally see my own truth in the mirror. I feel like I've failed myself, and in doing so, failed the planet. I cannot believe that I have been so arrogant and ignorant for spending so much of my time sleepwalking through life.

Do not chastise yourself. There is a positive and transformational element to guilt that can become a powerful force. There is always the grace of a second chance. That is the beauty and magic of redemption. We all get to challenge our so-called mistakes and redeem our careless actions. We all get the chance to right our wrongs. Therefore, do not give yourself a hard time over this. And do not be self-condemning, for that was the past. Instead, rejoice that you have finally awakened to the truth of what needs to be done. Celebrate that you have finally woken up and became conscious of the vital role that you can play. You are finally opening your eyes to an all-new paradigm, one that will become your savior.

Thirty-One

*A*lthough I was ashamed that I had been so blind to these truths, I knew that I wasn't alone in burying my head in the sand.

Please help me out here because there is something I need to grasp. Why are so many of us sleepwalking through these truths that threaten our own existence? If the planet is reaching such a critical point in its evolution, then why are we still strolling through the park as if everything is sweet? If what you say is true, then why aren't more people picking up this deep feeling of unease and restlessness?

Oh, but they are, in more ways than you would ever realize. People the world over are feeling this deep sense of anxiety and fear. They are tuning into the distress call being drummed out by the planet. That is why connecting to our own emotions will be so important in the years ahead. This is why empathy will play such a key role in our recovery as a race.

Both emotion and empathy are pivotal to how we bring the outside world inside of us. And they are critical in that they also enable us to bring our inner world to the surface. Empathy and emotions are the soul's way of shouting to the world, "Yes, I am here right now, and I feel deeply alive." In that way, emotion and empathy gift us with the unique ability to establish what it is to be a spiritual being, to be human.

Our emotions also serve other important functions. They show up in the body to help us define the world, and in doing so, define ourselves. When your destructive emotions appear to be running out of control, listen to them carefully, for they are valuable signs. They are signals that point us to where we must change our lives and our thinking.

How can we possibly alter our thinking? Our thoughts just show up randomly at any time, don't they? How can we control and manipulate our thoughts?

By realizing that we are all in the driving seat of our own lives. Life cannot do for you that which you do not allow through you. You can spend an entire lifetime believing that you are the helpless victim of your thoughts, emotions and others' intentions. You can berate every person who shows up in your life, believing that he or she has in some way wronged you. But it will change nothing. For only when you discover that there is something much deeper and more profound going on here will you fully appreciate that you are infinitely more than just your mind.

Once you recognize that you are a co-creator, you will not only take full responsibility of your life actions and everything that shows up, you will also see the divine truth that no part of creation is ever apart from you because it is part of you.

So life is not just happening to us?

No, at every moment, your life story is happening through you. It is happening through your emotions and thoughts. It is happening through every event that you experience. That is why you feel most alive and connected to life when you are in touch with your emotions.

So, fully acknowledging our trapped and often denied emotions is an essential part of our life process?

Yes. All your emotions are the result of your intentions as a fully creative being. They are the combined sum of all your thoughts in a physical form, whether they show up as good or bad emotions.

Why are you emphasizing good and bad?

Because you are the one who is labeling an emotion. It is your perspective on whether an emotion is good or bad. What you may see today as a bad emotion could well turn out to be a positive turning point in your life. Let me give you a good example. Imagine that you had a "clear-the-air discussion" with one of your directors. And try to imagine that this discussion evolved into a heated and honest exchange of opinions. Before long, you are both expressing your absolute truths. Now, how would this heated confrontation make you feel?

Knowing that I hate confrontation, it would make me feel apprehensive and agitated.

Even if you knew that your point needed to be made?

Yes.

And how would you view the situation if you had told your director exactly what you thought of him? Would you see this as a plus or a minus?

I would be angry with myself for losing control. And then, yes, to answer your question, I would view that emotion as negative and destructive.

Even though it was your absolute truth, you would still see it as negative and destructive?

Well, yes, I suppose so.

Then you are not seeing or appreciating what all emotions can do for us. Regardless of whether you see some emotions as negative or not, they still serve a vital evolutionary function. They give your emotions the perfect opportunity of expressing how you feel and who you are. They do this by igniting the true feelings inside of you. Internal growth of the self will only ever be born from a place of absolute truth, and to touch this truth involves honoring your emotions.

Even the bad, painful and awkward ones?

Especially what you would view as negative emotions.

What is "absolute truth?"

The essence of your true self. Live out in the open and express your emotions as they arise, and a true liberation will come into your presence. At this point, you will, without question, know what your absolute truth is. Your essence is that still and loving part of you that you simply know to be true. You may not know how you know, but you will. It will be sensed within every cell of your body.

Now let us move it on a stage. Let's get back to your discussions with your director. Imagine that you made comments to him that led to your dismissal from your position. Try to imagine that your heated discussions led to you joining another company, one where you are able to fully express your creative talent. In hindsight, how would you now view your verbal emotional outburst?

I think I am joining up the dots. I get your point. What you're saying is that what first appears as a negative life situation and emotion can actually turn out to be a positive. If I wouldn't have had the courage to stand up for my own beliefs and express my true feelings, then that argument wouldn't have taken place. And if the argument hadn't happened, then it would never had inspired me to seek alternative employment.

What you are getting at is that we shouldn't become too attached to everything that is happening to us, especially if the experiences showing up appear at first to be negative and painful.

There you have it. You have answered yourself. What may at first appear to be a disaster is often a stepping stone toward something far greater.

And what exactly is "greater?"

A greater expression of who and what we are. In the context of how I have used the word greater, I am referring to self-growth, and not just as an individual. I'm talking about our cultural community as a whole.

Do you mean collective consciousness?

That's correct. Remember, the one place where you are standing in life only gifts you with a limited picture. It is as if you are pressing your face up against the tapestry of life. Draw back, however, and you will then begin to see the whole picture. In most cases, it's wildly different from what you envisioned. Even those seemingly undesired life events gift us with enormous personal growth down the line.

This point really resonates with me. As I've mentioned before, there have been several situations when it has felt like my whole world is caving in. But later on, and with the chance to reflect, I've discovered that what I imagined to be a disaster was a blessing in disguise.

It is not what we are most comfortable with that offers us the best life lessons. Our greatest teachings and wisdom come from the people and situations where we least expected it.

I remember something that a past manager always said to me. She said that we often learn just as much wisdom from what someone is doing wrong as we do from watching someone do something right.

Only someone who has fully lived will appreciate that statement. Mistakes are not always bad. They help us to see where something can be improved.

But we live in a culture that hides away its mistakes. We are part of a society that condemns mistakes and gives little opportunity for second chances. One example is the way that the media and press hound a person once a mistake comes to light. They chase, bully and blackball somebody until he or she does the "honorable thing" by resigning. The insane thing is that once a person has been broken and has resigned, it is then assumed that the original problem just vanishes. It doesn't. I've seen this time and again.

So what would you do?

I'd give the person another chance to put everything right. After all, in most cases, the person is the most equipped person to resolve the problems. He or she is not likely to make the same mistake twice.

Only an unenlightened race would judge all mistakes as bad. Most of our emotional and personal growth derives from one form of mistake or another. True growth is born out of adversity.

So if my negative and repressed emotions hadn't burst to the surface, I'd never have gone on to find the right job where I could express my creativity to the maximum.

It is not healthy to only express your positive emotions and deny those angry ones. Act in this manner, and you will be denying a large part of who you are. That is why all emotions should be brought up to the light and observed. Lying under those emotions is the truth, not only how you feel, but also the many thought forms that feed those emotions.

The reason why all emotions are important is that they form a vital crossover between your inner spiritual world and your outer physical reality. Our emotions are the important bridge linking the unmanifested potential of the universe with the physical reality of your everyday life. What many have not yet fully fathomed is that emotions are the junction where your true spiritual essence and matter merge together.

You could say that our emotions are physical representations of the divine spirit that resides within each and every one of us. They are the equivalent of all your thoughts in a physical form.

Or, as Einstein stated with his $E=mc^2$, energy is the equivalent of matter squared.

Thank you. See, you are now filling in the gaps for yourself. Emotion is sacred, universal energy becoming real in the world. Or, put more succinctly, divine life force becoming physical in the world of matter in which we live.

This is phenomenal. You describe this in simple ways that are easy to grasp.

Hang on. I think I am just beginning to work out the divine process here. We are the instruments helping the divine to become real, aren't we? And a huge part of this ever-evolving process is our emotions. They help us to feel alive. They enable us to bring our inner world into reality. That's what is going on with this wonderful dance of energy, isn't it? As co-creators, we are creating heaven on earth.

My beloved and cherished friend, you are seeing the truth of life's miracle from an all-new plane. You have joined up the dots to the divine matrix that is unfolding. You, and everyone else on this planet, are calling forth the divine potential of the universe. As the divine makers in this cosmic equation, you are all manifesting the unseen potential of the universe. You, my friend, are the creator. We are all squeezing the infinite possibilities of the universe out into the physical world by the power of our own thoughts and emotions, our actions and reactions. That is how important we all are in this cosmic dance of the heavens. We are not only here to experience the essence of a spiritual life in a physical form. We're also on this planet to learn and remember how to become divine creators of the universe.

Thirty-Two

*T*his was incredible, the notion that we are all co-creators. I felt like I was ready to burst at the seams, as if I had just been given the golden keys to the universe.

So, we are not just some evolutionary accident within the fabric of the universe. And we are not some machine detached from the unfolding process. We are fundamentally a team player in this universal game. We are the director, producer and actor of this creation on earth.

My son, you have not even touched the tip of the iceberg of understanding yet. We are still a young race of souls and are only skimming along the surface here. When we all discover how infinitely powerful we are, everything will change. We will change. Then we will usher in a new paradigm that will render the old one meaningless and obsolete.

If all of this is true, then this means that we *all* have the potential to create heaven *or* hell on earth. We all hold the reins to what is happening in the world.

If you wish to refer to it in those terms, then yes. We are creating heaven or hell on earth. The thoughts we invite into the world decide what we create. We are all contributing to what happens on this planet, whether we are consciously aware of it or not.

But, hang on. Does that mean that there is no heaven or hell out there somewhere? Is there no nirvana or eternal damnation waiting for us? Is there no paradise or place of enlightenment?

How can heaven or hell be out there somewhere? If so, then where is "somewhere"?

I don't know. That's why I was asking you. I was holding onto my childhood belief that there was a heaven or hell.

First, there is no "out there," only what we create inside and outside of us. You can easily create a hell for yourself if you so wish. It is simple. All you need to do is spend your entire life not listening to yourself.

I'm not sure I get what you mean.

Creating a hell for yourself is easy if you continue to believe that your whole life revolves around being a helpless victim. Trap yourself in the false belief that all human beings are bad, and your trust for humanity will go out the window. This type of negative thinking is another way of living out your own hell. For if you cannot trust another person, then what you are really saying is that you cannot trust yourself. And if you do not trust life, then you will not trust yourself. But listening to the soft, loving and compassionate voice of your conscience will lead you away from any self-constructed hell.

And what about our emotions in this equation?

Listening to the emotions in your body is equally important to listening to your own conscience. Combined, they give you a powerful tool of transformation to live and express your life fully. But deny both, and you deny the essence of who you are. If you have ever blanked out your conscience and emotions, then you will know exactly what I mean.

I have spent most of my working life shutting out that niggling little irritation at the back of my mind. Whenever I have done something that a tiny part of me instinctively knows is not right, I have this annoying voice sitting on my shoulder.

When I was about seven or eight years old, I once pinched some chocolate bars from the local candy shop that was owned by my best friend's father. I felt so guilty afterward that it made me sick with worry. Because I was so young and naive, I convinced myself that somehow the police would discover my crimes and arrest me. I spent weeks not being able to sleep properly. It was ridiculous. In the end, I made up my mind to confess to my friend and his father. But every time I entered the shop to apologize and pay up, sheer panic swept through me. I just couldn't bring myself to come clean.

Why?

I was too afraid of losing the trust of my best friend.

So what happened in the end? How long did you remain gripped by guilt?

It was no good. Eventually, my conscience got the better of me. I had to do something. It was driving me nuts. In the end, I went along to another candy shop and bought the same number of identical chocolate bars that I had stolen. Then I went back to my friend's shop with them stuffed up my sleeve. When nobody was looking, I shook the chocolate bars back onto the shelf. No one ever found out.

The sense of relief afterward was incredible. I remember sleeping like a baby that night. I can't tell you how wonderful it felt. It may have only been something trivial, but back then it was if I had stolen the crown jewels.

The more sensitive and still you are, the more you will become aware of your conscience. The greater awareness you have of your emotions, the more in tune you will become with your underlying thoughts.

I always remember back to that week before I finally put right my wrong. The feelings and stress I experienced in my body completely shocked me. They had come from nowhere. On some days, my entire body would be in agony. I didn't appreciate what was going on at the time, but on reflection I now know that my emotions were sending me on a massive guilt trip. The worst thing was that my guilt seemed to follow me around everywhere. It was always at my side, whatever I did. It was sheer relief after I'd decided to give that chocolate back. And, funny enough, all my pains then suddenly vanished.

That is a wonderful story. It perfectly depicts the power that repressed emotions can have on your life. Deny the guidance of your conscience, and you do more than just create a sense of unease. You also turn down the opportunity for massive personal growth.

I want to add something. I've not yet mentioned how my conscience affected my schoolwork. The nagging and incessant voice of my conscience sat on my shoulder like an unwelcome guest. I hated it. It wouldn't shut up, and it drove me mad.

Our conscience is our great truth-teller. Be awake to its message and guidance, for it will free up the mind. Deny and ignore it, however, and you will be continually plagued with self-doubt. Your conscience will never leave you alone because it is an essence of who and what you are. To run away from your conscience is no different from running away from yourself. Sooner or later, you'll discover that you are chained to yourself.

As I've grown up, I have become a master of self-deception. I now know how to turn down the volume of my conscience and even block it out completely. I'm not proud of this behavior, but over the past several years, I have practically blunted the voice of my conscience.

Then you have denied an essential part of who you are as a human being. You have denied your true identity. By blunting your conscience, you are refusing the help of the greatest guidance you have within you. You are, in effect, going through life blind with no guidance system to fall back on.

But I was doing it for my own sanity. The tiny, niggling voice at the back of my head was often condemning, criticizing and abusive. I had to shut it down to survive.

If the mental stream of thoughts in your head constantly condemns you, then it is most definitely not the voice of your own higher guidance. When your own internal guidance communicates with you, it is often wise, insightful and softly spoken. This tone is gentle and undemanding, unlike that of its counterpart, your fearful self. That ego part of your self is forever whining and critical.

You are confusing the voice of your higher self with that of your fearful ego. Please try to discern between these two because one will lead you to your truth. The other will lead you to a state of constant fear, paranoia and indecision.

I've had enough destructive experience in living from my ego state to last a lifetime. My past five or six years have been lived in this place. I have wasted too much time *not* listening to my conscience. Instead, I purposely shut it out and ignored its wisdom.

You never completely shut out your conscience. You just mute it and suspend it. This is exactly the same for any unwanted emotions that you do not wish to face up to. You may deceive yourself in the illusion that certain emotions have evaporated, but they are causing havoc in your body under the surface. It is a grave mistake to believe that if an emotion is out of sight, it is out of mind.

I don't think I like the sound of this. What type of havoc are you referring to?

Emotions that are not healed, resolved or brought through into consciousness sit under the surface of your life, waiting to pounce. They are prowling for the perfect opportunity to arise when they can finally break into the light of your conscious mind. Remember, your emotions are the combined life force of source energy, manifesting in a physical form. They often have messages for you, which you may not always wish to acknowledge. Sadly, because it is often neglected and denied, repressed emotion explodes at the most inappropriate time. It is very often misdirected toward an issue or person who is unrelated to the root of your core anger.

I think most of us have been on the receiving end of that treatment before. We've all experienced the wrath of someone's intense anger and then realized in hindsight that his or her fury must have originated from misplaced emotion.

Displaced emotion, especially in the form of anger and rage, will continue to become a more common occurrence in the decades ahead. If we don't learn how to resolve and heal our emotional trauma in a controlled fashion, then we will all feel the damaging effects of society's repressed emotion. This will cause chaos and have devastating consequences for the fabric of society as a whole, particularly if this fundamental issue is not tackled.

But what must happen for us to avoid this situation from tumbling into chaos?

It is almost so simple that you could literally look right through the answer: be more in tune with the emotions in your body.

In tune?

Be consciously aware of what your emotions are trying to show you. And stop harbouring and repressing damaging emotions that, if not dealt with correctly, will cause havoc to your own body, society and the future of the planet.

Boy, you are really going strong with this emotions thing. From what you have said before, I know they are important. But you talk as if understanding our emotions is paramount to our very survival as a species. The way you elevate this topic, anyone would think that emotions are more important than terrorism, the warming of the planet, or even economics and growth.

There will soon reach a point in your evolution as a race when you will know this simple fact to be absolutely true. Getting a grip on our emotions and understanding what they represent will be one of humanity's greatest challenges in the years ahead. Only when we appreciate that life energy feeds through our emotions will we come to see the truth of what is going on in this cosmic evolution. Emotions are the life-force energy in our bodies. They are a mirror of our combined thoughts in a physical form. Not a single emotion shows up in the body without a prompt or cause.

So every single one of our emotions is born from a cause? And it is possible to control all of these emotions?

Yes, but only once you understand the process of emotions in the bigger picture of life creation. Master this process, and you will gain one of the greatest truths throughout the universe.

This sounds like it is about to become heavy.

It may well be important to our very survival, yet it is also simple to grasp. Even a child can understand the vital role that emotion plays in the matrix of life creation, for it is not difficult to master. The hardest part is convincing your mind that the process of creation can work for you. The only way you can discover this truth is by experiencing it for yourself.

On one level of creation or another, we are the ones who have created our emotions. We have called them forward in response to how we think and where we say we wish to go. No emotion is just an accident. All emotions can be traced back to a definitive cause.

Which is?

Our thoughts. They ultimately create the emotions inside our body. They are the prime cause. They are the original ignition. I want to make some undeniable points here because many hold the false notion that thoughts and feelings are uncontrollable. This is one of the largest mistruths holding back our evolution as a planet. Thoughts may carry significantly less life-force energy than emotions, but they are still a vital function in the whole process of what we create in our lives. They are the match that lights the creative process, and our emotions are the fuel that powers this.

But how do we control our thoughts? I have a million and one different thoughts passing through my mind every day, and I suspect it is the same for the majority of people. How can we choose what thoughts to hold onto, and what thoughts we should let fall away?

You are correct. Most people have a non-stop passing parade of thoughts filling their heads. For some, this is a severe handicap, especially if the majority of those thoughts are damning, self-critical and negative. But do not for a moment believe that you are only your thoughts. Doing so will deny yourself that greater part of you that is linked to the invisible and the divine. If you let this incessant mind chatter rule your life, then it will exhaust and crush you sooner or later.

I can vouch for that. Some days, I arrive home from work and collapse in the chair, absolutely shattered, even though I've barely moved out of my car seat all day. It feels as if my agitation and constant worrying about sales orders, budgets and staff problems are completely draining my energy.

That's because they are. Thoughts demand energy from you to stay alive and thrive in your mind. But if you become addicted to your thoughts, you will soon collapse from mental exhaustion.

As I have discovered to my cost already.

You wouldn't expect to read every news story in every single paper that was published. Well, it is no different with your thoughts. There is no way that you would have the time or energy to attend to every thought. It would be an impossible task, not to mention life-draining. Try it and see what happens. You will discover, at your peril, that incessant thinking will eventually damage your health.

So letting my thoughts run amok in my life is actually bad for my health?

Yes. Your mental, emotional and physiological states all suffer when your thinking takes you over. If you constantly live in your head and deny those other parts of self that need attending to, you will very quickly find your life draining away.

And another point: This behavior also blocks the portal that injects you with creative energy from the divine source. Stay imprisoned in your mind for long periods, and you will very quickly discover that you are obscuring your creativity and inspiration.

Why is this?

Divine inspiration and creativity are the pure essence energy of the divine. This is the life-force energy that wants to break through into the physical world. But it cannot become real if there is something blocking its path.

So, our constant thinking is standing in the way then?

More than standing in the way. Your incessant thinking is obliterating any chance that divine source inspiration has to manifest itself in the world of reality. Please remember, in a harsh sense, you are an instrument of the unseen and the invisible. As a co-creator, you are the perfect tool, the paintbrush that enables the potential of the divine to manifest. Block that channel, however, as many people do, and you refuse all divine essence the chance to break through and to become real. And, worse than that, you actually snuff out any chance you have to be a creative being. There is nobody in this world that cannot be creative. In every single moment, we are all creating something.

But how can we all be creating something in every single moment? You have just told me that some people block out this life-force energy.

You are missing the point. Yes, many do shut off their creative channels that feed divine source into our world. But that doesn't mean that they are not still creating. Let me paint an example. If you spent all your time ignoring Alison and paid her no attention whatsoever, what would you create?

I should imagine that if it went on for too long, I would soon create a divorce.

That is exactly my point. You haven't done anything, but you have still created something unconsciously with your inaction. You have created disharmony, anger and, I suspect, great frustration.

Right, I get it. We are all creating, even if we don't *think* we are creating.

There, see, now you have it. You don't realize that you are creating something because it's not at the front of your mind. Most forms of creating are achieved in this way. Most of what we create in the world is actually done unconsciously, without us even being aware of what the consequences will be. If somebody shuts a door in your face without thinking, do you judge that person to be rude and obnoxious, or do you reach a more enlightened conclusion? Do you see that he or she is really unconscious and therefore unaware of the actions? Or do you criticize and condemn the person for the behavior?

I get your point. People aren't always necessarily rude on purpose. It may just be that they have something else on their minds.

Very few people are rude and ignorant on purpose. I know this is hard to accept, especially if you are on the receiving end of a person's ignorance. But look at the larger picture, and you will see that it is deep unconsciousness that creates what you may judge to be rude behavior. Many people have so many pressing issues and anxiety on their mind that they are often unconscious of what's happening around them. You could also say that most accidents are created in the same way. They happen because a person's mind is someplace else while the person's body is in the here and now. And because the person is not fully concentrating on what he or she is doing, an accident occurs.

Thirty-Three

I now realized that most accidents aren't really accidents at all. They are situations where a person has let his or her conscious attention wander off to another place. I wanted to understand this better.

Does this mean, then, that there is no such thing as an accident?

Now you are beginning to understand the truth of this situation. You are correct. There are no accidents because somewhere there is a definitive cause. Accidents have been created often by a person's inaction, and what he or she hasn't done. And they are caused by a person's body being in one place, but his or her mind and thoughts being in another.

World-class athletes and those at the top of their profession know this principle. They know that they need to focus 100 percent of their conscious attention on any given situation. Only then will they perform to their optimum level.

So even our indecision and inaction are creating something in the world. It's creating the space in which something that we cherish can fall away and die. In my case, it's my marriage.

Precisely. Your ignorance and unconscious awareness of what is really happening still creates a powerful force. You may not be aware that you are starving your marriage of love and attention, but it doesn't take away the undeniable fact that you are still creating something negative. We are still creators, whether we choose to manifest something consciously or unconsciously. The creation program inside us still runs whether we are aware of it or not.

This is what happens when you are unconscious of the fact that your creativity and inspiration are being stifled. On one level of awareness, you don't even recognize what you are doing. You don't realize that you are denying yourself something because you don't even know that something else exists.

Presumably, this is because we are so caught up in our thoughts. We are addicted to them.

Yes. You are trapped in the illusion that you are only your mind.

And what you are saying is that we are infinitely more than our thoughts.

You have no idea how much more. Break free of this contained way of thinking, and you will see that the entire universe opens up before you, and inside of you. It is a tragedy that so many people spend most of their time trapped in this contained way of existing throughout life. They are so convinced that there is nothing more than their minds that they waste their lives churning over the same old thoughts. They are so addicted to their thoughts and entrenched beliefs that they look right through the great unseen and the perfection of the divine.

Then, one day, something extraordinary happens. They suddenly realize, to their amazement, that they had forgotten about creativity. They may have neglected to attend to their creative urges, but when they reappear, people are astonished. They're shocked because it's as if a whole new universe has opened up for them. And, of course, that's exactly what has occurred. An entirely new universe of wonderment, curiosity and inspiration suddenly comes flooding back into their presence.

This is all blowing me away. Everything you are pointing out could be directly attributed to my life story. I can't remember the last time I let my imagination wander. And I certainly cannot recall when I last read a good book that inspired or challenged me.

Then you have not lived your life fully, my friend. You have been trapped inside your head for way too long. You have become addicted to your thoughts and believed that nothing else exists outside of them.

Nothing will take you farther away from who you are as a human being than neglecting your creative side. For when you create, you welcome in the pure divine essence of life force.

The way you describe it, you make it sound as if we can all be creative. But I have a few friends who clearly don't have a creative bone in their body.

Have I not already said that we are all creative beings? We are all master technicians in this whole cosmic construction. The only travesty is that most people have lost the importance of this divine truth. They have fallen into a dream and forgotten the gift of their divine connection to the universe. When we are children, we still have this gift. We know or imagine that the whole world resonates along with us. But as we develop social conditioning and become adults, we let the mind dominate us. We let it become the master instead of the servant.

It is impossible to disengage from this human function as creator, even if we were to choose to. We can't, for we are all creative beings with the potential to bring the unseen, unmanifested and invisible into the physical reality.

I find that hard to believe that every one of us is creative. I've been on courses linked to work where some people were so lacking in creativity that it was embarrassing.

It is imagination and courage that they lack, not creativity. We are all born creative. It's in our nature to be creators. That's what we know best. I'm afraid you are wildly off the mark with this one. For starters, you cannot teach creativity because we are creativity. We cannot become creative because we are already creative. At best, you can teach people how to switch off their suffocating thoughts, which will then allow the light of their creativity to breathe and blossom again. There is not a tiny cell in the entire body that is not already creative. Even the cells in your body are creatively evolving, growing and morphing as one whole system.

I like the idea that we are all creative.

Why do you imagine that the soul incarnates into a physical body? Why do you think that the spirit slows down its vibration and enters into a physical being? It wishes to experience the glorious feeling of being a co-creator on this extraordinary planet. Not the passive spectator, but the co-creator.

If a person vehemently denies he or she is creative, then that is simply not true. The person is denying the miracle of who he or she is. Not everybody may be keen to openly express this, but we are all creative. And we are being creative in every single moment, and with every action of our lives.

Wow! That's incredible.

It most certainly is something worth celebrating, isn't it?

So the only object blocking our own creativity is our mind?

Or the thoughts and constant static that roll through your mind. Clear a lot of the unnecessary mind stuff from your head, and you will soon discover the secret of becoming a fully creative being. All you ever need to do is to get out of the way and let the life force work through you. Artists, sages, spiritual teachers and masters know this truth. They appreciate that they must first step aside, get out of the way, shut down the mind static, and then let the divine life force work through them. Healers are also familiar with this divine process. They instinctively know that all healing is not directly attributable to a special gift that they own. Healing is present because healers learn that they are only the transformers in the whole process. They are the conduits, which offer pure grace and compassionate love.

It all seems too simple. That would mean that we, as human bodies, are nothing more than a physical channel.

You are drawing closer to the truth here. You are beginning to see that we are all paintbrushes in this whole cosmic picture. The way that you brush your strokes and choose your colors determines the kind of the life picture you create.

So if I am a paintbrush of the divine, who is creating the picture?

Source is the energy creating the painting, and the universal consciousness and collective force that constitutes the universe is the artist.

Do you mean God?

If you wish to interpret universal consciousness or the divine in that form, then yes. The painter of the universe is the collective spirit, life force, divine energy, source, God…call it whatever you so wish. But know this much, my dear friend, the combined energy and potential of this force is greater, larger and more expanded than you could ever hope for or imagine in your wildest dreams.
I can feel that something is troubling you.

In one sense, I am elated. This somehow confirms what I have always suspected. Yet, in another way, I don't know what to feel. I'm confused. In my mind, I always imagined that if there was a God, then it would be somewhere *out* there. I imagined that God was untouchable, unquantifiable and immeasurable.

The infinite is unquantifiable and immeasurable. For how can you measure something that is constantly evolving and becoming bigger than you know? How can you conceptualize something that is larger than your mind could understand? Do not try to grasp what I am saying here with only the mind because this is a concept too large for the mind alone to embrace.

You are right. And, sadly, what we cannot understand and conceptualize, we usually condemn.

That may well be woven into the nature of the human mind. It may well be the language of how we have been conditioned. But it is not part of the nature of the soul. Your soul knows that you are more than your body and mind. It already knows that you are connected to something far greater than the tiny physical self that you imagine to be you. If you live in the mind alone, then your life will remain barren and deeply unfulfilled. That is why you must always listen to your feelings, for they are the echo and vibration of your soul. They are the truth of who and what you are as a complete and whole being of light.

My beloved friend, what you may not yet understand is that we are all essences of God in varying forms. We are all uniquely special parts of the great unseen potential of the universe, becoming real.

Thirty-Four

*T*his new concept of God was a revelation to me. It was far different from what I had perceived and believed as a child.

So there is no God out there because it is inside of us. It is part of everything. All that we see around us is an essence of God, manifesting in a physical form.

Yes, in every physical and nonphysical form that you can wrap your understanding around. But, please, do not take my word for it. See it, and then feel it for yourself. Then a theory will become knowing. And when you truly know something deep in your heart, it will override any construct of the mind.

The divine is in the stranger that you come across in the street. It is in the wild animal of the forest. And it is present in the water that you drink, the food that you devour. There is no place or thing that is not the divine. God, spirit, energy are all of it. We are all a fragment of God, and yet we are all of God. There is no part of this delicious cake that you are not, my friend. We belong to all of it because we are all of it. Can you not see the implications of this truth?

I think I'm just beginning to grasp it. If we are connected to everything, it would completely change how we view the rest of the world. It would shatter all beliefs and religions that hold onto doctrine that we are all separate. The ramifications of this are too numerous to mention. This understanding would completely demolish our present worldview and the ideologies that prop it up. This belief would change everything.

219

This is more than a belief. This is a deep knowing that we have always felt in the heart. But as I have constantly said, do not go on my word alone. Point your conscious awareness inward, and feel it in every cell of your body. Only then does a truth become real.

I think you are right. A deep part of me has always believed that this is the case. Since I was young, I knew that we were all linked to one another in some way.

Please don't think. Feel it instead. Your feelings are where you will touch the divine truth of the invisible and unseen. Go with your emotions here and not your intellect. One will lead you to your truth. The other will falsely lead you to the truth of others.

Is it always wise to side with the heart over the head?

You do not have to choose one above the other. What I am portraying is that you must be highly conscious. And this entails listening to what is going on inside of you, not another person's thoughts external to you.

Shouldn't we be cautious of letting our hearts rule our heads? I mean, if we constantly let our feelings run the show, then wouldn't we overreact to those issues that we feel most passionate about? I need some clarity here because there are some huge gaps in my understanding. Much of what you're saying resonates with me strongly, but there is still something missing. The jigsaw is not complete.

I read a recent newspaper report about a Palestinian suicide bomber. A widow with two young children wandered into a crowded square in Israel and blew up dozens of innocent civilians. It was shocking. Many of them were young children. There was universal outrage and anger from the authorities, and the Israeli government wanted instant retaliation. The very next day, a videotape, recorded hours before the bomber blew herself up, turned up at the offices of a local newspaper. In the background were several hooded extremists lined up against the wall, brandishing machine guns. The shocking video gave an indication as to what emotional state the suicide bomber was in.

The tape showed a broken human being pouring out her heart to the camera. She was highly emotional and passionate about her cause.

Which was?

To maim and destroy what she viewed as an oppressive and unjust people. Her sole passion in life had become the destruction of a government that she viewed to be evil.

My point is this: If we are to honor and express our emotions openly, like you say, then shouldn't we be prepared for more demonstrations of terror such as that which is seen in Israel?

Nearly all of us have angry emotions at one time or another. We surely can't express all of them openly. Otherwise, there would be untold carnage and anarchy in the world, wouldn't there?

You have brought up a good point, one that I will try to answer as best I can. First, do not ever underestimate the power that emotions have over us as human beings. Whether deployed productively or destructively, emotions still carry an immeasurable force. The case you mentioned is a typical example of how the broken human spirit reacts when all hope has disintegrated. Drive the spirit to the very brink of annihilation, and fear will engulf a person's conscious mind. All clarity and reason will then be obscured by feelings of anger and revenge.

So how can we refrain from letting our emotions completely overwhelm us? How can we pull back in time before unleashing trapped and denied emotions, especially if they are angry and bitter emotions?

Being overly emotional is every bit as dangerous as being totally detached from your emotions. They are two sides of the same coin. Either one of them robs you of your true essence. The key here, as always, is balance and discernment. Applying reason and intellect to your feelings will bring the grace of discernment into your presence, and it will help you to determine between the guidance that is coming from your true self, and the fear that derives from that ego part of you. One is life-supporting, while the other is life-destructive.

221

And using discernment will enable us to decipher between the two?

Discernment is an attribute and filter that you must apply to every one of your life situations, especially if your goal is to enjoy a balanced, free and fulfilled life. This is the only way that you will arrive at your truth, and not the truth of another. It is not best practice to simply follow your heart and ignore the head. To do so can render you emotionally unstable, especially if you let your feelings run wildly out of control.

Is that what the suicide bomber had done? Let her feelings run out of control?

Yes. She had overreacted to her emotions without first filtering them through her conscience. Had she deployed discernment, the human side of her would never have allowed her to carry out such an act of terror. That is because, on a deep and profound cellular level, all human beings feel the pain of their fellow kin. This is a natural law that is imbued into our genetic makeup. It is woven into our cells, and it is what makes one part of our organism react to the other in distress.

So we *are* an organism, not a race. This conversation becomes ever more bewildering.

Does describing our race as an organism make you feel uneasy?

Not so much uneasy, just strange. I've never quite thought of humanity in those terms before.

And not only humanity. Try to imagine that the entire ecological system is one gigantic organism, interconnected, interrelated, and joined together by the miracle threads of life force.
If you are sensitive enough, you will feel the pain of death in others, even those who are on the other side of the world, whom you have never met. However, if you are ruled by your mind and shut off from your feelings, then I doubt that you will feel anything.

Relating that back to the suicide bomber, it didn't matter whether she was overemotional or detached from her emotions.

Both could be equally destructive, in very different ways.

This whole emotions issue is considerably more complex than I ever envisioned. On the one hand, you are suggesting that we should honor our instincts and feelings. Yet, on the other, you are saying that we should contain them and use discernment. I am now mystified.

Let me clarify something important here. Fact number one: Your emotions are your truth, but that doesn't necessarily mean that the thoughts feeding those emotions have originated from you.

Now you have lost me.

Let us take a few steps back. Otherwise you are likely to tie yourself up in knots. Every single one of your emotions originates from the thoughts in your head. Your emotions ignite depending on the intensity of your thoughts. They are the collective cause of your emotions. Your emotions are a physical mirror that demonstrates what is going on inside your head. Are you still with me?

Yes, this is straightforward. Our emotions in the body are a direct reflection of the combined thoughts inside us.

Good. Now let us move it on another stage. I mentioned that your thoughts are the fuel and drivers of your emotions, be it whether you have negative or positive thoughts.

I'm with you all the way so far. And you've also previously said that we create and manifest whether we are conscious of it or not.

That's correct. Now back to your thoughts. Where do you imagine that most of your thoughts originate from?

Inside my head. My thoughts are stimulated inside my brain.

Not totally correct, but anywhere else?

From universal source energy in the form of inspiration.

Very good. I'm impressed. Any others?

Not that I can think of.

What about nature and the environment? What about the natural beauty that is all around you? Do creative thoughts not originate from these sources?

I accept that nature and beauty inspire my creative process. They certainly stimulate my thoughts, but I wouldn't go so far as to say that my ideas *come* from those sources.

They don't? Are you sure about that?

I'm positive. How on earth can creative thoughts come out of nature, and then be fed into me?

By the transfer of information. Tiny light particles or waves carry the information that passes between you and nature. And between beauty and you. Has it never crossed your mind to wonder why a walk in the country can be so inspiring? Have you never found it extraordinary why so many ideas enter your head while you are walking by the sea? These are mere external stimulations. In purely biological terms, they should in no way affect your inner world, the world of your imagination and creativity. Yet they do, and often in the most profound ways. What's happening here is that an energy exchange is taking place. You are transferring some of your thoughts and ideas with those of nature. This is what inspiration implies. You are literally breathing in the positive light particles via all your senses. Not just your sense of sight, but all your senses. And there's more to this miracle of life. The wonder of this story is that nature also reacts to your vibrations and emotions. The exchange and inspiration works both ways.

This is incredible. So nature is not only inspiring me with ideas, but it is soaking up my own thoughts, too. I'm literally inspiring the outside world and nature to become more. This is fascinating, but also hard to comprehend.

Not when you come to understand that everything is connected by a universal web. When you begin to see that we are dealing with a highly intelligent organism with infinite possibilities for growth and connection, you begin to acknowledge that nothing is ever apart. We are all connected, on one invisible level or another. We are all part of the same cosmic soup. We always have been, since the dawn of time.

Gardeners and farmers, who spend most of their time out in the open, know that this law exists. They may not openly express it, but subtly they appreciate the power that kindness, love and conscious attention can have on their flowers and crops. They know full well that the amount of love and caring they administer will be directly attributable to the yield they produce.

This is like something out of science fiction. I'd occasionally heard about gardeners talking to their plants. Apparently, it helped with the growth. But I never for a moment imagined that there was any truth to it.

Again, try it and see. All truth is born out of experience, not just what your culture leads you to believe.

I've just had a thought. What does that mean to genetically modified crops? They are produced on such a large scale that there is practically no human intervention involved in the growing process. If your theory aligned with what you are saying, then wouldn't the crops look withered instead of bright and healthy? I've seen some genetically modified foods. They look flawless and perfect.

But what do they taste like? And what nutritional benefits are they bringing to you—or not? Do not be fooled by appearances. Would you trust somebody with a cruel demeanor simply because he or she had undertaken cosmetic surgery? Would you always judge a book only by its cover?

Okay, I get the point. Beauty is only skin deep, but goodness goes right to the bone.

Precisely. Just because an apple shines does not render it nutritionally perfect. Just because a vegetable looks physically healthy does not mean that it contains all the required nutrients of the more traditionally grown variety.

How come?

Because of the speed and manner in which these genetic crops are grown, not to mention the lack of human involvement in producing the crops. If crops are fed nothing but artificial fertilizers, derived from a lethal petroleum cocktail of chemicals, then that is exactly what will be harvested—crops that are devoid of the necessary goodness that our bodies require. Modern agriculture may be deriving excellent yields, and the produce may well look decent and presentable, but ask yourself these questions: Are the chemicals that I am allowing into my body life-sustaining or life-destructing? And are the soils that my foods are grown in naturally fertile or artificially fertile?

This is shocking. Why are these important facts not made available to every single person?

It doesn't suit our culture to know the full story. Presently, we much prefer to believe what we see on the surface. What suits us.

No different to society then. We're happy to believe all the gloss, but often have no idea what the real issues are underneath.

Exactly. If we did discover the full truth of how our food is produced, there would be outrage. When it is discovered that we are taking into our bodies harmful chemical concoctions, there would be a mutiny on this ship. Our bodies absorb lethal combinations of drugs that may be harmful enough alone, but add all these together and we create a time bomb waiting to go off. As extraordinarily agile as it is, the body cannot sustain a constant barrage of toxic poisons.
Please, do not get me wrong. The human body is an incredible piece of equipment. It can endure horrendous abuse, and yet it still gets up in the morning and goes on its way, even allowing for all the toxins we flood it with and the poisons that gradually break down our genetic immunity. What I'm pointing you toward here is awareness. If you want

to discover why so many new diseases and cancers are taking hold, you needn't look much further than the food chain.

So what kind of damaging effects do these toxic pollutants have on our minds then? If they affect our bodies in some way, then surely they must affect us psychologically and emotionally, too.

They do, and in more ways than you can envision. Your thinking capacity can be severely hampered if and when the wrong combination of chemicals is blended together. And, in the wrong person, it can dramatically influence how he or she thinks, acts and creates. It can stimulate mood swings, depression. Not to mention an inability to focus properly.

But surely chemicals have to be tested rigorously before they slip into the food chain?

Yes, but the tests undertaken are for the effects of a single chemical. What is not factored into the equation is the lethal combination that is created when several hundred different chemicals come together in the body.

This is all frightening. In this case, then, we are nothing more than a gigantic Petri dish.

A Petri dish that is stirring up lethal cocktails that cannot be found anywhere else in the natural universe.

Dying for a Change

Thirty-Five

*O*f course, I'd always known that chemicals could be hazardous, but I'd never really concerned myself with them too much. I was beginning to realize I should have paid more attention to their effects.

I've just thought of something. If we are receiving inspiration from nature and the environment, then how is this affected by these hundreds of different chemicals in our bodies?

The signals that your cells transmit and receive are scrambled and thrown out of alignment, and if a dangerous combination of chemicals come together, it is even possible that your cellular growth can be severely affected. It can affect a deficiency in the production of your proteins, which are the building blocks of life.

You mentioned other external sources of thoughts coming into our heads. How are these affected by the chemicals in the body?

In the same way that the signals of nature's inspiration are disrupted by chemicals, so too are the other sources of external thoughts interrupted. Normally, you should be able to connect to and tune in to someone who is emotionally close to you. This ability is wired into us on a genetic level. But, again, this connection between your cells and the cells of the other person can be distorted by chemical poisons. It's as if you are smearing oil over a copper conductor. You are blocking out all chance of meaningful connection. You will have witnessed this if a person close to you is on several forms of medication. You may notice that your relationship doesn't seem to quite hit its normal peaks. It can't. There is an imbalance in the cellular makeup.

This is no different for someone who is prescribed a course of medication for depression. I have experienced this firsthand with a close friend of mine. The treatment may have stabilized his emotions and temporarily shut out his distress, but the consequence was that our friendship never seemed to have the same degree of depth and intimacy. The drugs made him less able to connect on his usual deep level. He sometimes felt detached and shut off from his emotions, which in turn made it nearly impossible for us to connect. This also left him feeling worse off in other ways. I know that the treatment was helping him to survive and hold it all together, but there was a tiny spark that went out in him. He was never the same person.

If the channels to our emotions are shut down purposely to avoid some kind of emotional trauma getting through to us, then it also blocks off the ability for someone to empathize in their normal manner. The exact same channel is used whether we express emotion or shut it out. And in the case of antidepressant drugs or chemicals, your emotive channel is numbed and closed down. If you stop the pain signals from reaching you, then you also stop the intense joy from coming in. Creative people who spend their lives in the arts can fully appreciate this. They know that there are several key factors to ensuring that inspiration, emotion and ideas are channeled through them effectively. Add drugs to their bodies, and they know that their creative urges will be more sporadic, unpredictable and, sometimes, creatively erratic.

And what do drugs do to our feelings and emotions in the long term?

It really depends on the type of drugs. But, essentially, and to varying degrees, they are the same. All artificially manufactured chemicals give you very brief and intense glimpses of bliss, physical comfort and satisfaction. But, ultimately, and in the long term, these drugs numb and deaden your emotional channels.

Just as sugar gives us a temporary high?

Yes. It is the same process. It eventually shuts down and blunts your feelings. And, in turn, these drugs will make it more difficult for you to connect on a level of empathy with anyone.

So it has a significant effect on our ability to get in touch with our emotions.

More than significant. It can be dramatic and destructive, especially when you consider that emotions are the divine energy that passes through us. You will already know from experience that being cut off from our emotions disconnects us from all other human beings.

For me, relating and connecting with others is the core of what is pivotal in being alive. Extinguish that by blunting my emotions and I'd become a robot devoid of feeling. It definitely makes you wonder what all these drugs will do to our bodies in the long term, doesn't it?

Not to mention to your relationships. It is nearly impossible to connect with someone on a deep and meaningful level if their emotional faculties are not firing correctly. But, unfortunately, there are many people who desperately need their medications to survive. The drugs have become a crutch to lean on.

That is not exactly a fair exchange, is it? If our ability to function in the world and connect properly with other human beings is compromised, then being addicted to medication is one huge sacrifice to make. If that is what drugs do to the body and the mind, then I'm not sure I would want that kind of hollow existence.

That is an easy assumption to make while you are fit and well. But what if you did require some form of daily medication to stay alive? Would you deny it and risk the consequences of not taking your medication? Would you have the courage to go it alone and put your complete faith in the power of self-healing?

That is an impossible question to answer. It's easy for me to say "yes" because I have been fortunate with my health. It might be a different situation had I inherited genetic deficiencies from my parents or contracted a life-threatening disease. I don't think I am in the position to say one way or the other. All I do know is that I have been blessed with my health. Even when I have become ill, I've used my positive attitude to try and rid myself of sickness. I know this may sound ridiculous, but I always pretended that I was fine, even when I was clearly showing the early symptoms of illness.

And how did you put this belief into action? What practical application did you apply?

First, I would shut out all my thoughts about the illness. I remember doing that ever since I was small. I used to spend a lot of time playing alone, but, fortunately, I had a fantastic imagination to keep me occupied. I created a game. Whenever I sensed an illness coming on, I would block out all thoughts about that illness.

How?

By changing my mind. Every time a thought of illness entered my head, I would close my eyes and pretend I was zapping it dead.

And what would you do if the thought moved on a stage further? What if your thoughts had jumped across the bridge to combine and become a strong feeling, an emotion that had developed itself into a physical pain in the body?

The moment an ache or pain arrived, I'd immediately pretend that it was a letter containing an image that I needed to see or a vital message for me to listen to.

What kind of message?

It could be anything. It was always the first thing that came into my head. I'll give you an example. If I was sniffing and felt a cold coming on, I would hear in my imagination, "Go out into the garden and get some fresh air." So I'd follow my imagination, and then I'd hear something like, "Sit quietly for a few minutes, close your eyes, breathe deeply, and then imagine that the sun is taking away your cold." It was extraordinary. And, amazingly, ninety-nine times out of a hundred, it worked. After a while, I was doing this so often that it became a learned habit. I didn't think anything of it because it became my natural response to any impending sickness.

When I was younger, I also used another imaginative method of zapping away all illnesses. I would often pretend that my head was divided in two halves, one full of positive thoughts, and the other, dark negative thoughts. I constructed a game where I pretended that all negative thoughts brought me illness, and all the good thoughts took them away. So every time I felt myself coming down with something, I would quickly obliterate all the negative and toxic thoughts.

And you still use this effective method of positive affirmations to this day?

Yes, although I've never dared to tell anyone. I'm not sure what people would make of it. They'd probably imagine that it was crazy. And, anyway, I'm not sure that others could handle the notion that they could heal themselves. The thought to some might appear ridiculous. I think it would both confuse and frighten most people.

First, let me make something clear. What you have explained is not ridiculous. As a highly intuitive and insightful child, you understood the infinite power the mind has over the physical body. As a young child, you may not have fully appreciated the divine process taking place, but you did know one undeniable truth. You knew without question that it worked for you, and you believed in it implicitly. It became part of your belief system. That is all that matters here. Your faith in self-healing was absolute.

And the strange thing is that this was a natural instinct, one I have always fully been aware of. I cannot remember a time when I didn't hold this belief. I know that I used to have an incredible imagination, and that definitely had a lot to do with it. As to what was really going on, I never gave it a thought. I never questioned it because it nearly always worked.

You never gave it a thought or questioned it. That was the secret as to why your belief was unflinching, my friend. You appreciated that your thoughts do control what you create.

Is this something that only a small number of people are naturally born with?

Most definitely not. We are all born with this natural ability to self-heal. It is woven into our genetic code and the cells in our body. As children, we instinctively know this. We don't question it. But as we develop and mature into teenagers and then adults, we forget about our own natural healing abilities. We very quickly detach ourselves from all beliefs that the mind is infinitely more powerful than the body.

When you have a cut on your skin, the cells and stem cells in your body go to work right away. They are consciously aware that your skin must be patched up immediately to avoid any chance of infection or bleeding to death. This intelligence and organism inside you knows precisely what must be done to heal you. There is no pause because your cellular system instinctually knows what its healing function is. It just gets on with the job at hand without any conscious interference from you. But with other external matters, it is wildly different. We falsely hold the outdated model that we cannot heal ourselves. This is something that our present culture abides to and honors. But, sadly, this false wisdom is not from actual experience. It's a belief that our young and immature culture has grown up with and adopted.

So why do we lose sight of this inherent natural ability to self-heal?

Because we are socially conditioned to believe that only doctors and medication can heal us. We are brought up with the false understanding that only pharmaceutical companies and modern medicine can "fix" us. *It never even enters our heads to question that something more profound is possibly going on here. We never think to look into what the power of the mind can do for our physical condition. Heck, the majority don't even use their minds, let alone tap into their infinite potential.*

Scientists who study the positive and yet bizarre effects of placebos know that something extraordinary is going on. They know, without question, that the majority of the healing taking place is actually due to the patient's own belief in the doctor's prescription when a placebo is administered. These scientists know that it is the patient's own self-healing that is curing his or her illness. After all, how else could somebody become completely cured by a placebo that is really nothing more than a harmless sugar tablet?

I've never really thought about belief and self-healing this way before. But if this is fact, then why isn't this information more widely available? Why is this understanding not taught in schools to all children? And why are the medical journals and scientific papers not awash with this new wisdom?

It all boils down to the commercial aspect. Can you imagine what this would do to the whole medical profession should it be proven true? Can you not see how this would fundamentally shatter all previous beliefs?

Not to mention the effect it would have on profits for pharmaceutical companies. I can't imagine they would be pleased if this wisdom was adopted by the medical fraternity as a whole.

If our culture discovered that, in most cases, they could actually control their own health patterns and well-being, then a lot of establishments would crumble. Can you imagine what consequences this would have on how we all view the world? If everybody knew that, in most situations, they could self-heal, just imagine what effect this would have on society.

So what is holding us back from adopting a more holistic vision for the future? What's preventing our education in schools from looking into this more deeply?

The answer is complex, but, in a few words, a great deal is invested in holding back the evolution of our race. There is much to lose commercially if the truth were known to all. It is very hard for a sector to change its ideas when the very act of change would threaten its own existence. The majority of the medical profession, not to mention the ballooning pharmaceutical industry, has much invested in our culture remaining tied to this model. They are not in the industry of enlightening their patients, for to do so would threaten their own professional existence.

But it doesn't make any sense. We haven't the social or financial resources to keep the health service growing. There isn't the budget available to find more doctors or medicine. I read in the papers that, as a nation, we could be bankrupt within the first few decades of this century. If we maintain the current growth patterns of medical dependency, then medical care would eclipse all other national spending by the middle of the 21st century.

And as you may well discover, it will then only become a viable service to the elite.

This mentality is ludicrous. If we continue on this road of blatantly holding back new understandings, then nobody will ever become self-reliant with regard to their health. And if the medical profession and drug companies are happy to withhold this new wisdom, then they're not just cheating us. They are actually holding back our evolution as a species. How are we ever going to evolve when the truth is being held back from us? It's not ethical.

Let's not get carried away here. There have been some extraordinary medical advances over the past two centuries. Medicine, with the aid of science, has taken a quantum leap forward in its understanding of the human mind and body. And these new discoveries have prevented millions of deaths. Do not forget this. But here is the crux. We have now reached a stage when human evolution needs to take its next leap. It needs to advance onto a higher level of vibration. Unfortunately, this new paradigm shift does not fit cosily into the thinking of the present paradigm. Medicine, science and the pharmaceutical companies have now constructed a dependence culture that is nearly impossible to change. They certainly do not want to see their power taken away and shattered, especially as it has taken hundreds of years for our cultural beliefs on medicine to reach this position.

But, come on, it's a no-brainer here. If the majority of drugs and medication are shutting down our ability to feel alive and connect with others, then we are doing more harm than good. All we're doing by becoming too reliant on the medical profession and medication is substituting one nightmare for another. We're simply pushing the bubble to another place. Okay, we may be resolving every tiny ailment in the body, but if that comes at the expense of my ability to connect deeply with others, then I'm not sure I'd want it. My emotions are important to me. They help me to truly feel what it means to be a human being.

And you've not mentioned that your emotions are your inner truth in physical form. Take that away, and you deprive yourself of the essential ability of touching your own soul.

If my emotions are severely disrupted by taking artificial chemicals into the body, then I'm nothing more than a walking zombie, detached from the rest of the world.

My friend, you are now beginning to open your eyes to the full picture. You are joining up the dots and seeing with great insight and wisdom the kind of world we will create for ourselves if nothing ever alters. When a culture becomes overly dependent on drugs and medication, then it produces a society that spends most of its time sleepwalking through life. And when a race relies on external material fixes, then it becomes deeply unconscious of its actions—a race that is detached from the possibilities of its inner, subjective world.

Not to mention a human race that is oblivious to what is going on all around itself. If we remain asleep and deeply unconscious of our emotions, then surely we will create a future society that is devoid of all feeling, won't we? If all forms of drugs do blunt off our emotional channels, then we will develop into a race where there is little compassion or reverence for anything.

As I have already intimated, living with your emotional channels fully open is vital to ensuring that you gain a sense of who and what you are. Take that function away, and yes, you are correct, we do create a half-asleep race that is deeply unconscious. You cannot express empathy and compassion to another if your own emotions are blunted by artificial chemicals.

Thirty-Six

I didn't think I wanted to take this conversation much further. I could hardly bear to think about all the consequences for an emotionally numb society.

Compassion, love, empathy, altruism. They are the glue that holds our society together. Lose these, and we would quickly slide into anarchy. If we do not have compassion for other human beings, then life stops having any meaning. I've seen firsthand what antidepressants can do to people's feelings and compassion. They may be shutting out their emotional trauma, but from another angle, they are depriving themselves of the much-needed connection to others. Their pills may be helping them to cope, but if their emotions are shut down, they won't have the benefit of living a full life.

There is another important issue that you have not mentioned here. If human beings deny themselves the ability to have deep and meaningful relationships, they throw away the largest reflection available to them.

Reflection? What do you mean?

We all need healthy relationships to help us define who we are as a person. Other people, and the relationships they bring to us, afford us the gift of reflection. Take these essential mirrors away, and we have no means to reflect back to us who we are and who we are not.

So other people are vital to our own growth?

Have you not heard the expression, "No man is an island"?

Yes.

Well, this is exactly what I am describing to you. You cannot know yourself in the absence of all other human beings. You cannot find out who you are if you do not first discover who you are not. All relationships demonstrate this by acting as your mirrors. All people coming into your life help bring you reflections. They enable you to discover those parts of self that are obscured. This process ultimately reveals the essence of your own soul. You are on a voyage of self-discovery on the choppy ocean of life. And each relationship you magnetize to you is another port of call.

Only by observing the behaviors and emotions of others around you can you then contextualize your own behaviors and emotions. Only by witnessing what you are not can you then decipher that which you are.

I've never fully appreciated the relevance or vital importance of relationships before. Like most men, I suppose I've have taken relationships for granted in the past. I've never seen them in the light that you have just painted.

Relationships, and the emotions they evoke, will always be the most critical essence of your living experience. Sadly, both are not given the attention they require. You have had several periods throughout your life when you have detached yourself from deep, meaningful relationships. This is not uncommon practice for most males, who will usually have many friends, but few deeper connections. You may have fulfilled a tiny requirement of your needs with your often fleeting friendships through work, but there was still an empty space waiting to be filled. You were still waiting for those richer and wider relationships to develop. But I tell you this: Without full emotional stability, you cannot nurture and cultivate deep and meaningful relationships. And in absence of these, you cannot discover the essence of what and who you are.

And, therefore, without relationships, we cannot work out where we wish to head.

Perfectly put. Many people feel lost not only because they are confused or desperate, but also because they are not in tune with their own emotions and, therefore, in tune with themselves. Most people don't listen to what their body is trying to communicate to them. Most are not conscious enough to patiently witness what their emotions are showing. Flooding the body with chemical concoctions that do not exist anywhere else in the universe may well temporarily shut down any painful emotional static. It may well cut off your anxiety and pain on a conscious level. But, unconsciously, the program of pain is still running. Your unease is still there. It's running under the surface of your life, causing untold damage.

You've talked a lot about relationships between people, but what about the other relationships in our lives? What about our relationships to the environment? If we are emotionally detached because of the excess chemicals and toxins in our bodies, then what does that do to our relationship with the environment and nature all around us?

You have an important point. But there are two other important factors that you have forgotten here. One is your vitally important relationship to the divine and source that inspires you. And two is the relationship that you have with yourself. These are both every bit as important as any of the others. For if you do not have a relationship to yourself and the universe, then you will increasingly find it difficult to connect with other people.

Sorry, I never even thought about that.

If your emotions are out of balance or detached, then you cannot in any way hope to understand the relationship you have toward yourself. And if you do not understand yourself, then, for sure, you will not connect with the divine. These are all fundamental pivots in how you set up your life. Deny even one of them, and the other aspects crumble.

In the case of divine source energy, creativity wants to move through you to manifest itself in a physical form. Remember, you are an instrument of the divine. You are a paintbrush of the universe that is creating a divine portrait on the canvas called life. Energy cannot move through you if your cellular body is choked up with toxins and drugs.

And what about our relationship with the environment?

This is one relationship that is constantly abused and taken for granted. What you may not appreciate is that we are a microcosm of the world. Just as our eclectic mix of cells, atoms and molecules help us to function as a human being, so the planet relies on every living cell and atom to maintain its overall health. In effect, we are the cells, and the planet is the body of the organism.

When you say "every living cell," are you meaning all of it, the microorganisms, nature, ecology, the environment?

Every single organism you can imagine. It is all part of the whole body of earth. There is nothing that is not part of this planetary system.

Wouldn't that suggest, though, that whatever we do to this planet, we also do to ourselves?

See, you are slowly coming to these conclusions without my help. The true picture is beginning to shine through. Just as we are a microcosm of the living world, so the planet is a macrocosm of us.

This is amazing. You are making this sound so straightforward and easy to grasp.

And the exciting fact is that you have only just skimmed the surface here. You are only seeing the gloss to this divine truth. There is significantly more going on here than you could hold in your present understanding. If the entire truth of the universe and its vastness opened up to you, then you would find it nearly impossible to hold such concepts in your present limited way.

This sounds exciting. It helps me to bring alive the universe within me, knowing that on earth I am a tiny part of some vast intergalactic, constantly evolving matrix.

You are not just a tiny part. You may be contained by the physical illusion that you are only one person, separate and detached from the rest of the world, but you are not. In a physical sense, we are skin,

242

bones, tissue, muscles, organs and blood. But what are these made up of?

Cells.

Yes, we are all made up of cells, which consist of molecules, which are made up of atoms. And what constitutes the atoms? Fast-moving subatomic particles that are made up of energy.

So we are nothing more than flashing pieces of light energy.

Yes, now you are coming closer to the truth of what we are. You are a cellular bundle of light energy particles, which are constantly exchanging information with other particles belonging to the organism. That's because you are the organism in a fragmented form. And at a sub-nuclear level, you are threaded to every other part of consciousness in this universe. Some religions and many spiritual teachings know this truth. They know that we are spiritual light beings in a physical body. We are energy, having a human and physical experience.

This is amazing. It's now making sense.

Everything in this universe is made up of the same energy. We are linked to the same universal energy field. That is why someone sensitive to this web can pick up the emotions of another. This helps to explain why we are able to become so intuitive to the feelings and thoughts of others. You are simply reading the data and information contained within the energy field.

If this is all true, then surely this understanding will revolutionize how we all connect to one another, won't it?

You cannot even begin to imagine how this will change the world. Think about it for a moment. Try imagining what this would do to the integrity of your relationships. Everything would change beyond measure. Can you envision what this would mean to any person, nation or corporation with an unethical approach?

Boy, can I. This would create havoc to begin with. If people continued to awaken and become more conscious, they would soon sense what is really going on under the surface. This new way of understanding would demand that politicians and governments exercised openness and transparency in everything they do. And if we could see right through every false proposal or recommendation, then nobody could ever be fooled. I can't even begin to imagine how this will alter the business and political environment.

Not to mention how we define our relationship toward the environment that sustains us. Begin to see that we are all linked on this interconnected web of energy, and we would never abuse the planet's environment again. We will then come to realize that nothing is separate from us. What we do to the planet, we do to ourselves.

I don't know what to say.

You have defined it well. Yes, it does go beyond words. It is intuitively that you will be able to separate integrity from falsehood and truth from deception. Words are not required when you use feelings as your compass to define truth. The ancients practiced this way of communicating for many thousands of years. They instinctively knew that words are the least reliable source of discovering the truth of a situation. Better to watch facial expressions, be aware of body language, and then observe the feelings in your own body. All of this will lead you to the truth more easily than mere words.

So what has driven this change forward? Why are we moving into a more nonverbal way of communicating?

Because our race has become tired of the shallow story we have created for ourselves. We've become exhausted by all the deception and corruption, the philandering and abuse. Culture is now calling out for a more honest and open society, one that is in tune with who and what we are. The illusions and deceptions of the past no longer serve us. We want a new way, a more truthful and honest way of living. This is why our species is evolving to the next stage. Our consciousness has cried out for change from the depths of our collective soul.

So we have instigated this shift ourselves? We've collectively manifested the early shoots of what will become a radical shift.

We hold the golden key. We are driving this vehicle forward toward a new and more enlightened way of living, connecting and being.

And this is actually due to the way that *we* are thinking.

Yes, with every thought you make, and every desire you wish for. Your actions, and sometimes inactions, are driving this evolution forward. Your hopes and wishes are the drivers here on this ever-continuing evolutionary journey. Know that you are a creative being with infinite potential. That's how powerful we all are, my beloved friend.

You mentioned inactions. How can my inactions drive forward evolution? It doesn't make sense.

If you are a deeply unconscious being, then your inactions often have the most effect on your life and the world you see around you. It is a common misconception to believe that only what you do can influence the state of the world. I want you to view it from another angle. I want you to know that if you are highly unconscious, then what you don't do most affects the world, in a negative way. If you were to ignore the plight of the starving and poverty-stricken, then on one level you would believe that you are not harming them. But on a deeper subconscious level, you would feel and somehow know that you are harming them. You are harming their ability to live by shutting out their pain from your mind. It may be easy to convince yourself that you have not contributed to their condition, but look deeper and you'll soon see that you have. By your sheer inaction, you've actually condemned them to death.

I've never seen it in that way before. I never realized that doing nothing and shutting it out of my mind were actually contributing to their distress.

But you never do completely shut out this humanitarian distress call. This is the great illusion being played out in the more affluent parts of the world. You falsely imagine that if something is out of sight, then it is out of mind. You believe that just because social deprivation is not on your doorstep, then it will not affect you. But here is the great secret: You do feel this emotional distress call from your kin. You do pick up signals from others in crisis. It may not be at the front of your conscious mind, but it is certainly sitting in that subconscious part of you. Why do you think that modern society is growing so anxious and restless? Why do you imagine that hundreds of millions of affluent people are suffering from deep depression and a complete loss of hope and optimism?

It's because of the pace of life in the world today. And it's, in part, due to the lack of meaning in our lives.

No. It is not only due to these factors. Trying to live and survive has been substantially harder in the past. Our race has had to endure far more emotional and physical pain than is evident in today's society.

So what is it then?

This emotional vibration we are sensing is the distress call going out from those who are on the brink of catastrophe. It is the SOS being sounded by those billions of beings who are close to annihilation. Have I not said before that we are all bonded to the same web of energy?

And this distress is being picked up by all of us on a cellular level?

On a deep energy level of vibration, yes. We may be able to pretend that global distress is not affecting our own energy, but this is not true. The cells that make up our bodies know this. They know it because they feel it on a subliminal wave frequency. Even a child could work out what is happening here. That's because so many children are presently being born with some kind of hypertension. Their young bodies are more sensitive and finely tuned into what is really happening on a level of energy. Their not yet fully formed cells are overloading and fusing.

Our inaction is not only causing us greater levels of internal pain and confusion. As we begin to pick up this heightened sense of unease and anxiety, it is also creating an energy imbalance in our emotions.

Which is presumably why so many of us find it easy to become emotionally fraught.

Yes.

But if science continues to keep energy, or life force, locked out of the equation, then we are never going to realize what is going on here. If we constantly refuse to acknowledge that we are all interconnected and interrelated, then our emotional restlessness will just keep on increasing, won't it?

If you are referring to the emotional frequency of the planet, then yes, this collective feeling of hopelessness and disconnection will continue to expand. And your emotions will continue to be your messengers here. Go inward and feel for what your emotions are trying to tell you. Then you will feel this unease for yourself.

This disquiet and sense that something is not right are already reaching critical proportions. The signals are clearly there. The proof is already evident. All you need do is peel back the false veneer and see where society really is right now. Look into the figures. Study the reports. Only then will you realize that we are a planet fracturing from the inside out.

Have you not felt this unease and restlessness in your own soul before? Have you not experienced moments when panic and anxiety sweep through your body for no apparent reason?

Yes, increasingly. But I had put it down to the hectic way that I live out my life. I tried not to pay too much attention to my emotions because doing so would leave me agitated and stressed. I found it better to shut out those emotions and ignore them.

I tell you this truth: If you were to become highly intuitive and sensitive, and then retire from your job, you would still pick up this deep sense of anxiety and unease. Even without your daily problems to overcome, you would still feel that something in your life is out of alignment.

This is shocking. I've just had a nasty thought. If I was retired, then I would sense this general unease even more. At least now, I can shut out this emotional anxiety by working hard. I can block out this restlessness by keeping busy. Take that away, and I'd feel the full force of this distress from others.

Please do not forget that you are a body of light resonating not only with the vibration of the cosmos, but also with other energy on this planet. No longer hold onto the false belief that you are detached from every other piece of living carbon. You are not. The universe is bonded to you, and through you, on the great energy web of life. This is why you will feel every vibration on the web.

Every single one of your relationships is holy. I mean this literally. It is whole and real to you, for if you abuse the relationship to the divine, to the environment or to strangers, know that you are actually harming yourself.

Thirty-Seven

I had heard the expression, "What we do unto others, we do unto ourselves," but it had never really resonated before…until now.

It all makes perfect sense to me now. If I harm, damage or neglect anything that is in relationship to me, then I am damaging myself.

Yes, that is because everything outside of you is a mirror. It is reflecting back events, choices and life situations that help you to define who you are. When you not only see this truth, but also feel it deep in your heart, then you will have evolved onto a whole new level. That is what we are doing here, my beloved human. We are creating a global organism that is slowly becoming conscious of itself. We are evolving the system that is gradually linking back up.

If we trust this fundamental shift and let go, then we will allow the world to move into a new gear. We are moving onto a completely new level of sensitivity and understanding. In the next few decades of the twenty-first century, we will witness emotions becoming more erratic. But please do not despair at the seemingly catastrophic events that you will witness. Instead, rejoice, for these are undeniable signs that we are evolving as a race.

I don't think I like the expression "catastrophic events." This sounds as if we are in for a rough ride.

It will be as rough or as smooth as you wish it to be. Everything solely depends on how fast our race awakens from its illusion of separation.

249

It depends on how quickly we become conscious and see that we are all part of the divine matrix. Make no mistake. There is now a new paradigm being ushered in. We are becoming more intuitive to the world around us. These are birthing pains we are suffering and nothing more. If you do witness the beginnings of social breakdown, terror and upheaval, do not despair and become despondent. Try to see it as a positive sign. This is the golden sign for humanity to go to work. It is our alarm call, shaking us to wake up and take our place.

Sorry to be a doom-monger, but what if we don't wake up in time? What if our race *doesn't* turn it around and become fully conscious before it is too late? If we don't stop being ignorant to what is really happening under the surface, then we really will invite in global disaster on a scale never witnessed before. And if we cannot pull all the nations together for a common cause, then we certainly will bring forward the end of our race—if not all of it, then certainly most of it.

Do not be so despondent here, my friend. Believe it or not, this is the age that we have been looking forward to. We are now on the most riveting chapter of this particular story. Let us not spoil the fun. Instead, let us write the final chapter ourselves.

Fun! I don't see the fun in the gradual degradation of our life-support systems on earth. I don't see any fun in witnessing the disintegration and breakdown of our social systems. I've seen some of the figures and projections for the next century. I've spoken to those who predict when the oil will run out and when water will become scarce. I know that it will not impact a great deal on my life, but what about my children? And their children? How are they going to cope with a warming planet and shortage of resources? So how can you say that this period of change will be exciting and fun? I see it more as terrifying. Watching us unconsciously stumble blindfolded into our own demise is not my idea of a great awakening taking place.

Then it is simple: Do something about it. Be the change that you want to see in the world.

That's what Mahatma Gandhi said. Be the change you want to see in the world.

Gandhi was a gifted and compassionate seer. He inspired hundreds of millions of people. He was a true leader and visionary. But he was just one person whom many lost souls have followed. One human being amongst the darkness of despair. Now try to imagine millions of other Mahatma Gandhis. All inspiring. All helping us to find the leader within.

So are you saying that we should all become leaders and get others to follow us? Are you implying that we should preach our ideals and ideologies, and hope that others will see sense and come on board?

No, that would be a disaster.

It would? Why? I thought this is what you were pointing toward.

The consciousness of this planet is now already edging into this new paradigm. What served the planet yesterday will not necessarily fit it today. The world has changed, and so have we. What we now desire is to be self-empowered, not led. What we now wish to become is a co-creator, not a follower.

So where do you suggest we start?

Start by going within and listening to your heart. Get in touch with yourself, and say hello to your soul. Only then will you truly begin to self-realize your potential. It is only at this point that you will awaken your being and truly discover who you are. Listen to that softly spoken conscience that is your compass, and watch for your emotions, too. They are both an essential element that will help you to get back in touch with yourself. You need to have a relationship with your higher self, for this is where your truth will be found.

What do you mean by "higher self"?

The true essence of who you really are. This is the divine essence that bonds you to all other life on this earth. Practice this often by giving yourself time, and it will soon lead you back to your own truth. And when you rediscover this secret, it will empower you beyond belief. Your life will awaken, and so will you, my friend.

What you are saying is that we should always go inside of ourselves first, before we listen to everything that is external to us.

Good, you are getting close to the core truth. By all means, observe another's truth. Give respect, listen and filter through what most resonates with you. This is how you will arrive at your own centered place. But do not make the mistake of swallowing whole a concept that another is forcing down your throat. Use discernment, always, and then you will arrive at your truth. Remember, just because another person deeply inspires and motivates you, it is not a signal to give away your own power. To do so is foolish, not to mention self-deluded.

This is what fundamentalists do, isn't it? They completely surrender their own beliefs to something or someone they view as a higher authority.

There is no higher authority. If you refer to "authority" as some untouchable, commanding and dominant force, then your whole understanding of the unseen and invisible is misconstrued. However, if you see this "higher force" as an energy extension of your own self, then you are correct. You are closer to the divine truth. The point I want to make is this: Never, ever give up your own power and integrity. For to do so will forever imprison your soul behind the gates of despair. Instead, always take care to listen to the higher truth resonating within you because it will always lead you back home.

I am constantly listening out for that quiet, still voice from within. But it's hard because there is so much mental static laid over it. My mind is filled with so many thoughts and concerns, worries and problems that I struggle to concentrate for long periods of time.

There are many reasons for this. That still and peaceful part of your being has to confront many of the distractions of the mind. One of those is the increasing mind chatter that is filling your head. This is a combination of all your worries, anxieties and stress. And it is your unhealed and unresolved emotional difficulties. But become conscious that something far more is happening here. You are also picking up the distress signals of many other external sources of energy.

But how do we power down this overactive mind static? What must I do to shut out these incessant thoughts in my head? I would give anything to create a gap in my thinking. If I could find a way of switching off this unwanted mind stream, then I could sleep properly. Relax more.

I'm sorry to pop your bubble, but a substantial amount of the mind static can be directly attributed to the distress signals being emitted by the earth. The planet is crying out for help, and you are subliminally picking up an SOS from earth energies.

So the anxiety building inside me is not all of my own making or the distress picked up from others?

Most definitely not. Why, did you think it was?

Well, yes.

Do you honestly believe that all the mental static and anxiety that is presently building in the human psyche is due to the frantic speed in which our lives are carried out today? Do you truly imagine that the depression and stress that is afflicting the majority in the affluent western world is totally due to today's hectic pace of life?

Actually, I did. Most of us try to squeeze so much out of the orange that it's no wonder our lives are coming apart at the seams. I even rush through my meals at the dinner table, and that's if I sit down at all. Most of the time, I eat on the go. I'm always too busy trying to get somewhere else. Or I'm too busy trying to become something else.

I can see how you have arrived at this conclusion, but you are wide off the mark. If you imagine that today's frantic pace and the vibrations you are picking up from others' distress is solely to blame, then you are not seeing the wider perspective. Much of what you are actually feeling is not due to the hours you work or the way you live. And it is not due to the empathy you feel for others. If that were true, then your ancestors from the past would have suffered significantly more stress and anxiety than is witnessed today. Look back barely a few centuries ago. Past generations endured poor working conditions, hunger, poverty and abuse that would make today's lifestyles look like a stroll in the park. Yet, for all this, they still didn't suffer anywhere near the level of mental anxiety and emotional suffering. Try working eighteen-hour days, seven days a week, without any holidays, and see how you would feel. You will discover that, in comparison, most westernized societies are pampered.

Then why is today's society suffering a sharp rise in mental-health problems and emotional difficulties? And how is it that depression and other anxiety-led illnesses are mushrooming out of control?

Have you not seen what is happening here yet? We are moving into a new and more enlightened age, when we will appreciate the infinite power of energy fields. We are about to peep into the creative process of how matter forms, and in doing so, discover the effect of our thoughts on the world. Once we come to realize that our emotions are an essence of divine source, one that we ourselves have called forward, then a whole new form of living will open up to us. The vibration of the planet has already begun to shift. A new frequency is being set. A new mindset is being ushered in, and this is affecting every living organism on planet earth.

One of the core reasons why we are now feeling this restlessness and unease is not just because of the manic pace of life or the distress signal from our kin in the developing world who are suffering at our expense. It is because we are all feeling the effects of the emotional watermark as it begins to rise. Our collective consciousness is evolving along with that of the planet. Have I not already said that we are all one? We are all interconnected to the web of life. And as we become more consciously evolved, our emotional antennae are being finely tuned.

And nobody, regardless of his or her emotional stability or economic prosperity, will escape from this sense of unease now rising? We'll all pick up the vibes of this distress call from humanity and the planet?

Nobody can escape from these changes, for the shift has already begun. And because we are linked on a universal web, we all feel this heightened sensitivity. We all tap into this collective pain. The planet is a self-regulating system, and our cellular bodies are crying out that this interconnected system is now beginning to fragment and break down. The signals we are picking up are telling us that the planet's life-support systems are under severe stress.

Hasn't the planet always passed through these dramatic shifts, though? Hasn't this always been a part of the changing cycles and altering patterns?

Over billions of years, there have been sudden and dramatic changes as the earth moves its body from one level of evolution to another. But today is a different story. Today, there are around six billion humans on the planet, each taking something from the planet. And each one needing to be clothed, fed, watered and kept warm.

In a roundabout way, are you trying to tell me that there will not be enough to go around? Is that what you are implying? Because if you are, then that's a similar case to what we see today.

No, you are wrong here, I'm afraid. There is more than enough to go around. There always has been, because we and the earth are one intelligent system. And that system knows that we work best together as a single organism. But we are now reaching a dangerous threshold in human evolution. We are arriving at the critical point where we are exceeding the natural carrying capacity of the earth and its support systems. Add to that the destruction that we are inflicting on the planet and its depleting resources, and you will begin to see where we are headed.

I once heard it described that humanity is like a cancer on the surface of the earth. We were portrayed as the disease that is slowly destroying the whole ecosystem.

The planet, its vital resources and its consciousness can never be destroyed. It may well change form, but planet earth always knows what to do if its very survival is threatened by any life form. The system will always protect itself. Life will always protect life.

That is so inspiring to know. Hearing you say that humanity will survive anything gives hope for the future.

Who said anything about humanity?

Oh.

I was referring to life and consciousness. If the planet's very survival is put at stake, then its life-force energy will simply retract back into a far more sustainable form of matter. And if any part of the system threatens the whole system, then that part will be cut off and starved of energy.

Are human beings "that part" you are referring to?

There is no discrimination here. If the earth is under attack and its systems threatened, then the organism and its cells will decide which part of the life system needs to close down. The planet's self-regulating life system will work out what cancerous cells are working against the whole system, what part is the most demanding on energy resources, and then take appropriate action. In the case of survival, if one species threatens the life of all other organisms, then it will be eradicated and killed off.

This is horrifying. *We* are these cancerous cells on the surface of the planet. It's humanity that will be cut off from the whole system, isn't it?

The planet will always balance its life systems accordingly. There is an intelligent organism at work here that most of your scientists have not yet come anywhere close to understanding. The earth regulates itself by changing, altering and adapting to conditions in its environment. And if one part of that environment is threatening the future of the whole planet, then its energy supply will be cut off.

Will there be any warning when and if this starts to happen?

My friend, it is already happening. Study the global statistics, and you will see the undeniable truth for yourself. The water, food and energy sources that humanity needs to survive are becoming scarcer every year. The planet is already realigning its ecological systems to maintain its long-term health. The weather patterns are already changing. The planet is warming. And water table levels are dramatically receding. All these are contributing toward providing the earth with the ability and balance to survive. Just as a tree drops all its leaves in winter to conserve vital energy, so the planet is drawing back to a functionary level where it can guarantee its long-term survival.

Thirty-Eight

*A*ll this talk about survival was really frightening me.

What you're saying is scary. What about human beings in this life equation? Where do we sit in the future?

It is the height of arrogance to believe that humans sit at the top of an evolutionary pyramid. We may well be the most conscious and technologically advanced, but that does not mean that the world will support our needs ahead of all other life needs. The planet's desire is to maintain its own survival, and it will do whatever it needs to do to ensure that. It will protect all of the system, and not only one part of it.

It certainly won't protect the one part that is causing it the most distress and poisoning it.

Do not get me wrong here. There is no agenda. The consciousness of the planet wants to maintain all of life, for life is what it is. But if we are not careful, we will tip the balance over the edge. We will reach a tipping point when the earth has no choice but to protect the well-being of the whole system, not just one part of it.

You are talking about the planet as if it were a real living person.

The earth is a living, breathing system. As I've already intimated, it is a macrocosm of our own bodies. Just as the cells in our bodies make up who we are, so the earth has a cellular system, and those cells are us.

So we are each an individual cellular body part of the earth?

Yes, you are a collection of cellular parts that make up the whole life system called earth.

This is amazing.

And you haven't even worked out a fraction of what is going on here. Peer into a microscope and look back the other way into reality, and you will see exactly the same construction. Stare up at the stars, and you will begin to appreciate that planet earth is only a tiny speck of the whole.

So earth is only a tiny cell in the whole body of the universe?

There you have it. You are beginning to see that life goes both ways.

And presumably, where we are standing determines how we see our place in this cosmic soup of consciousness.

Infinity goes both ways, not only up. Biologists and quantum physicists know this. They know that, at the deepest level, we are all one of the same energy. We all consist of the same matter, all relating and interconnecting. There is nothing in this cosmic soup that is not attached to us. That's because we are all of it. We are a microcosm of the world in which we live.

This is unbelievable. I don't know why, but on some deeper level of understanding, I have always felt this to be true.

Of course you do, because the world lives inside of you. Anything that happens to the planet will be echoed through you. If there is a devastating loss of the Amazon rainforests, a part of you feels it. That is because, on a larger scale, those forests are the lungs of the world. And in being so they are your lungs, too. This is why cancer, disease and famine will thrive in the years ahead. They are simply mirrors of what is going on at the macro level. If the planet's living systems begin to break down, then physically so do ours.

This is because all energy is interwoven.

Yes. We are a mirror of what happens to the world.

I still find this whole concept extraordinary. If we are struggling to maintain the needs of billions of people around the world already, then what is going to happen in the future? The planet is projected to reach nine billion people by the middle of this century, which is half again of what it already sustains. Hypothetically, what's going to happen if this coincides with the planet gradually cutting off our water and food sources?

First, this is not a hypothetical theory. This is a fact if we remain on the same course. The figures are there. The statistics are in. Make no mistake. If we sleepwalk and remain chained to the path we're on, these events will happen.

This is chilling.

Second, there is enough food, water and shelter for everyone because the life system on earth already provides for it. There is also enough love, compassion, peace and friendship to go around, although there are many who do not wish to believe this. The shortages you witness and the statistics you find, however, still don't come close to painting the true picture. They do not tell the real story.

Which is?

That half of the so-called impoverished world could live off just half of what the other affluent part of the world throws away.

Oh! That hits it home for me. I don't know what to say.

Do not go searching for words. It is what you are feeling that I am most interested in.

I feel nothing but absolutely ashamed. And I feel so helpless and useless, too.

Feeling ashamed and useless will not help you wake up to what is really happening in the world because it closes down your own emotions. Better that we all use less and enable other parts of the world to thrive and survive.

When we are ashamed, we block out the vibration of the world, and in doing so, our connection to it. Only when you let go of shame and get in touch with yourself through your emotions will you then feel inspired into action. Shame is something that torments you and keeps you entrenched in self-pity. It will keep you small. Action, passion and inspiration will drive you forward.

But if, like many, I haven't yet woken up and seen what is really happening in the world, then what will make us sit up and take notice of these changes that need to be made?

The desperation and poverty that you presently witness in most of the poor and developing nations is soon coming to a town near you. The affluent west has enjoyed a favored lifestyle that would be revered by our ancestors of the past. But in the first half of this twenty-first century, everything is about to tip upside down. Everything is about to change.

What do you mean? Are you talking about a global recession, social breakdown, or what?

Not as such, although what you see as westernized economies will suffer a major slide backward in their living standards. Just as the developing nations will thrive and grow, so the established nations will fight to keep hold of what they have.

So what are you predicting with this shift? Are the roles of our global society about to be reversed? Will our western society shrink as the developing nations expand?

I will just say this: Our whole way of living and communicating is about to receive a huge jolt. Sooner or later, we will awaken, and only then will we realize that the eastern economies of the world are overtaking, outbidding and developing well ahead of the west.

This is going to have an enormous effect on how the world's natural resources, energy and economic growth will be shared. If the emerging nations try to maintain their prosperity, then we are in for some seismic shift of attitudes.

Then the westernized societies had better hope that the emerging nations treat them better than the west has treated them in the past. What you call the west should hope that the developing nations are more compassionate and sharing.

I think I can see what is going on here. This global role reversal of economics is to give us, in the affluent west, a taste of our own medicine, isn't it? We are about to experience firsthand what it feels like to be neglected and forgotten, abused and tormented. We've had it so good in the past, but now we're about to discover what it means to be the poor cousin of the global family. The words that keep filling my head are, "What goes around comes around."

Do not become so despondent. There is no absolute reason to suggest that there will be some kind of payback here. If you wish to imagine that the emerging economies of the east will treat you as you have treated them, then fine, live with that paranoia. But it does not serve you in the long run.

Why do you think that the affluent and established nations are desperately holding onto all the power? Why do you imagine that they are maintaining such large armored forces, even though we are living through relatively peaceful times? The few and select power-broking nations that control the world trade movements know that this shift is happening. They can foresee that an economic upheaval is about to unravel within the next two decades. And because they will not hand over power easily, they will fight to keep their privileges and what they have enjoyed.

We are now moving well beyond the natural carrying capacity of the world. The subject of population figures will again be a major discussion point in the years ahead. And with the emerging nations striding toward a westernized way of living, we will very soon reach a tipping point.

Tipping point?

A period when the natural resources available will not be enough to service the planet's needs and requirements. The irony here is that the affluent commercial lifestyles that the emerging nations crave are not physically achievable. There are not enough global natural resources for the east to live up to the sometimes wasteful standards of the west.

Do you mean that they are chasing an illusion that can never be fulfilled?

Put that way, then yes, you are correct. The emerging and developing nations are sprinting after a dream that is both impossible and unsustainable. There would need to be three times the amount of the available planetary resources for the east to achieve westernized living standards.

Boy, this is sure going to create global friction on an unprecedented scale. I bet nobody has pointed it out to the east that they are wasting their time. If the natural resources will not be available, then their dream of attaining a westernized lifestyle will never materialize.

What makes you naively assume that the east will be the region that goes without? If members of those emerging nation states work double the hours for only a fraction of the pay afforded in the west, then what makes you assume that the west will not be the loser?

You are right. That's shocking. Most of our production now comes from China, India, Russia and many other countries in that region. And workers from these countries are prepared to put in substantially more effort for significantly smaller returns. But if this is the case, then what will this do to our western markets? Are you saying that, eventually, the east will outbid us for most of the natural available resources? If much of the east and the developing world charges toward living the "American dream," then there are not going to be enough natural resources to go around.

With limited energy, food and water available in the world, it has been a dream to imagine that the entire world can live a westernized lifestyle. We are the ones who have been living that dream. We have constructed a culture and throwaway lifestyle that cannot in any way be maintained indefinitely. We have been living on borrowed time, and it will soon be time to pay that debt back.

Does that mean that we are in for a sudden awakening in the west?

Please do not keep separating the issues between the eastern and western parts of the globe. There is no divide here, only what you imagine. Depleting resources and a warming climate coupled with a populace under increasing levels of emotional distress affect everyone around the world, whether they are fully conscious or deeply unconscious to it. Remember, we are all bonded to the web of life. We are all one. Whatever another feels, even on a subliminal and subconscious level, is vibrated back to us. That's because we are all part of life.

This is all really scary. I'm beginning to see where our culture is heading in the future. Please tell me, is there any hope for us at all? Can we wake up in time and turn this around?

There is always hope, so long as we awaken and honor the true feelings inside us. Get in touch with the essence of our true identity, and we will feel the collective pain of the nightmare that is being created. And only by feeling this collective pain will we then feel empowered to act.

The emotion of empathy is hard-wired into our genetic makeup. It is something imbued into our cellular system so that we can protect the whole system. You could say that it is a survival mechanism of the whole earth system.

I hear what you are saying, but I'm uncertain whether we have the ability to see the full picture before it is too late.

Do not despair when this shift first appears to show a complete breakdown in our social, political and economic systems. Although this shift may appear to be dangerous, be consciously aware that this is part of the much-needed transformation process. It is the chrysalis that needs to happen. This quantum shift is not something to fear, for we first need to see and own a problem before it can be healed.

We are moving through an incredible age when a new birth of humanity is taking place. A new global consciousness is rushing in because this is precisely what we have collectively called forward. Humanity is stepping up a gear as the old world order breaks down and falls away. This is a time of great change to welcome in because the heightened emotions now witnessed in society are clear evidence that we are becoming more in tune with the planet. And, in doing so, we will feel more connected to one another.

Why is this shift seen as such a dangerous time in our evolution?

If we do not become consciously aware that this quantum shift is happening, then we will become more confused and riddled with despair. Fear will overtake us, and our emotions will become wildly out of balance. Only when we see and appreciate the whole story will these changes empower and inspire us, rather than deceive and depress us.

So we need this global shift in consciousness to happen, and we need it now.

For the sake of our race, it's now essential that we move into a new gear, but most of us, at present, are still stuck in neutral. Many are so paralyzed by social and economic change that they choose to ignore the environmental signals or signs of social breakdown. Much easier to bury the head in the sand and hope that this visual demonstration of global distress will disappear.

Most half-intelligent people can see that our present capitalist and consumerist way of living is not working for the benefit of all. Admittedly, it's considerably better than the alternative of communism or socialism, but that's not exactly saying much. You only have to witness the ever-increasing divide between the rich and the poor, and between the haves and have-nots, to see why we are in such a mess. You only have to hear that prisons are full to capacity, or that all illnesses, stress and depression are becoming a global epidemic, to see what is really going on. There are so many statistics showing that life is clearly not working in its present format. Yet politicians, governments and corporate leaders continue to tell us otherwise. We kid ourselves and pretend that everything is fine by closing our eyes to the truth.

After twenty years out on the road selling to clients, I have seen this gradual restlessness take a hold. I've seen how people are slowly becoming more despondent and depressed with their lives. The pace of life is becoming too much. I think most of us are seeing that technology has made us all busier and more stressed. It may have benefited the workplace in some ways, but, in others, this infatuation with speed and figures is driving us close to the edge. It's ridiculous to say it, but I am now suffering from an information overload.

After getting to know my clients well over the years, most of them feel the same way as I do. They are crying out for a new way of living, sharing and communicating. They're desperate for more integrity, honesty and truth in their lives. And yet we still keep on living out this illusion that modern living is working for us. I sometimes feel that we are all playing out the scene where the emperor has no clothes on. Everyone is paralyzed by fear and not standing up and telling the truth of how they feel.

It's almost as if the collective pain we feel is so intense and deep that we don't wish to face it, let alone try to articulate it. I think we are so terrified of what we may discover under the surface of our emotions that fear takes us over.

Then the question, as always, is this: What are you prepared to do about it? Are you happy to just sit back and see your world come apart? Are you able to contain your emotional discomfort and pretend that nothing needs changing? Or are you prepared to let your heart and truth finally find the surface?

Thirty-Nine

I felt as if I'd just been issued a challenge. I wanted to break free from the inertia that afflicted me and so many others, and yet the thought of it was daunting.

Like many people I know well, I can feel this deep anxiety and irritation building inside me. Some days, my negative emotions are like a distant hum, barely audible. Yet, on others, they engulf me and fill me with dread. I have had occasions recently when I simply cannot see a way through. It's almost as if a thick mist has surrounded my life and snatched away all hope for the future.

Then if this is the case, celebrate, my friend. Take it as a blessing that your emotions are waking you up to your truth.

How can I celebrate when this deep, dark depression takes me over? I should be trying to run away from this emotional disquiet and pain, not inviting more of the same into my presence.

I'm afraid that this is the very same behavior that will take you farther away from your truth and, therefore, your freedom. Denying, repressing and hiding away from this emotional distress are the very actions that have trapped our society where it is. Do not believe that you have to follow the crowd. Shutting out your internal pain is not right, regardless of what social conditioning teaches you. Instead, open up to your pain. Invite it in and listen to it, for a voice heard and understood will not then keep knocking on your door.

This is the greatest misunderstanding our culture has adopted. We should not hide away our collective pain. Being open to our feelings is where our salvation will be found. Do not try to mask your painful feelings, for all emotions are your messengers. They are bringing you the vital signposts needed on your personal journey.

What you have done in the past is not uncommon. You have always glossed over your negative emotions, plastering them over with positive thinking. Another way you've coped with it has been to keep yourself busy. But I tell you this: You should not run away and disregard your sadness or negative emotions, for they carry the antidote that you need to help move you to another level of understanding. And they carry the key that will open the door to a more enlightened way of living.

I thought I was doing the right thing by blocking out my negative emotions. But from what you are saying, I have got this wrong.

There is something noble in trying to extinguish all of your unwanted feelings, but this behavior will not serve you. It never has, and it never will. You have believed wrongly, for way too much of your life, that the makings of a human being are dependent on how much pain he or she can disguise. And you have constructed a false theory that the gauge of a person's inner strength is to be measured by how he or she grins and bears suffering. My friend, you are not on your own with this belief. This is an affliction that has infected the thinking and behavior of most males, not to mention a rising number of females, too. But you need to understand what this is doing to our race. You must see that this is destroying our very spirit.

Please help me here. Everything you are saying is ringing a bell with me. I can feel in my heart where I have made so many mistakes. I used to be so proud that I could bottle up all my negative and destructive emotions. I imagined that I was doing so well that I could put on a brave face, grin and bear it. But now I know that this was wrong. I should have been more transparent and open. And I should have shared my feelings with others, including Alison.

If you do not listen to and resolve your emotions properly, then they will simply boomerang back at another time, and often in a far more destructive way. Therefore, always listen with your heart to what you interpret as your negative emotions. They carry far more important messages than any positive emotion will bring you. In truth, there are no negative or positive emotions, only those that you label as such.

How can that be? I know whether an emotion is good or bad. I know whether an emotion brings me joy or pain.

Let me repeat this because it is important: All your emotions are messengers from your higher self. They are signposts that give a perfect contour to the inner realm of your soul. All emotions that show up in the body are there for a perfectly good reason. They are present to help you find your way back home.

Find my way back home?

To the truth of who you really are. That's what emotions are designed to do. They are your truth-tellers and your way-showers. And emotions are magnified thoughts that show up in the body. They are a physical representation of your spiritual self. Know that your emotions will give you the most accurate portrait of what is happening in both your heart and your head.

Are you telling me that I should honor *all* of my emotions, even those negative ones that bring me excruciating pain?

Especially those painful emotions. The disease that our culture has contracted, and then passed along down the line of our culture, is that painful emotion should be avoided at all costs. We live in a society that does not wish to face up to its personal or collective pain and responsibilities. Yet I tell this undeniable fact: Until we do, nothing will ever alter. And until we stop blocking out this emotional distress, our race will never awaken to a new way of living and feeling.

What do you mean by a "new way of living and feeling"?

Our race is crying out from the depths of its collective soul for living a new way of feeling in the world. Through desperation and collective desire, we are drawing toward us a new age of connecting, empathizing and kinship—one that has been long overdue. But none of this can happen until we take the next quantum leap in our evolution. And at the core of this shift is interpreting the purpose and function of emotions. It is the heightened faculty of feeling that will enable human consciousness to flower, blossom and finally awaken. And to ensure that that happens, we must start opening up our emotional channels. We must get more in touch with our feelings, which are the language of the soul.

I think I'm beginning to understand why our culture is calling forward a more empathic, compassionate and caring society. We only have to acknowledge the sheer number of human beings who have been slaughtered throughout much of this century. Tens of millions of lives have been snuffed out because of wars and disagreements over trade, land and resources. So much suffering has been endured by those power-hungry leaderships that want to control the will of the people.

I connect with what you are saying, but shouldn't we just concentrate on creating more positive emotions in our lives, rather than listening to the bad emotions? Wouldn't it be better if we adopted more positive thinking and therefore shut out the negativity?

First, no amount of positive thinking in the world will change anything if practical action is not brought into the picture. You could pray for peace every day of your existence, but until your life becomes a visual demonstration of that peace within you, then nothing will ever alter in your world. Second, do not imagine that positive thinking alone can resolve the suffering felt by your soul. To believe that you can suffocate your emotional pain under a thin gloss of positive thoughts will still not make your soul's pain vanish. This practice simply mutes your internal pain. It suspends it, but definitely does not eradicate it. All positive thinking does is block off your emotional pain until you are ready to pick up your trauma once again and deal with it.

Emotional hunger is really a disguise for the hunger of the soul that wishes to express itself in a physical form. Your emotions are your truth, and in every moment of your life, they want to be heard.

Thank you. Now I realize why listening to my negative emotions is so important. These emotional messages are helping to point me back to where I say I wish to go. And by listening to *all* emotions, I am touching the essence of my soul, the truth of who and what I am as a human being.

Good, you are beginning to bring this all together now. Let me give you an example that relates to your own life. Can you tell me what your intention has been since leaving school? I want to know what has driven you since you were sixteen years old.

What's driven me is the desire to succeed and prove some of my teachers wrong. I was despondent because of some of the things I was being taught. I wanted to prove to myself and others that I could make a success of my life. This desire was unflinching, and I would say that it has become an obsession.

So you knew with absolute conviction where you wanted to head?

Without question. Like the majority of teenagers leaving school, I may not have been focused on one particular career, but deep down, I knew that I was going to make a success of my working life. If nothing else, my deep desire was to prove some of my teachers wrong.

And what about any self-doubt that crept in? Did this not throw you off your intended path?

No, I would say the reverse. Every time a negative emotion popped up with "You're not good enough" or "You don't deserve this," I simply used it to drive myself on. This negative emotion became a powerful inspiration to me. I used it to my advantage, and it worked.

The prominent meaning behind this process is your desire and your will to succeed, for when desire mixes with emotion, you can transform any negative emotion into positive action. It is at this junction that the power of creation comes into play. Believe in something enough, back

273

it up with emotion, and all things are achievable. You can exterminate any negative emotion felt in the body when desire is the fuel driving you on.

And there's another reason why's it's important to clear up, resolve and heal your "negative" feelings: Doing so is vital to ensure that your emotional channels are left fully open and clear. Only then can the world resonate through us. It is only at this point that our infinite possibilities can be self-realized.

All emotions move through these energy channels, which bridge both your spiritual essence and your physical body. Shut off these channels by blocking them with the energy force of unresolved emotions and, very soon, even joyful and positive emotions will struggle to break through to the surface. Always remember this: The degree to which you let all emotions into your presence is equal to how alive you will feel.

This is why some people become addicted to certain painful relationships, isn't it? And why certain people hold onto emotions that make them suffer. It's because all emotions help us to feel alive. If all emotions help to make us fully conscious, then this explains why certain people become addicted to pain. They don't know any other way to properly feel alive, so they desperately grab onto the second best thing.

Which is pain. Whether you experience pain or joy through your emotions, the outcome is the same. On a level of the soul, you still feel alive.

But it seems insane to wish for painful emotions instead of those wrapped in joy. Why would anyone want to do that?

Some people do not feel they are worthy of receiving joy. Their self-confidence and self-esteem are shattered and downtrodden.

So they settle for the next best things.

Which are negative and painful emotions. Better to feel some emotions than none. Better to feel half-alive than nothing at all.

Even if that portal is through pain.

Believe it or not, some people have lived their whole lives in this way. They have become trapped and addicted to a contained and painful way of living, which no longer serves their higher purpose.

Which is?

For the soul to experience the joy and love of living in a physical body.

But if so many people are living their lives in this way, then this is criminal. To live tormented by painful emotions sacrifices everything that makes us human. I may have experienced some dark periods when my emotions were blunted and shut down, but to have endured that for most of my life doesn't bear thinking about.

And you would be horrified to discover how many human beings presently live this way. You could say that it is a social problem of endemic proportions. More people are living the nightmare of emotional torment than you realize.

That is shocking. So, getting back to the point, blocking out unwanted emotions has a detrimental effect on our feelings of joy and bliss. On a personal level, this makes so much sense to me. I have spent huge amounts of my life cut off from my deep feelings of pain, and never once has it served me. With hindsight, I can now see those periods when I have gone so drastically off course.

Feeling your emotions of pain and working through them are essential. It is vital because all feelings and emotions travel through this energy channel inside you. You have been wise not to succumb to antidepressants because it could well have stunted your ability to connect with others on an emotional level, not to mention halted your spiritual and psychic evolution.

One of my best friends recently signed up for a round of antidepressant medication, and the results initially seemed to be marvelous. This goes completely against what you are describing to me, so I'm confused. Whereas he was practically suicidal, he now seems upbeat and able to function. He laughs, jokes and says that, finally, he can face the world again.

But is he fully present and conscious of his life? Does he express great feeling toward others, the environment or nature? Does he pay much attention to the present state of the world?

No, not exactly. He doesn't seem to care much about anything now. Issues that once used to bother him don't even register on his radar. Nothing seems to faze him, be it work-related problems, difficulties in his marriage, finances. It all goes completely over his head. I sometimes envy his ability to shut it all out and get on with his life.

I want to make the most important point of our conversation here, so please listen to me carefully. Your good friend may very well be shutting out his emotional difficulties and trauma, but please let me assure you of this fact: His emotional problems are still alive under the surface of this charade being played out. His negative and destructive feelings are still eating into him, even though he may not be consciously aware of it. Just because the nerve receptor that alerts him to his emotional pain is blocked off does not mean that the pain impulse has subsided. It is still present and waiting for him to pick up the call. Just as a computer program can be running at the same time that you have something else on the screen, so do destructive and denied emotions cause havoc when you are not fully conscious.

All your friend is doing by closing down these emotional channels is condemning himself to a life devoid of deep connection with others. And because our connection to others is so important to help us define who we are, I'm afraid that your friend may spend a lifetime lost and confused.

You cannot spiritually evolve and grow as a human being if you constantly deny certain unwanted emotions. All emotions are sacred. They are messengers from the soul, helping you to make sense of your living experience on earth. Shut this feeder channel down, however, by numbing his feelings, and your friend will remain forever trapped in a self-created hell of No Feeling.

The true bliss of living a deeply compassionate, loving and joy-filled existence cannot be revealed to you if you throw away the mirror that reflects back what you are. All emotions help you to feel fully alive, and they are there for a reason. Emotions are life-force energy from divine source that we have called forward by our own thoughts. And they're the messengers of the soul. Deny them, and you will lose your connection to the world.

This is why there is such a deep hunger and longing for a new way of living and connecting. We have reached a critical point in our evolution when we want to take our emotional frequency up to a new, heightened level.

Dying for a Change

Forty

*E*motions. Everything always seemed to come back to emotions.

I don't think I ever imagined that emotions could play such an important role in our lives. Had I realized that, I certainly would have given the whole area more attention.

Emotions are important because they enable our spiritual presence to experience the feelings of living in a carbon body. They are the lifeblood of how we interpret and feel the physical world of form that is all around us. However, disconnect from your feelings, and you are nothing more than a dead, empty shell, devoid of all life. It is no coincidence that most of the greatest atrocities ever carried out by humans upon other humans can all be directly attributed back to those who were emotionally numb. Look into most cases of murder, and you will inevitably see that the perpetrator's emotions were blunted and not present. No human beings who are fully alive, conscious and in touch with their deep emotions would ever dream of harming their fellow kin. They could never imagine physically or emotionally harming one of their own. This is because, on a level of interconnected energy, they know that they are really harming themselves.

It's just dawned on me. If people are unconscious of their feelings, then wouldn't that mean they are also unaware of the feelings of others? If a person did use some form of drugs or alcohol to shut out emotional pain, then surely he or she would care little for others, nature or the environment.

Now we are coming to what will become the making or breaking of our society. What I am about to show you will determine whether, as a race, we break through or break down.

This sounds scary. You've taken me on so many roller coasters here. I'm not certain I want to hear this.

As I've implied in many different ways, before we can resolve something, we must first open our eyes to the truth. You cannot fix that which you cannot bear to look at. You cannot heal that which you deny.
No matter how much pain and sadness you will have to endure in the process of self-healing and self-realization, it is nothing compared to what humanity will face if it sits on its hands and closes its eyes to what is happening. Just as a person must go through the pain barrier to face up to and heal his or her emotional pain, so humanity must own up to where it has drifted wildly off course. Of all things, as a society we must be true to ourselves.

That is so true. No pain, no gain. Funny enough, I heard that on the radio today.

That is a wonderful, blessed statement. I like that. No pain, no gain. Without fully facing up to the pain, humanity cannot move onto its next stage of evolution. And without becoming conscious of the nightmare we have now created, we cannot change course.

So what is this big change you are talking about?

I have already demonstrated to you the important role that understanding emotions will play in the decades ahead. And there is an essential part to understanding our emotions, which will be the key to the survival of this race.

Which is?

Empathy. Empathy will bring salvation to our race and help turn everything around.

Empathy?

Yes. Fully appreciate the power that empathy has to shift the global consciousness, and you will look at this whole topic through new eyes.

That is a very strong statement. What do you mean by, "Empathy will bring salvation to our race"?

Just as the impending climate crisis, social breakdown, global poverty and future energy shortage will force us all to awaken, so will our understanding of empathy help humanity to finally wake up and reconnect. This is what will potentially prevent our race from cascading into a cycle of self-destruction. I hope it will save our race from imploding. Do not underestimate the power of empathy to hold humanity together. What we are about to witness is a quantum shift back to community, reverence and connectedness. Our race has the potential to wake up to the sacred that is within us all. And at the heart of this global shift will be our deep appreciation for our fellow kin, of which empathy will play a key role.

And empathy is the tool that will bring us all together.

Empathy is the glue that bonds us all together. It is the divine channel that enables us to touch, feel and experience the love and pain of others as if it were our own. This is what empathy brings to our presence. It enables us to be emotionally intuitive to the feelings of all other living things.

Including human beings. But why would we want to physically experience the emotional pain of what another person is going through? If we are highly intuitive and tuned into the painful emotions of another, then why would we ever wish to feel that pain as if it belonged to us?

On a deeper level of existence, your soul knows that it is part of something greater and larger than itself. It instinctively knows without question that you are but an essence of all life. This is why your soul wishes to experience life from other perspectives. Its mission on earth is to feel the totality of life, and thus to feel whole again.

And the best way of achieving this is through the emotion of empathy.

Empathy enables the soul to feel, appreciate and connect to the life of another person. It enables the soul to look at the world from a new and more expanded window. Let me give you an example. Try to remember what you felt when you were knocked down by that car as a child.

I can get straight back into that moment. It makes me shudder. The sudden and abrupt shock left me confused and traumatized.

The personal trauma you experienced was bad enough, but please now cast your consciousness back to what you felt when you experienced the accident from the woman's perspective. Remember how she felt when you saw the world through her pain, through her eyes.

That experience was ten times worse. Feeling everything from her perspective helped me to appreciate what pain I had inflicted on her. For the first time ever, it made me fully understand the consequences of my actions.

I want to share something with you that you have not been fully aware of until this point. Ever since that accident, your soul has craved to experience the suffering and pain of that driver. You may not have been consciously aware of this, but on a deep spiritual level, it was something that your soul has always wanted to experience.

I wouldn't wish that experience on my worst enemy. Experiencing the feelings that the driver had been put through, and seeing the world from inside her body, was unbearable. It was torture to witness the whole thing. I'd never appreciated what pain and anxiety she had endured, not until I had felt her feelings for myself.

Empathy gets you closer to the truth of another's feelings and experiences, more than anything else. For the sake of your own spiritual and emotional evolution, you needed to feel a sense of what that driver had suffered. Only then could you come to see the true reflection of compassion. Only at that point could you empathize fully.

Everything boomerangs back to emotions, doesn't it?

Now you, too, can see the relevance of why understanding emotion is so critical throughout our society. And you can now fully appreciate why this topic will dominate much of the social vision for the future.

It's all beginning to make sense. This explains why our global culture has such an insatiable desire for storytelling, doesn't it? It's because we all want to briefly experience what other people feel. We want to step inside another's shoes and see how we would react given the very same circumstances. We all want to try on another person's life for size.

And storytelling from every genre, and every cultural and religious background, gives you this unique ability. Storytelling helps us to get inside another person's feelings. And stories identify the consequences of actions. They give us a brief insight into others' life experiences and help us to learn from those experiences.

Without actually going through the life experience ourselves.

That is the grace and beauty of storytelling. It is no coincidence that the most inspirational and successful writers alive are also those with the greatest ability to feel empathy for others. Writers can be intuitive about the feelings and emotions of the characters they create by completely shutting down their own identities.

I'm not sure I fully understand what you mean by "shutting down their own identities."

Conscious writers will be able to lose themselves in both the story and the characters they are writing about. And one of the core reasons why readers connect deeply with books is because writers put their own ego to the side. They briefly lose their own personalities and adopt the feelings of their characters' life situations.

So being a better empathizer really does make for a better writer?

Not just a better writer. It makes you a more complete and rounded human being, too. If you can identify with and actually feel the emotions of what another person is going through, then it will help you to understand your own feelings. This is because everything showing up in our lives is really an outer manifestation of our inner world, the world of our thoughts.

Understand your own feelings, implicitly, and you will make better sense of who you are as a person. And when you tap into other people's feelings, you will discover one of the great secrets of life's sacred journey. You will find that another's emotions are really a mirror reflecting back to you, feelings that are your own. This is why an angry person always seems to show up in your life at exactly the same time that you are feeling angry inside. You are simply magnetizing people and events toward you that mirror your own internal feelings.

That makes sense. From my own life, that situation always happens. If I'm feeling happy and joyful, by coincidence, happy people just seem to turn up in my life.

Know that they don't just show up. It is not coincidence. The energy vibration inside you is literally drawing them toward you. The world is a perfect mirror of your inner world.

And this happens all because our feelings are magnets?

Yes.

Incredible. This process is so simple.

Life is easy to understand once you have mastered the basics.

I now appreciate that empathy brings us much closer to what another feels than any other life experience.

Empathy fulfills an insatiable thirst for life that is woven into our DNA. And it enables us to feel part of something infinitely larger and greater than ourselves. Empathy helps us to arrive home and see that we are not just a single entity in the world. We are an integral part of something infinite, immeasurable. We are divine essence belonging to the body of the universe.

And as part of something whole, we all have an insatiable desire to see how we would react, given another person's life situation. I think that seeing how another person lives and reacts is something that we're all born with.

Now that you are aware of this truth, always ask these questions when a new life situation or person shows up in your life. What has this person come to teach me about myself? And, in return, what can this relationship help to teach to the other person? The key with all new relationships is to look for the life lessons. All relationships have come into our lives for a divine purpose. They have shown up to offer an opportunity for personal growth and self-development. That is the purpose of relationship: to show us who we really are.

Forty-One

I now understood the importance of establishing and engaging in relationships, but it still seemed easier said than done to me.

We live in a world where fear prevails, and most of us are petrified of forming new relationships. Heck, most people are even terrified of striking up a conversation with strangers, let alone forming new friendships.

Then you will never discover the true essence of who you are as a human being. Relationships, and those who bring you these vital life lessons, are your mirrors in life. Cover these mirrors, and you will never realize your full potential.

Are you saying that we can never fulfill our creative potential as a human being if we don't get our relationships right?

It is not about getting relationships right or wrong. What I'm saying is that you should be fully conscious that all relationships will bring you gifts. They will all help you to grow, even those that you may judge to be destructive.

Because I have avoided confrontation most of my life, I have tended to steer clear of any person or relationship that dares to threaten how I see the world. And I've kept a wide berth from anyone who sees the world from a different perspective to that of my own.

Then you have denied yourself life. You have thrown away relationships that could have brought you numerable opportunities for personal growth. You will often learn more about yourself from negative relationships than from those that are comfortable.

I never looked at it this way before.

That is because you were always keen to surround yourself with like-minded people. It may be easy to rely on comfortable relationships that do not threaten your thinking or ideology, but ask yourself this: What are my existing relationships bringing to me? Are they challenging and inspiring me? Or are they causing me to stagnate as a person? From the life you have lived over the past few years, I would guess the latter.

You have absolutely nailed it. I couldn't agree more. I have stagnated as a person by constricting myself to only relationships that are safe and comfortable.

And has it served your growth? Has this enabled you to step outside your comfort zone?

Not at all. In fact, probably the opposite.

You cannot hope to fulfill the vital need of all human beings if you do not step outside of your box. Remaining in your comfort zone will not offer you the chance to experience alternative feelings to those of your own. And it certainly will not help to expand your perspective on the world.

I'm not sure I agree. I *do* get to experience what others feel. That is what my closest friendships bring to me—the opportunity to share what they are feeling so I can view life from other perspectives.

You are missing my point. Close friends may well offer you alternative perspectives on life, but if their viewpoints are very similar to your own, then where is the growth coming from? If their opinions correlate with much of your own thinking, then will their thoughts and feelings differ much from yours?

I get the point. We need to share experiences and feelings with people who come from completely different social, religious and cultural backgrounds. Only then can we truly appreciate the wide spectrum of life experiences.

Never turn down the opportunity to feel what another person is feeling. All relationships grant you the wisdom to feel life from an altogether more expanded perspective. This is why empathy will become such a key component in the future. It will enable human beings to go beyond all language and cultural differences. And it will help communication between all religious backgrounds. Regardless of creed, all human beings share the same wants and desires. At a deeper level, we all want to be loved, and we want to share our love.

Will our modern culture ever reach a time when none of us will need to use words? In future societies, will we just communicate via telepathy, intuition and our feelings?

That time is a long way off, although we are now seeing the early signs that we are becoming more telepathic and intuitive. There will reach a period when a significantly greater part of communication will be through feelings and telepathy. But, for now, we are seeing the foundation stones laid down for the future. You only have to recall your own experiences to realize that this heightened awareness of the feelings of others is already happening. The psychic and emotional bonds that a child and parent demonstrate through intuition and empathy clearly identify this. This is no longer theory, but fact. We are waking up to a new level of communication.

Two of my best friends at school were twins. They were so tuned into one another that they could always guess what the other one was thinking. It may have been a bit spooky, but I was fascinated by this. Again, it proved to me that something mysterious was going on.

There is nothing mysterious about using the emotional channels of love to tune into someone you are close to. This happens to most people already, although they may not always be conscious of it. The only reason you paid this more attention was because of the intensity of your own feelings. What you experienced with your mother made you more aware of this psychic and intuitive bond. You knew that something more was happening.

But if most people aren't even conscious of their psychic abilities, then surely nothing will ever change in our culture. And if the majority of us are sleepwalking through life, then we will continue to deny that we are anything more than a physical body.

This will not always be the case. There is a massive awakening beginning to take place. And when this evolution of consciousness does take hold, the majority will come to realize that they are indeed spiritual beings, living out a physical life.

When even greater numbers of our global community awaken, we will begin to appreciate with growing intensity that we are linked to one another on a huge web of energy.

So, if more people believe that this shift in consciousness is taking place, it will further ignite our intuitive and empathic abilities?

On a global scale, yes. We will be able to experience firsthand what this expanded version of consciousness will mean to our everyday lives. People will become more intuitive to the world the moment they wake up and realize what is happening. And our ability to become better empathizers will increase when we see that our energy is constantly tuned into a global community.

Much like a psychic version of the electronic internet.

Yes.

And our feelings will be the instrument that enables us to plug into this divine web that feeds energy to everyone?

Feelings are everything, which is why it's crucial that you listen to what your feelings are communicating. They are not only your soul's messenger. They are also your connection to creativity and source energy from the divine. Your individual feelings in the body are tools that will tune you back into the world. Cut off your feelings, and you sever your lifeline to not only divine source, but also every other living thing.

And no matter what emotions I try to mask, others will always pick up these emotions on a deeper level of understanding?

Yes. You cannot hide anything because the connection between you and the rest of life is always open. Trust that others are always subtly picking up your internal feelings, and you will begin to understand why they sometimes react the way they do.

And this is because every one of our thoughts and feelings are being pushed out into the world.

All thoughts and feelings are energy, and the strongest energy charge that you emit out into the ether is your trapped and unexpressed emotions. This is why you will intuitively feel if another person is not telling you the entire truth. That person may tell you he or she is fine, but you know differently on an energy level.

Because our bodies are picking up an energy vibration from that person's magnetic field.

That's it. All emotions are energy. They are energy that in one way or another is connected to you. Just because you are not consciously aware of these vibrations does not mean that they do not exist. It could simply be that the mind static of worry and anxiety is so strong that it obscures your intuitive feelings.

Or our minds are so full and confused that we cannot even begin to break through the crust and decipher what the body is desperately trying to tell us.

This is why it is so imperative that you have other relationships around you at times when you are going through emotional trauma. Not only do they offer you vital mirrors, but they also offer an avenue to express your denied feelings. Just as a powerful magnet will vacuum up iron filings, so your trapped emotions are being drawn to the surface by the presence of a caring and compassionate loved one.

We act as magnets to one another then? We help each other to draw out emotion?

Yes, from a healing aspect, the presence of another helps to draw out our sometimes repressed and denied emotion. It enables us to bring emotions into the light that we have not perhaps dealt with or reflected upon before. This is the great gift of compassion and empathy. They are essential life tools if we are to help heal the pain of those we love dearly.

But as men, we are not very good at sharing and expressing our deepest emotions. We don't always wish to bring the inner world of our feelings out into the open.

Then you miss one of the greatest gifts that the life experience bestows on you. And you throw away any chance you have of becoming a deeply fulfilled and satisfied human being. What you do not realize is that if you don't take responsibility for your emotions, then other outside forces will.

What outside forces are you talking about?

The energy of all life. If you believe that you can go through your entire life without sharing parts of your inner world with others, then you have no idea what power your emotions possess. And you have no idea of what you are missing. Emotions are the life-force energy of creation that has been drawn to you, by you. They have been magnetized toward you by your thoughts, that creative energy force that wishes to manifest itself in a physical form. Choose to ignore your emotions by keeping them hidden away, and you will soon discover that all trapped energy goes to work on your physical body.

Do you mean that it will harm us?

Not intentionally. Remember, all emotion wants to do is to find the light and become creative. This is one of the main purposes of emotion—to bring through the unmanifested divine and replicate it in the physical world. Try to recall a time when you have harbored unexpressed emotion. How did it make you feel?

I've been a master at holding my emotions in and pretending that everything is okay. There are so many times when I have just wanted to explode at an obnoxious and awkward client. But I couldn't. I'm a director, and it wouldn't reflect well on the company or its reputation.

So you bite your tongue and hold it all in?

I do. But it's painful, and it hurts. I can almost feel the pressure building up in my stomach and around my back. I hate it that I cannot express how I truly feel. I know this causes my neck aches and the pains around my chest, but I just have to put up with it because it's part of the job.

Is it part of the job description to bring on a heart attack or stroke? Is it your job to leave your wife without a husband and your children without a father? Does your job description say that you must physically damage your body at the expense of holding in your true feelings?

I get the point.

But will you do anything about it? That is the big question. Given a second chance at life, would you change your behavior? Will you respect yourself enough to tell others how you are really feeling about those negative emotions, which bring pains to your physical body? And will you ever stop trying to sit on the fence all of the time in business? Confrontation is good if it produces the only tool to help pry open your denied and repressed emotions.

You have a great way of shining the torch into corners of my life that I haven't ever wanted to face. Thank you. I cannot express to you how grateful I am.

Sometimes, we have to be cornered before the real truth comes out. We have to face annihilation before we break down the ego's barrier and discover what is really getting to us. Know that whatever unexpressed emotions you hold in your body will eventually find the surface, whether you choose to bring them out or you leave it to life. Either way, emotion will eventually become real.

What you are implying is that there is always a conscious choice to make. We can either be open with our emotions, in which case we remain healthy and balanced, or we can ignore them, pretend they don't matter, and suffer the consequences.

Consequences that, over time, will manifest themselves as a physical or mental illness.

This entire conversation is all about emotion and changing how we perceive ourselves in the world, isn't it? It's about understanding why we are here and what our purpose is.

And how would you answer your own questions?

I'd say that we're here as spiritual beings to experience life fully in a physical body.

And…

Our purpose on earth as a co-creator is to learn how to manifest the unseen mystery of the divine through our creativity. To bring through the divine and create the beauty of that infinite potential here on planet earth. That's why we are here.

Anything else?

Use emotions and feelings to help us contextualize what it means to live in a physical body. And, in doing so, to realize that we are never separated or apart from everything else out there. I now understand that we are all fragments of the same divine energy. We are all one.

This has been an incredible journey, my good friend.

You are telling me. You have blessed me with such wisdom and insight that I don't know how I can begin to thank you. You have filled my heart and soul with such an abundance of joy, love and wonder. I thank you for that. I thank you for helping me to wake up.

No thanks are necessary. If you do wish to thank anyone, then thank yourself. And if you want to thank life, then it is simple. Go out and let your living experience be an example of your highest truth. And give thanks that your curiosity has brought you to this wonderful place in your life. Give gratitude that you had the presence of mind to see where you have gone so drastically off course.

But I didn't find the answers, you did.

No, it was you, my beloved friend, who discovered your own treasure. You revealed your greatest hidden secrets. Every answer that you ever need is always there waiting for you. Please remember that. And all you ever need do is go within. That is where your salvation will be found.

Dying for a Change

Forty-Two

I was standing at the back of my long hallway at home, looking toward the front door. There was absolute silence. Where were the waves? Why wasn't I cold? Why was I in my own house? I couldn't figure out what was going on. How did I get here? Why was I not in the sea? Why had the voice of the presence abruptly stopped, our conversation ended?

The presence that had gifted me with such wisdom, insight and love had vanished. Suddenly, I felt more alone than ever. I knew the presence had left me because every cell in my body could feel it. Low-level anxiety rippled through me. My feelings of serenity and calm had disappeared.

I became acutely aware of the intensity of everything around me. The colors were brighter, more vivid. Whatever I fixed my gaze upon suddenly became more clear and defined. I'd look away from something for the briefest moment, and the reverse happened. The image would disintegrate.

Not knowing what to make of it all, I tried calming myself by reconnecting with some of the wisdom I had just been taught by the presence. I was looking for guidance, help, a clue…anything. But something was blocking me from recapturing any memories of our dialogue. I knew that I was being made to focus on this scene alone.

I glanced up and suddenly noticed that Alison, Jenna and Olivia were standing motionless by the front door. Alison was in the middle, with Olivia and Jenna on either side of her. They had their backs to me, and they were holding hands. They seemed to be waiting for something. I don't know how long they'd been there, but I had not noticed them up to that point. I tried to move toward them, but I was paralyzed. Some form of energy was blocking me. Frustrated and angry, I yelled out, but no sound came from my mouth. What was happening to me? And why was I being shown this?

A loud knock sounded on the front door. The vibration of the knocking penetrated me. The door opened by itself, and two police officers filled the door frame. One was a very tall man, and the other a much shorter woman. The man was first to speak.

"Mrs. Murtha," he paused as if waiting for something, "we regret to inform you that we believe we've located your husband's remains. A body has just been recovered from a beach five miles along the coast. Unfortunately, it is badly decomposed. We'll need you to come along to the station with us and formally identify some of his clothing."

Alison and the girls immediately broke down and started to sob uncontrollably. Dazed and shocked by what I was witnessing, I felt as if someone had drained the life force from me. I was spinning and felt sick. I didn't know what to do next.

Overwhelmed by an intense emotional pain now flooding my veins, I tried to switch it off. To my annoyance, nothing happened. The girls continued to wail, and the pain I was picking up from them seemed to intensify. The noise was echoing through me. I wanted it to stop, but I was helpless to make it happen.

Then it dawned on me: Have I actually died? Is this why I am seeing and experiencing this scene? I became completely overtaken by the horrifying thought that my life had been terminated. "This is the end," I told myself. "I *have* died. And I am now experiencing events as they are actually happening."

With my heart thumping and my soul aching, I looked again toward Alison and my daughters. From where I was standing, I couldn't see their faces, but I could feel the presence of their pain. It felt as if it was inside me, around me. I couldn't escape from it. I was linked to it, part of it. The noise of the wailing gradually grew louder and louder. I couldn't bear the pain anymore. I tried to cover my ears, but it failed to mute the sound.

"Turn around, girls," I pleaded. "Please let me see you one last time." But they wouldn't turn around. They couldn't hear me. I was certain they didn't even sense I was there. I continued to try and draw their attention with my thoughts, which seemed to be the only way I could possibly communicate with them, but it was useless. They continued to ignore me, and then their image began to fade. At the same time, they began moving farther away from me. In sheer desperation, I reached out with my arm in a last-ditch attempt to touch them, but it did no good.

Crying, I turned my attention away from them and focused back on the light beaming from the table lamp. Its brightness was now also fading, as were my energy levels. I screamed out in one last call for help, but my voice only echoed inside me.

Then, everything seemed to stop. All the painful emotions I had been feeling, the wailing, the scene by the front door with the police officers… it all appeared to be suspended in time, as if the entire universe had been put on hold.

With blinding clarity, absolute truth suddenly flowed into my awareness. Information seemed to download into my consciousness in a fraction of a second. I knew without a doubt that I *hadn't* died. And I *wasn't* witnessing the aftermath of a foregone conclusion. This was a premonition. There were still other life options open to me, over which I had absolute and total control.

I glanced toward the front door again, but everybody had disappeared. And, bizarrely, so had all the emotional feelings I had for my family. I felt numb and empty at first, but this soon changed as the powerful and immense presence came back to me. It filled the gap left by the love that I had felt for Ali and the girls. This loving presence was inside me, engulfing me. Filling and comforting me. I could sense that it was here for a definite purpose. It wanted an answer from me.

I understood. It was time to make a decision. I had to decide whether to go forward or pull back. I had to choose between life and physical death.

I felt like my soul was being pulled in two directions. One part of my spirit wanted to let go of all the constrictions of living inside a physical body. It wanted to be set free and return to the divine essence of source, of which I absolutely knew I was an integral part.

But the other part of my spirit—the higher part—knew that I still had major life challenges to overcome and to learn from. This part of me didn't want to move forward. It wanted to hold back and return to the physical realm. It wanted to complete its calling on earth.

A strong tingling, like an electric shock, rippled through my body, but the sensation was pleasant. A wave of heavy emotion trickled through every cell of my body, and I knew that I needed to go back and fulfill my life promise. Even though the desire to shed my physical body was overwhelming, I needed to complete what I had come to this earth to do. I had never been so certain of anything in my entire life.

At the moment I made a conscious decision to stay with my body, everything inside me shifted. The presence left me once again. Immediately, I was back in the freezing water! Shocked and disoriented, all my physical sensations suddenly rushed back as the images of the hallway evaporated. It felt as if the volume to my senses, all the dials to my pain, had been turned right back up again. The crashing waves. The intensely cold wind. The darkness. The feeling of hyperthermia in my bones. I shuddered as a wave caught me full in the face.

Treading water and shaking violently, I looked up toward the full moon, which was growing brighter. That, and the increasing number of stars that were now punching through, seemed to be my only companions. Although the sun had now disappeared into the sea, I was shocked to realize that some light was still fanning across the sky. The sunset was at exactly the same position as it had been just before my conversation had begun with the presence. Nothing had changed, and yet I felt as if I had been communicating with the presence for days.

I tilted my head away from the crashing waves and tried to refocus on pulling myself back together. There was no more time to reflect on the extraordinary events in the hallway or the conversation. I knew I needed to muster up every bit of attention and willpower to stay afloat.

Conscious of the pains in my legs and arms, I took several deep breaths and tried to relax. I kicked my legs back up to the surface in an attempt to float horizontally. After experiencing the wonderful feelings of weightlessness and freedom, I now felt heavy and constricted. Every bone in my body felt like a lead weight. Struggling to stay afloat, I let my legs fall back beneath the surface as I righted myself.

With little energy left to fight, I considered what would happen next. I had made a decision to come back into my body, but how was I to be rescued? Something incredible would have to happen, and quickly, or else I would be dead within minutes.

I began to panic. I had made the wrong decision. What had I been thinking? How could I have been so stupid? I had the opportunity to leave all the pain behind me. I had the chance to let go of my physical body and go forward to whatever was waiting for me. But I hadn't taken it. For a brief moment, I entertained the thought that I had dreamt the whole thing. Perhaps I hadn't had a choice to make after all. But I knew implicitly that what I'd experienced in the hallway had really happened. What I had seen and felt was real.

Although I'd nearly given up hope of being rescued, I prayed furiously for something, anything, to save me. I became so focused on praying that even the feeling of cold briefly evaporated. I prayed for the presence to return and save me. I prayed for the universe to take pity on me.

Memories of Alison and the girls began to fill my head again, and this seemed to inject my prayers with a greater and more intense energy. I craved the experience of oneness that I had felt earlier in the water. I wanted to feel connected to something again, to be part of something infinitely greater than myself.

Looking up toward the coast, across the railway line, I noticed a strong light shining in a top-floor window of an apartment building. I could just make out a shadow. Someone was moving around in the window. It was all the inspiration I needed. The presence of that person was enough to lift my spirits. Focusing all of my attention on that window, I continued to pray furiously. I prayed that I would be seen. I prayed that the person would come and rescue me. I prayed like mad because, whoever that was, he was my only connection to another living being. He was my only link to life.

Second by second, I urged this person to look out and see me. I willed him to look down toward the sea. My total attention was fixed on that silhouette.

Still upright in the water, I became aware that I was struggling to stay afloat, and I looked around to see whether the tide was turning. I had glanced away from the window for only a second, but the connection was broken. All the positive energy that I had been directing toward the person in the window had evaporated.

Surely, it was complete madness to hang onto the notion that I could ever be saved. It was dark. I was in the sea. This person was in a top-floor apartment, unaware of my presence. Whoever it was could never have seen me.

I looked up at the window again, but it was empty this time. The person had vanished from sight. My heart dropped like a stone in my chest. I stared in disbelief at the empty space. My last thread of hope had been cut.

Drifting aimlessly, I closed my eyes and tried to ignore the biting cold that was eating into my bones. I was sick of the rollercoaster ride I had been on and tired of false hope. I thought about swallowing seawater and filling my lungs, but I was too much of a coward. I couldn't go through with it.

I became acutely aware of the sound of the crashing waves slamming into the seawall. It was as if the volume had been turned up. All of my attention was now focused on the roar and crash of the water hitting the wall. No other sound in the world mattered.

Forty-Three

*S*uddenly, I thought I heard another sound, one that was different from the noise of the waves. It was higher-pitched. I strained to listen. I was certain it was a man's voice. Was I hearing things? I wondered whether my imagination was playing tricks on me. But it *was* a man's voice, which punched through again, loud and clear. This time, I could hear him yelling.

"Do you need help?"

Terrified that it was another figment of my imagination, that it would just create more false hope, I was too scared to look in the direction of the seawall from where the voice was originating. But I could still hear him shouting, "Do you need help?"

I had to look. I couldn't believe it. Somebody was actually standing there on the pathway. A man was madly waving his arms around. Petrified that I was hallucinating, I glanced away before looking back and checking again. I wasn't imagining the man. He was real.

I was elated. Instantly, I felt stronger and lighter. I shouted out loud again and again, "He is here to save me! He's here to rescue me!" Against all the odds, and to my utter amazement, my prayers had been answered.

"Are you in trouble?" the person yelled out, continuing to wave.

I couldn't believe what I had just heard. Of course, I was in trouble. Did he honestly believe that I was swimming in the freezing sea by choice? My throat may have been on fire, but I still managed to scream out, "Help me, quick! I'm struggling to stay afloat." My voice was broken, and I wasn't certain whether the man had heard me.

"I'm going to get you out," he shouted back. "Trust me. Hang in there, mate." I wanted to trust him. I wanted to trust this stranger more than I had trusted anyone else. He was all the hope I had left.

"I need something to hold onto! I need to stay afloat!" I was amazed my voice was strong as I yelled back to him.

I knew I didn't have long. I felt dizzy, and I had a paralyzing cramp in my legs. Peering over the top of the waves, I saw something orange being thrown up into the air. I presumed it was a small buoyancy aid. I could just make out that a rope was attached to it. My heart sank as I watched the orange object plunge into the water. It landed miserably short of where I was, barely a stone's throw from the seawall.

I lunged desperately toward it and tried to swim closer, but it was a waste of time. Every muscle in my body ached. My saturated clothing was heavy and dragging me down. I didn't have the strength to swim a single stroke.

I could see people gathering on the seawall. Some of them had flashlights. They were shouting and waving. Why were they just standing there? Why wasn't anyone jumping in to save me?

"Help is on its way. Swim toward the orange buoy," a woman bellowed, pointing toward it. Of course, I knew where the buoy was. I didn't need to be told. Didn't she realize that I could do nothing about it? I couldn't swim all that way. I couldn't swim at all anymore. In fact, it was a struggle just to stay afloat.

If help was on its way, what kind of help was it? A helicopter? A lifeboat? Whatever help she meant, it had better be soon. I couldn't hang on much longer. "Do something!" I managed to scream out. "Don't just stand there!"

Wave after wave slapped me in the face. After each battering, I frantically searched for that one lifeline, to see the flash of orange against all the grey. Closing my eyes, I began praying furiously once again. "If there is a God in the universe, then please, please help me."

Opening my eyes, I saw that the buoy seemed to be closer. Perhaps my imagination was playing tricks on me. Or maybe the changing tide had dragged me nearer to the wall. But all that mattered now was that I had a better chance of reaching it. It was the spark of hope I needed.

Everyone on the seawall was shouting, screaming, willing me on. Their sheer presence seemed to inject me with incredible belief. I began to think that I could make it. The fact that others cared about my survival fuelled my sense of hope. This was no longer just about me. I wanted to do it for me *and* for them. I didn't want to let them down. I didn't want to let my family down.

Determined to stay conscious, I desperately scanned the horizon for signs that a helicopter or rescue boat was on its way. But I couldn't hear or see anything. Nothing but stars and a fat moon filled the sky. I wondered whether anybody had actually called the emergency line. What if they hadn't? What if everyone had presumed that somebody else had made the call?

"Try grabbing the buoy!" a man screamed out repeatedly.

I looked around. I couldn't believe what I was seeing. The buoyancy aid was closer. The changing tide had drifted it over within spitting distance of my reach. I had to get closer to it. I had no energy left to swim forward, so I flipped over onto my back and began kicking and thrashing my legs. I had a cramp in my thighs and every single kick was torture, but there was no way I was going to give up. Not now.

"Grab the rope!" someone yelled. I turned instinctively and snatched at the blue rope attached to the buoy. Somehow, I managed to grab the rope the first time. I couldn't believe it. I tried to squeeze the rope tightly in my hands, but my fingers felt brittle and numb. The rope sliced through my hands like a hot knife going through butter.

Somebody on the seawall obviously thought I had hold of the rope properly because I heard someone yell, "Pull him in now!" Jerked out of my hands, the air-filled buoy skipped up into the air and landed some distance from me.

"No!" I screamed.

"No!" somebody else shouted. "Stop! He's not got hold of it yet."

I desperately lunged forward and tried to kick my legs. Somehow, I managed to scramble closer to my lifeline again. This time, I was determined not to let go. I reached out and clawed at a small rope-loop that was hanging from the buoy and instinctively slipped my arm through it.

"I've got it," I tried shouting, but my voice had almost gone. Nothing happened. I didn't move. They obviously couldn't hear me. "Pull!" I shouted louder, my voice cracking. Suddenly, there was a jolt, and I was partially lifted out of the water. I could just make out the figures of two men who were reeling me in. I had no energy to do anything. I had no choice but to lie back, exhausted.

I was ecstatic. *I'm going to be saved. I'm going to live.* Like a mantra, I kept repeating these words over and over in my head. I was being rescued. Then I could tell everyone everything.

Finally, reaching the bottom of the seawall, I looked up at the two men who were hauling me in. I didn't want to lose our connection. I recognized both of them. They were local lads. I had passed them on the street many times before. Only then, they hadn't meant anything to me. But now it was different. Now they were everything.

"Tug hard," shouted someone in the crowd.

My right arm was almost wrenched from its socket as I started to be winched up. The wind was howling as they pulled hard. I was being bashed against the algae-covered wall. Sopping wet, I dangled there like a motionless puppet.

"I'm falling backwards," I cried out, as I felt the loop slipping from my arm. "I'm losing the rope." I tried desperately to grab hold, but I couldn't feel anything. My fingers were too numb. I slipped from the nylon loop that was coiled around my arm and shoulder. Powerless to stop it, I somersaulted backward into the sea. I blamed myself. I hadn't been able to hold on. I heard a woman gasp just before I plunged back into the sea, close to the rocks.

"Help!" I screeched as I resurfaced. "Help me!" I stretched out both arms in front of me in a vain attempt to stop the waves from pounding me against the bottom of the wall.

"Grab the buoy as tightly as you can," someone yelled as they tossed it back down to me. "We're going to pull you alongside the wall."

The orange buoy practically landed on my head. I lashed out wildly and tried to hook the trailing rope with my forearm. I managed to catch it and slip my arm through the loop. It was now wrapped around my shoulder.

"Okay, pull!" yelled one of the men, yanking hard on the rope. Again, I was partially lifted out of the water. Staring up, I saw a line of faces peering down at me from the top of the seawall. They were all straining to get a better look at what was going on. I felt like an animal being stared at in the zoo.

"Get out of the way!" bellowed a man as he shunted the crowd back from the edge and toward the railway line. "We need to drag him along to one of the breakpoints in the wall."

I felt a sudden jolt as I started to be pulled along the wall. In the feeble light, and from where I was at the bottom of the wall, I couldn't make out who was tugging on the rope. However many there were, they must have been running because I was practically skimming along the surface of the waves. I wondered how far they would have to pull me. I felt my ribs knock against something solid. I presumed it was rocks, but I was too numb and exhausted to care.

"Keep going," I heard a male voice shout. "Almost there."

We finally reached a breakpoint along the seawall. I saw a gap and a concrete ramp that disappeared into the sea. As I was dragged onto the ramp, I recognized it. It was close to a café where small boats and canoes usually pushed off.

"That's enough," someone shouted. "Stop pulling him." I was lying on my back in shallow water. I caught a glimpse of some of the people lined up along the ramp. Now, no one was shouting. No one moved. There was an eerie silence. Finally, two men waded into the freezing water and dragged me out. I couldn't stop shaking. One of the men tried to haul me onto my feet, but my legs gave way.

"We'll have to carry him," he said. I felt certain that I was going to pass out, so I flung both my arms around one of them.

"You'll...never...believe...what...has...happened," I tried to whisper, but my throat was on fire, and I could barely get the words out. I knew I wasn't making any sense. I couldn't string one sentence together, let alone make myself understood.

A waiting paramedic took control. "Save your energy, son." He threw a padded silver blanket around me. Then, with the help of a colleague, he grabbed hold of me and held me up. "There'll be plenty of time for that in the hospital. What's your name, and where do you live?"

"Bill. Bill Murtha," I stammered, clutching tightly onto both of them. 'I live at...'" It was ridiculous. I couldn't even remember my own address.

"Don't worry," said one of them. "Take your time." Finally remembering my home address, I blurted it out and then broke down in tears. I couldn't stop myself. I wasn't embarrassed that everyone was only yards away, watching me. I just wanted to get home where I would be safe and warm. I wanted to see my family again.

"Right. We need to get you to the hospital fast." The paramedics, one on either side of me, hurriedly began carrying my dead weight up the stone steps. The path that weaved around the cliff face seemed to go on forever. Both of the men were puffing and panting.

We finally reached the top of the steps by the road. One of the men shouted out, "Please, everyone, stand back!" A small crowd of people was gathered around the ambulance.

I must have passed out at that point. The next thing I was conscious of was lying in the back of the ambulance, strapped onto a stretcher, which rattled and bounced around as the vehicle negotiated sharp bends. One of the paramedics was at my side. He was looking away from me, checking one of the monitors. I glanced down and saw that I was attached to several tubes. I wanted to ask a hundred questions, but I couldn't. My jaw was aching, and I had a splitting headache. I didn't have the energy to open my mouth.

"We don't want to lose this one to hyperthermia." The paramedic sounded worried as he shouted to the driver. He obviously didn't realize that I was awake. "Put your foot down," he told the driver.

Lose me? I felt a surge of anxiety and anger race through me. There was absolutely no way I was going to give in, not after everything that had happened. The paramedic's words injected me with an urgent desire to live. I was determined. I *wasn't* going to die. Not in the back of an ambulance, and certainly not alone with someone I didn't know. I *was* going to make it.

Forty-Four

*T*he next thing I knew, I was being raced through a narrow corridor and into a small cubicle. I was in the emergency department of the hospital. Everyone around me seemed to be in a hurry. I could hear lots of talking. I felt a sharp jab in my forearm, and I was out cold again.

When I opened my eyes, my right leg was shaking furiously. It was knocking against the metal bars at the side of my bed. I tried pinning my leg down with my hand, but I was too weak. Unable to fight the fatigue, I drifted back to sleep.

"You're an extremely lucky man, Mr. Murtha," said a friendly female voice. I opened my eyes. The busyness had now been replaced by calm. I noticed that several more tubes had been attached to me.

"You are fortunate to be here." I looked up. A nurse was standing by my bed, smiling. I didn't know what to say, so I just smiled back at her. My eyes felt so heavy, and I struggled to keep them open.

"Your wife will be here in a short while," said the nurse, checking one of the monitors. "She's been contacted and is already on her way." Speechless, I just lay there, trying to piece everything together.

"How long have I been out cold?" I finally asked.

"Less than an hour," answered the nurse, puffing up my pillows. There was an awkward silence before she carried on. "You gave everyone quite a fright, you know. It was touch and go for a while."

"I can't remember much about it," I eventually replied, clearing my throat.

"Put it this way," she added. "We had trouble getting your core body temperature back up to safe levels." I couldn't answer. I had no idea that it had been that bad. Neither one of us said anything for what seemed like an eternity. Then, thankfully, the nurse broke the silence.

"Someone up there was clearly looking out for you tonight," she winked. A cold shiver rippled down the entire length of my spine, and all the hairs on the back of my neck stood up. I immediately remembered the presence in the sea and everything I had been through.

"The paramedics who brought you in told us how you'd been saved," she said.

"They did?"

"Yes, and what an incredible story…" The nurse stopped mid-sentence. I sensed that she was holding something back. She stopped what she was doing, sat on the chair and looked straight at me. "The chances of that man spotting you in the sea from where he lived must have been a billion to one. I would go and buy a lottery ticket this weekend if I were you."

I didn't know what she was talking about. What man? What place? Perhaps she meant the man who had first shouted to me from the seawall. Maybe he had spotted me from his home. But what was his name? Where did he live? I was desperate to ask the nurse everything she knew. I wanted the full story, to fill in the gaps. But I held back. I didn't want to ask because that would mean explaining my side of the story, and I didn't want to relive the entire thing all over again. Maybe later, but not now.

"How am I?" I asked, changing the subject. Clutching my ribs, I winced as I tried to sit up in bed.

"Apart from all the cuts and bruises, and a few fractured ribs, you have no problems whatsoever." The nurse gently took hold of my arm and helped me sit up. "Don't worry. It looks a lot worse than it is." I gently pulled down the covers on my bed. Where I could see, my body was black and blue.

"What about my right leg?" I asked, looking down. It was shaking uncontrollably.

"That's fine. It's just the severe shock to your body. The painkillers and sedatives should calm you down. Now, please, get some sleep before your wife arrives."

When the nurse left, I managed to kick off my bed sheets. Although parts of my body were bandaged, I could see that my legs were cut to shreds. I had several lacerations on my shoulder and right arm. The pain had been numbed, but the marks still looked awful.

I tried to drift off to sleep, but it was useless. Images of fighting for my life in the sea kept flooding back to me. All I could think about was how close I had come to dying. As I began to relive it again, I experienced a rising sense of panic. I tried to think about something else, anything to take my mind off what I'd been through, but it was a waste of time. All I could picture was me struggling in the cold sea, trying to stay afloat. Even though I was safe now, I kept reliving it all over and over again. I could still taste the rancid seawater in my mouth.

By now, my mind was racing. What would have happened if that person hadn't spotted me in the water? How much longer could I have held on to life? What if I had never seen my family again?

Breathing heavily and shaking, I couldn't switch off the memories of my experience. I lay back and stared up at the bright lights on the ceiling. Ever since my childhood road accident, I had lived with the fear that my life would end without warning. And, in particular, I'd had an unshakable and inexplicable fear of drowning.

I began to question the incredible things that had happened to me in the sea. The feelings of connectedness. The unexplainable visits to my past. The emotions, the memories. How could it all have happened in such a short span of time? I thought about the presence I had felt with me in the water. This loving entity had encouraged, guided, and supported me. And what about the phenomenal conversation we'd had? I had gained so much wisdom and had learned more than I had ever learned in my entire life. How could I begin to explain that away? I would not have been able to survive without that experience. It had helped me to make it through.

I worried about what I was going to say to Alison. She'd be arriving at the hospital any minute. What was I going to tell her? All of it? Some of it? None of it? I couldn't decide what was best, but I had to make up my mind quickly. If I did mention everything about my conversation with the presence, then where should I begin? And if I did pluck up the courage to tell her, would she believe me? Perhaps it would be better if I kept quiet. I could drip-feed everything to her gradually. It was probably better to wait until I had made better sense of it myself.

I didn't fully understand everything that I had been told by the presence, but I knew deep in my heart and in the depths of my soul that it was vitally important information. I had been given the wisdom and insight that I had been searching for ever since I was a child. So much of what I had been taught in that extraordinary conversation had been in direct response to the biggest questions I had ever asked about life. It was as if all the missing jigsaw pieces had come to me all at once.

I desperately wanted to experience once again that wonderful feeling of oneness and connectedness. I wanted to touch that place where everything had felt so balanced and right. A place where I had felt an overwhelming sense of belonging. The intense love I had experienced was unlike anything else I had ever felt. What the all-seeing, all-loving and all-knowing presence had shown me was that I am infinitely more than just the physical shell I thought I was. I now understood that I was part of something greater than I ever knew existed.

I was desperate to find something that came remotely close to the incredible feelings I'd had in the water. For some reason, I remembered those moments in my past when I had been high on drugs, when I had *thought* I was feeling calm and at one with life. As I stared around the brightly lit cubicle, it dawned on me why I had gotten caught up with drugs and drinking. In my frantically busy, stressed-filled life, they had brought temporary escape from all of the insanity and demands. The drugs had allowed me to push the pause button, to create an artificial feeling of happiness.

I wondered if it was the same for everyone who was addicted to drugs or alcohol. Had they also been searching for short-term escape? For that feeling of oneness and connectedness that, deep down, we all long for? Perhaps that was why my father had gone out drinking, rather than staying home with my brothers and me. Maybe he had needed to escape.

When I was with the presence in the water, I came to understand how important it is to experience true feeling and emotion. All feelings, good and bad, are vital to our learning and growing, I was told. This made me realize that I had spent much of my life pushing away anything that felt unpleasant. I had been denying the most fundamental life force, my own feelings. I had welcomed in positive emotions, but the moment I experienced anything negative, I would ignore it. It was my way of dealing with things, but now I knew that was wrong. I should have listened to *all* of my emotions.

I wondered whether I should share this extraordinary insight with

312

my friends. If I did find the courage to tell Alison, then surely I owed it to the others to do the same. After all, I was very close to some of my friends. But if I did bring everything out into the open, would any of them believe me? And if they did, could they ever appreciate all that I had been through? Petrified that I could jeopardize every friendship I had, I decided to say very little. I wasn't prepared to throw away the friendships that had taken me almost a lifetime to develop.

Suddenly, I heard Alison's voice coming from the corridor. I froze. I hadn't made up my mind what to say to her yet. I heard Alison ask which cubicle I was in. I could hear her footsteps getting closer. Why was I so worried? *Alison's my wife, for God's sake. I should be able to share everything with her.* But where was I going to start? It may have been only hours ago that I waved good-bye to her, but it felt like several lifetimes ago. And now I was no longer the same person. Everything had changed. How could I even begin to tell her about the presence in the sea or what we'd discussed?

Alison pulled back the curtain to my cubicle. She stood there for a moment, not saying a word. Then she rushed over, kissed me and gave me a hug. I started to cry. I couldn't hold back. No words were needed. I was so glad to see her. I had thought that I would never see her again.

Alison sat down and squeezed my hand. I managed to ask her where the children were, and she said that a neighbor was babysitting. When I eventually stopped crying, I began telling Alison about the accident. I told her how the freak wave had swept me off the seawall. I told her how terrifying it was to be alone in the dark. To be marooned in the freezing water and certain that I was going to die. I told her about the man who had suddenly appeared from nowhere and rescued me. Alison said nothing. She just sat there, listening to every word. I told her about the people who had pulled me along the seawall to safety. Then, finally, I told her what the nurse had been told by the paramedics—that a person had somehow spotted me from a long way off. The nurse had inferred that my rescue was down to a billion-to-one chance of being spotted. Alison wanted to know more about this person, but I didn't know any other facts. The nurse had only given me half the story.

Exhausted, I slumped back on the pillow. I may not have known anything more about who had rescued me, but I did know a lot more about what had happened in the sea. I tried to convince myself that I was

313

too shattered to share any other details about what I had experienced, but tiredness wasn't the only reason. I was too much of a coward. I held back most of the important details. I said nothing about the presence. I couldn't. I didn't want Alison to think that I was mad. What I had experienced was far too important. I couldn't risk being doubted. And I didn't want the whole thing devalued. What I'd been part of was miraculous.

I flashed back to when I was in the hallway of our home and had "witnessed" the police turning up to tell Alison and the girls that my body had been washed up on the shore.

"Are you okay?" Alison asked. She could see that my attention was elsewhere. I kept seeing, over and over again, me standing at the back of the hall, looking at the police officers. I heard myself telling Alison that I was fine, but I was shaking with fear.

"A policeman and policewoman came to the house," Alison said. "They came to tell me what had happened to you. I was worried sick."

I shuddered. The hair on my arms stood up. I just stared at her. I didn't know what to say. I couldn't shift the image of Alison and the girls crying from my head. Last night, it had actually felt as if I'd been there with them in the hallway, living every moment.

"Come on, what's wrong?" Alison said. She clearly knew something was bothering me.

"Nothing," I snapped. "I'm telling you I'm fine, okay?" Alison obviously didn't believe me, but said nothing. I felt guilty for snapping at her and not telling her the truth.

At that moment, my best friend Simon arrived at my bedside. It was a convenient distraction. The second I saw him, I broke down in tears again. I didn't know what to say. He was like a brother to me. We'd been through so much together. I was just so relieved to see him again.

Simon wanted to know all the details. He wanted to find out for himself what it had been like to come that close to dying. I told him the same as I had told Alison. The last thing I wanted him thinking was that his best friend had lost his mind.

The nurse came back and checked all the monitors next to my bed. Then she dimmed the lights and said it was time for visitors to leave. I didn't want Alison and Simon to go. I didn't want to be left all alone in the dark.

Simon said good-bye and promised to ring me the next day. Alison leaned over and kissed me. I smiled. She said that she would ring my work colleagues and explain what had happened. I waved good-bye and said I would see her in the morning. I told her to give Jenna and Olivia a hug from me. I couldn't wait to see them.

Dying for a Change

Forty-Five

Although I tried to stay awake, just to reassure myself that I was still alive, I must have drifted off. The next thing I knew, the sun was rising. I realized that I had been moved onto a main ward. It was quiet. Other patients were still asleep. For a few moments, I just lay there, looking around and taking it all in. Sunlight was pouring in from the large windows at the other end of the room. The enormity of what I had been through suddenly hit me. My stomach churned at the thought of it all. I immediately recognized how fortunate I was to be alive.

Lying perfectly still, I stared up in awe at the sun as it rose slowly above the hill beyond the town. It was the most stunning sight I had ever seen. This was the very same sun that I had said good-bye to while I was in the water. I hadn't thought I would ever see it come up again. I could feel a warmth building inside my chest. I lay there, crying quietly. I didn't want anyone in the ward to hear a grown man cry.

I watched an elderly man as he hauled himself up out of bed and shuffled toward the window. I guessed he'd recently had major surgery. He was using a portable drip-feed machine to balance himself. The man stood there, motionless, also gazing out at the sun.

Clutching at my sore ribs, I put both feet down on the cold floor. Dizziness assailed me, and I stood still for a moment until it had subsided. Slowly, I made my way over to the window to join the man. He acknowledged me with a nod, and then smiled. It felt as if I had known this man all of my life. There was a connection between us. I could sense it. And I was certain that he could, too.

I liked this man. There was a sense of peace and serenity about him that instantly attracted me. I knew that this man was open and honest. I sensed I could trust him. As odd as it seemed, he immediately felt like a friend. I had an urge to speak, but something told me not to. Instead, we just looked at each other in total silence. Then we both turned and stared at the sun as it rose over the town. There was no need for words.

What needed to be communicated was nonverbal. It was universal. A language that we both recognized. Every cell in my body sensed it. I knew without question that I was returning to being in touch with my sixth sense. I felt this man's appreciation for being alive. His kindness, his compassion. The love and joy he felt. And even some of the pain that he had recently endured. Momentarily, his feelings belonged to me. They were part of me.

I was tuning into a higher frequency. This was exactly how I had picked up the feelings of my mother all those years ago. It was the same intensity. Only this time, it was with a total stranger. Yet, somehow, I felt he was familiar. A friend.

Gazing out of the window, I remembered some of the insight and wisdom that the presence had passed onto me about emotions and empathy. I had been taught so much. I now appreciated that *all* emotion was the glue that bonded us together. And now I realized that it *was* possible for everyone to tune into other people's emotions. All we needed to do was simply focus our entire attention on the other person and concentrate on nothing else.

I'd honestly never given it a thought that others might also be able to feel what was going on inside of me. I turned to my new friend, standing beside me, and wondered if he, too, could sense what I was feeling.

The presence had told me that the more aware we are of our own feelings, the more aware we are of the feelings of others. The two were linked, intertwined. Somehow, ever since I had been a child, I had known this.

I was able to pick up the loving and compassionate feelings of my new friend next to me because my mind was open and clear of all thoughts. It wasn't choked up with the nagging worries that frequently clouded my thinking or the incessant "mind chatter" that usually filled my head. I also recognized that turning off the negativity in my head made it far easier to connect with others.

A surge of love raced through my veins and around my chest, filling me completely. I instantly knew that the old man could feel my emotion, too. I desperately wanted him to acknowledge that he could feel the love and kinship I was projecting toward him. But, too embarrassed to say anything, I turned and started to make my way back toward my bed. I didn't want to sound like a fool.

Then, just as I was cursing myself for being such a chicken, I heard him whisper something.

"I can feel it, too," he said.

I froze. I turned around and looked at him. We held each other's gaze for a few moments. He was smiling. That was the sign I needed. I knew right then that he could feel my love, just as I could feel his.

The ward began to stir as patients wakened. Nurses bustled in and out, getting everyone ready for breakfast. As I lay on my bed, I thought deeply about what had just happened. There had been a link, a bond, a soul connection.

For the rest of that morning, I managed to hold onto my heightened sense of love, peace and serenity. I didn't want to lose it. It made me feel more alive, more in tune with the world.

I wanted to sit quietly and watch everybody coming and going in the ward. This was unusual for me. I was normally the first one to strike up a conversation. But today was different. I wasn't in the mood for talking or rushing around. I just wanted to take it all in.

I enjoyed my newfound curiosity for observing life. I was fascinated by what I was learning about people's body language, conversations and expressions. There were so many nonverbal clues about how people were feeling.

Suddenly, all feelings of calm vanished. What about work? How would they manage without me? I thought about the meetings I was missing. The orders I wasn't taking. I didn't want to let down any of my big clients. Then it hit me. What was I doing? I had nearly died last night. For once in my life, work and business would have to play second fiddle. I was surprised. This was the first time since I had been plucked from the water that I had given work even a passing thought. I felt the stillness return. Now I realized that work was not the center of my universe. Other things were infinitely more important.

Sometime later that morning, one of the nurses came over to my bed. She said that a local newspaper reporter was downstairs in the reception area. He was refusing to go away. I played part-time for one of the local soccer teams and thought he'd come to interview me about my accident. Perhaps he'd come for a story for the back sports pages because I wouldn't be playing for a while. I agreed to see him.

Sitting down together in the television room, I discovered that he wasn't after a sports story at all. He just wanted to know about my accident. He must have had a tip-off from somewhere. He had already been to interview the person who had first spotted me in the sea. I told the reporter what I remembered the nurse telling me the night before. This must be the same man that the paramedics had mentioned to her while I was being brought through the emergency department.

"So, who is he?" I impatiently asked. "He's a local person, isn't he?"

"Yes," said the reporter, not even looking up from his notepad. "His name is Nathan. He lives in the apartments behind the railway line. It was from there he spotted you in the water. He was first on the scene. It was him, along with a few others, who pulled you to safety."

I vaguely remembered the faces of two of the men who had pulled me along by the wall. It started coming back to me. I could picture what Nathan looked like. I felt compelled to find out everything I could about him. I wanted to know Nathan's address, telephone number, contact details. What he did for a living. And I desperately needed to meet him. To thank him.

"It's no good trying to get in touch with him today," the reporter said. "He is down at the seawall being interviewed and having his photo taken. I was lucky to get in first. Now he's giving the rest of the press all the details."

"Details to what?" I asked.

It didn't make sense. I couldn't understand what all the fuss was about. There must be hundreds of people every day up and down the country who came close to drowning or dying. What was so special about this story?

"You haven't heard, have you?" The reporter glanced up, stopped writing and smiled. He looked slightly surprised. "Nobody's told you anything yet, have they…"

"Told me what?"

320

"How Nathan spotted you in the sea."

"No," I said. "The nurse said very little."

"Nathan spotted you through a telescope," he said. "That's the only reason you are here. Even though it was getting dark, he spotted you struggling in the sea. That's why all the papers are after the story."

I was speechless. I had no idea. A telescope. A telescope had saved my life.

After the interview, I went back to bed with my head spinning. Full of questions. I was already worrying. What had I said to the reporter? His questions had been relentless. I had felt dizzy throughout our meeting. I couldn't remember what I had said. I just hoped that I hadn't told him anything that I would later come to regret.

All I could think about was Nathan and the telescope.

Alison arrived later that morning to take me home. Before we left the ward, I went to find the old man. I wanted to get his name and to see how he was faring. His curtain was partially drawn, and he was asleep in his chair. I didn't want to disturb him. I was disappointed not to say good-bye, but I left him sleeping.

On the way home, Alison and I discussed what the reporter had told me about Nathan. She had already heard about Nathan and the telescope. Word had gone round the small town where we lived. I told her that I wanted to invite Nathan to the house.

When we arrived home, the phone didn't stop ringing. Friends, family, newspaper reporters…they all wanted to know how I was. The whole media circus was unbelievable. Local and national newspaper reporters were ringing persistently, hungry for my story. I'd never experienced anything like it. I was absolutely exhausted. But none of them seemed to have given that a thought. They insisted that I speak to them. I was so disoriented that I didn't think to tell them to leave me alone. Their questions were all the same. What had I thought about the telescope? How had it felt to almost die? Did I have a message for Nathan? Although I was shattered, I lay on the sofa and somehow spoke to all of them, snatching sleep between phone calls.

A few close friends dropped by to say hello in the afternoon. Simon popped in again to see how I was doing. I told him that I felt like a fraud. Apart from all the cuts, bruises and broken ribs, there was nothing wrong with me. It would all heal.

"Regardless, you should still take it easy," Simon insisted. "There's no need to rush back to work. Allow yourself plenty of time to digest what has happened to you."

I told him that I didn't want any fuss. I wanted everything to return to normal as quickly as possible. There was a business to run. I didn't have the luxury of time or the patience to sit around just thinking. In truth, I was frightened. I was petrified of revisiting it all. Perhaps it would be better to focus my attention on work. To push out the enormity of everything that had happened while I was in the sea. I didn't want to hold everything back, but I just couldn't bring myself to talk about it, even to my best friend. Simon sensed that something was wrong. He could see that I was in a terrible state. Naturally, he believed it was to do with the fact I had almost drowned, and the trauma of it all. Simon asked whether I might consider having any therapy or counseling. He didn't even know the half of it, but now wasn't the right time to tell him.

"Absolutely no chance," I replied. "I will deal with this myself." There was no way that I was going to talk to some counselor or therapist. What was the point? Nobody would understand what I had been through.

I had been home barely a few hours, and I was aware that I was already sliding back into my old ways. I felt edgy and tense. I struggled to relax. Simon could see that I needed to rest and went to talk to Alison.

The incredible feeling of calm and peace I had felt that morning in the hospital ward had now evaporated. What had changed in only a few hours? I had noticed something shift the very moment we had arrived home. Coming through the front door, I had been thrown back into the real world, one I'd grown accustomed to. But now, part of it felt strangely alien.

I looked around in a desperate attempt to ground myself. I wanted to appreciate all the lovely things around me. Our home. Everything that was in it. Two new cars parked outside on the drive. I was lucky. But instead of feeling grateful, I started to panic. I should be getting back to work. I needed to earn the bonuses to pay for all of this.

When Simon came back in to talk to me, I told him that the first thing I did when I came home was phone my Managing Director. I said we had discussed returning to work when I felt ready.

"How long will you be off?" Simon asked. "Weeks? Months?"

"Three days," I said.

"What! Are you mad?"

"Positive," I said. "I want my whole life back to normal by the middle of next week."

Simon looked surprised. Shaking his head, he smiled.

"What's wrong?" I asked him.

"I think you are insane," he said. "If it was me, I would take a lot more time off to take stock of everything, especially after everything that's happened."

I looked up at Simon without answering. He could see that I was serious.

Later, Alison went to pick up Jenna and Olivia from school, and Simon left me to get some sleep. I dozed on and off. All afternoon I had been waiting for the girls to come home. I don't know why, but I was nervous and excited at the same time. I wasn't sure how I would react when I saw them.

When the girls finally came bursting through the door, I couldn't hold it together. I started crying, and so did they. I was so glad to see them. Last night, I had almost died. I had honestly believed that I would never see either of them again. Cuddling them both, I didn't want to let them go.

Forty-Six

*T*he next morning, I woke up early. My ribs were sore, and I ached all over. It was Saturday. Alison had already walked down to the local shop with the girls to pick up a few of the newspapers. Nathan's picture was featured in several of them, along with the full story. I read every one of them several times. It was incredible. I still found it hard to believe that it had actually happened to me.

Alison had spoken to Nathan and arranged for him to come over and meet us. We were desperate to thank him, and so were the girls. They had already made Nathan a card.

Dear Mr. Nathan,
Thank you very, very much for saving my daddy's life.
Lots of love, Jenna Olivia Murtha (aged 8 6)

Alison and I cried when they showed it to us. They had written it without any help. It said everything.

I was apprehensive all morning about meeting Nathan for the first time. I had never needed to thank anyone for saving my life before. What was I going to say to him? How could I find the right words? Alison and I talked about what I should do for Nathan. I wondered whether it would best to give him a gift of some sort. Perhaps money? It seemed inappropriate. How could I ever put a price on my life?

I worried all morning about it. But then a phone call from a friend said that Nathan's girlfriend was expecting their first child very soon. So Alison and I settled on the idea of giving Nathan some money as a gift for the baby.

A few of the local newspapers rang up in the morning, offering to send a photographer and reporter to witness the meeting between Nathan and me. I turned them down flat. I wanted my family to meet Nathan without any photos being taken.

Every time the doorbell rang, I had butterflies in my stomach. Thankfully, Nathan arrived mid-afternoon and put me out of my misery. I think we both felt a bit awkward at first. There was so much I wanted to say. And perhaps so much that he would have liked to tell me, too. For a while, I couldn't say anything. I was too choked up. All I kept thinking was that "thank you" just didn't seem adequate.

Nathan and I shook hands and began to talk. I was ecstatic to be able to look into the face of the man who had saved my life. He was just as I had remembered him down by the seawall. We looked at the newspaper reports together, and then took turns telling our side of the story. I repeated everything that I had told Alison and Simon. He sat quietly while I told him.

Then it was Nathan's turn. The first thing he asked me was whether I wanted my bike back. It had been washed up on the shore at low tide, and Nathan had recovered it the morning after my accident. I said that the bike hadn't brought me much luck, so he was more than welcome to keep it.

Nathan then described to me exactly where his apartment was located. It was from his-top floor apartment that he had first spotted me with his telescope. I couldn't believe it. It was the same apartment where I had seen the silhouette in the window. The very same place where I had prayed furiously while struggling in the sea. I wanted to tell Nathan that I had seen his shadow at the window. That I had willed him, by some miracle, to see me. I could scarcely believe that he had spotted me and saved my life. But I kept silent because I didn't want to interrupt him.

Then Nathan told an even more astonishing and remarkable part of the whole rescue story. The telescope he had seen me through wasn't actually his. It had been borrowed from a friend who lived close by. Nathan went on to explain that he had been asking his friend to borrow that telescope for a number of months. And by a sheer fluke of coincidence, Nathan's friend had finally decided to take it round only a few hours before dark that very same day.

By twilight, Nathan had it set up, ready to look at the full moon. He went off to make a cup of tea but, when he came back, the telescope had dropped and was now pointing at the sea instead of the sky. Rather than adjust the telescope back to the correct position, he looked through it first instead. Even though he knew there would be nothing but black sea for miles around, Nathan said that he felt compelled to look through the telescope. His initial impression had been that he could see a seagull flapping on the surface of the waves. Then, with a start of disbelief, he realized it was someone in trouble in the sea.

Nathan rang 999 and told them what was happening. Then, realizing that I was struggling to stay afloat, he ran out of his apartment, asking for a neighbor's help along the way. Thinking that the Coast Guard would be a while, he wanted to see what he could do to help. As he and his neighbor ran down to the seawall, Nathan called for others to help him because he couldn't swim.

I sat on the sofa listening to Nathan as he told me all this. All the hairs on the back of my neck were standing on end. I was absolutely stunned. I could hardly take in what he had just told me. It was just too incredible. Too much of a miracle.

Having heard about Nathan's critical role in my survival, having lived through what I had lived through, now I *had* to believe the unbelievable: Miracles do exist.

How could my life ever be the same again?

Epilogue

*A*nd nothing *was* ever the same again.

Much to the bewilderment of my friends, family and work colleagues, I did return to my job only a few days later. It was my way of coping with the accident. My extraordinary experiences were just too big to absorb into the everyday normality of my life. So I reverted to my previous behaviors. I squashed down my experiences and buried them away.

I didn't tell Alison or Simon about the incredible conversation in the water, but it soon became apparent that it was useless to hide from the truth. My heightened conscience constantly nagged at me. I had searing headaches. I couldn't sleep properly. Several months after the accident, I started realizing that I couldn't shut it all out. Very quickly, my life slid back into a depressing cycle of drinking, drugs and denial. I was fully aware that my addictions and trapped emotions were slowly killing me. Something had to give.

My epiphany, my real awakening, took place in a dimly lit basement bar in Amsterdam a year after my accident. I was in Holland on a business trip, entertaining a group of major clients. It was three in the morning, and we'd been drinking heavily all day and night. Suddenly, as if spoken from inside every cell of my body, I heard the words:

Bill, you are wasting your life away. This is not who you are or where you're meant to be.

Shocked by the blinding clarity of the message, and afraid that I was finally losing my mind, I instantly sobered up. I thought, "What *am* I doing with the rest of my life?" I was fortunate to be saved by a one-in-a-billion real life miracle, but now I was throwing away my one chance to wake up and change my whole life around.

That one pivotal moment was the ignition I'd been waiting for. I was tired of my self-destructive behaviors. I was sick of hiding away the truth of my ordeal in the raging sea. Returning home from that trip, I finally knew that something had to change. *I* had to change. So I put the brakes on the drinking and entertaining. I cut out the drugs. And, slowly, I began to wake up to reality. For once in my life, I dug deep and mustered up the courage to face the responsibility for my own actions.

I didn't tell a single soul about everything right away. Even though there had been a dam-burst in my emotions, I still couldn't. There was far too much to tell. The full details of my ordeal dribbled out over the next few years, a bit at a time. Explaining what had happened, what I'd been through and what I had seen wasn't easy. But, over much time, I slowly built up the confidence to dole out parts of my story.

A year after that trip to Holland, I resigned from the company where I worked and, with the assistance of financial backers, co-founded a brand-new company. That first year was mentally draining and exhausting, but it enabled me to spend most weekends with Alison and the girls. I started carving out a new life.

Around that same time, I picked up a spiritual book, *The Road Less Traveled*, by M. Scott Peck. It was the first book I had read cover-to-cover for more than twenty-five years. Reading something that was a million miles away from financial reports or business plans was a revelation. That one book alone went a long way toward helping me understand the phenomenal wisdom and insight I had been shown in the water. It enabled me to fall back in love with reading. And most rewardingly, it reunited the deep passion and childhood thirst I had for writing and storytelling. After taking a test, I found out that I was both dyslexic and dyspraxic. Now I knew why I had always lacked the confidence as a child to read to the class.

Twelve months later, in 2002, I was given the green light after a lengthy and complicated operation to try for children again. The specialist had said that our chances were slim, but Alison miraculously became pregnant after only six weeks. Later that year, Kitty, our third and youngest daughter, was born. After a ten-year gap, it was great having the chance to be an older parent. This time, I was determined not to mess up and miss out.

Seeing Kitty grow up, taking her to school most days during those first all important years, and watching her develop her character, has made me fully appreciate what I'd missed out the first time around with Jenna and Olivia. Yes, there'll always be a huge part of me that feels guilty and saddened. After all, I wasn't able to dedicate anywhere near the same amount of attention, time and love toward my older children's childhoods. But every day I try to relieve this guilt by telling myself that I'm working hard to fill in the gaps. I may not be able to change or recapture the past, but I can try to gradually heal it by making it up to them in numerous other ways.

Kitty's arrival coincided with the rediscovery of my childhood love for storytelling. This ignited a desire within me to write down the bones of my unusual life experiences. More than anything, I needed to make sense of what had happened on that terrifying yet enlightening time out at sea. I began frantically jotting down in a journal many of the astonishing and amazing things I had learned during that phenomenal conversation with the presence. I tried recalling word for word, and sentence by sentence, many of the incredible insights with which I had been gifted. To my utter astonishment, I found that once I had started, I couldn't stop. The words just kept flowing. The floodgates burst open, and a torrent of denied emotion, built up over half a lifetime, gushed out onto the paper. Writing by hand, page after page was filled almost faster than I could take down what was coming into my head. Bizarrely, I wasn't remembering only key points. I was actually recalling the contents of that entire conversation in the water. It was as though I was really back there, reliving it all over again.

The cathartic process of writing turned out to be precisely what I needed. I could literally feel myself being healed from the inside out. That's the beauty of writing down the truth. The whole experience was liberating. Life-enhancing. Finding a creative outlet to release my unexpressed feelings let me view life from a new and higher perspective. As I started to see everything through an expanded lens, life began to make more sense. It took on new meaning and purpose. My consciousness changed, and so did I. Self-reflection offered me a unique opportunity for development, self-growth and healing. Before I knew it, I was writing every single evening after my family had gone to bed, often well into the early hours.

An early inspiration for my writing was the renowned crime-writer, Agatha Christie. Her riverside family home was close to where we lived at that time in Devon. Fascinated by the way she had overcame huge adversity to become a universal writing success, I began sending letters to her daughter, Rosalind. I wanted to meet her and talk through some ideas I had for a children's creative writing competition. After several letters, and after most people told me that I was wasting my time, Rosalind finally rang me one day and agreed to meet. I was pleasantly shocked. She actually invited me to tea at the family home, Greenway House.

Meeting Rosalind, and hearing about Agatha's early life as a budding writer, inspired my own writing even more. I returned home later that evening, energized and bubbling with enthusiasm. I knew what needed to be done. Quickly pulling together notes from my journal, I now had a fixed intention: to turn everything I had captured in my journal into a book. It is the book you are now holding in your hands.

When the first draft for *Dying for a Change* was complete, I spent months wondering what to do with it next. I wasn't a confident or accomplished writer, far from it. And I wasn't even certain whether anyone would be the slightest bit interested in hearing about my personal story. No matter how extraordinary it appeared to me, the finished manuscript was raw. I knew that it still needed major surgery to bring it up to an acceptable level for submission to publishers. So it just sat there, going nowhere, while I procrastinated.

As so often happens, opportunities presented themselves out of the blue. Life gave me a kick up the pants. At work one day, I was throwing out old newspapers from my office when an advertisement caught my eye. It was one of those spooky, crazy coincidences when the right newspaper item, person, and event show up at the perfect time. The ad had been placed by Katy Clarke, a professional author and writing tutor. She was offering one-on-one tutoring for aspiring writers. Taking this as a sign, I nervously dialed the number, while thinking all the time, "What am I doing? Who am I to think that I am a writer?"

Fortunately, a warm, bubbly Scottish tone answered my call. I didn't realize it at the time, but this would be the beginning of what would later blossom into one of the most important and caring friendships of my life. A week later, Katy and I met. We connected from day one. I realized within ten seconds of our first meeting that she was the perfect person to help me get my story down in a professional way.

For a year, Katy and I met at her home one afternoon a week after work. With sensitivity and generosity of spirit, she helped to painstakingly guide me at every juncture. The process was hard and long, and the learning curve steep. But, together, and with patience, we slowly chiselled my manuscript into shape.

Twelve months after meeting Katy, I reached a crossroads where the writing was taking over my life. It had become an obsession, one that my addictive personality couldn't easily switch off. Trying to balance the demands of a challenging business, coupled with the commitment needed to write for several hours most evenings, were exhausting me. For months, I was surviving on little more than four hours of sleep a night. It quickly became apparent that something would have to give way. I couldn't be all and do it all. Deeply concerned that I wasn't giving 100 percent to either work or my new insatiable passion, I had a critically important decision to make.

In September 2004, the dam finally broke. I woke up early one morning and intuitively knew what had to be done. There was absolutely no doubt in my mind. I needed to resign my position as head of the company I had jointly founded. I needed time to focus on the book and several other writing projects that were now filling my head.

Telling Alison, my staff and other directors of the company wouldn't be easy. I was afraid they would think I had completely cracked up. After all, I had spent my entire working life up to that point in the development and construction industry. It was all I knew. On the surface, however, everyone took the news well, even if they privately thought I had totally lost my mind.

Alison and I had been together since we were teenagers, and she knew that nothing could sway me off course once I was locked in. She may not have totally agreed with my self-belief, but with the utmost respect, compassion and deep understanding, she also realized that I would never be able to find inner peace until the book was out in the marketplace. She knew that if I didn't try, I would spend the rest of my days living with a deep and bitter resentment.

Shortly before the Christmas holidays of 2004, I finally waved good-bye to my old life in sales. Driving home from work, my cell phone rang. It was my bank confirming that the extra consolidation loan had been approved. Thankfully, I'd managed to draw some more equity out of the house. We now had the financial resources in place to fund both my writing and her planned new career at a local university, where she would be studying to be a primary school teacher.

Punching down these final words of the epilogue, I can't help thinking what an incredible life-changing journey these last several years have been. Some ten years on from my initial accident in the sea, I'm still left in awe at those experiences and the enlightening conversation that took place. Looking back, I now better appreciate that I needed that near-brush with death to finally awaken me to my highest and greatest potential. Near death encounters have that power. They enable us to reframe our lives, and in doing so, give them more meaning and purpose.

I don't profess to totally understand what happened to me on that evening out at sea. All I do know is that it still remains a mystery. All I am assured of is that, in some miraculous way, it radically altered my life, in every conceivable and imaginable way. It changed how I see the world, how I interact with others. Best of all, it radically altered every previous held conception I ever had of what it means to be a human being. You may interpret my experiences as an awakening of my soul, or an encounter with God- whatever God is. You may even see it as a brief glimpse into the immeasurable divine spirit that is inherent in each and every one of us. I think my personal experiences were all of those, and much, much more.

A close friend recently asked whether I now had any strongly held beliefs about what God or divine spirit is? This is a hard question to answer, especially bearing in mind that, only several years ago, I was an out-and-out atheist. Even today, after everything that's now happened, and after the incredible miracle that saved me, I still have some tiny doubts. I still have many unanswered questions about who and what we are, and our real purpose on earth. Perhaps these doubts are supposed to remain with us throughout life. Maybe we're conditioned from birth to spend our entire lives trying to work out exactly what God is and what God is not. Perhaps the joy of life is actually to be found with living in the mystery. Perhaps it was intended that God, or what we each perceive to be God, should be broader, wider and deeper than any of the organized religions know or can know.

Somebody recently asked me, "What if this writing project fails miserably and comes to nothing? What if you've sacrificed everything to a book project that risks your home, security, pension, and marriage. Your sanity even."

I answered him with the same belief that I have answered everyone else over these past several years. There was no option, not unless I wanted to spend the rest of my life living with deep regret and anger. All of it pointed inwards.

Sadly, back in November 2008, Alison and I did finally split up. The following May we should have celebrated our 20th wedding anniversary. I was devastated, yet strangely, liberated at the same time. I'd always imagined that our partnership was rock solid, a marriage that could weather every approaching storm. But it clearly wasn't. Come the end, I think we simply fell out of love. We started neglecting one another, no longer respecting each other, and before long, our marriage crumbled and we went our separate ways. It's tragic to watch what was once a deeply loving relationship, break up before your very eyes. The loss, pain and grief of it all shoots deep into the soul. Especially when there are children involved. But thankfully, and with the love of grace, we are just managing to keep our separation amicable.

From day one, when I took up the challenge to get my fascinating story written down, I've believed with all my heart and soul that this work has to get out there. I needed to risk and do anything humanly possible to make that happen. Even if it did contribute partly toward our marriage failing. Getting down my experiences on paper felt as though I had no other choice. I was compelled to write this book and, in doing so, answer my calling. And that's all I know.

Maybe the whole thing *will* come to nothing. Perhaps sometime in the future, I may end up full of remorse that my constant addiction to finishing this project led partly to the break-up of my family. Although I don't believe that is the whole picture. I think our marriage had already started to derail many, many years ago. Ever since we'd been forced to spend increasingly more time apart, due to our work commitments. And ever since I started looking at my life differently after the accident.

Throughout this entire process, I have followed my gut instinct and listened to my soul. I wrote down every part of the story I could remember. My story.

And that's all I could do.

Dawlish, Devon, UK June 2009
###

William Murtha Bio

William Murtha is a writer, philanthropist and global activist for issues related to personal, social and global transformation, the environment and social responsibility. *Dying for a Change* is his first book. Several years after his life-changing incident in 1999, Murtha left behind everything that he'd ever worked hard to achieve to pursue his dream of becoming a writer. Selling his business and turning away from a successful career in sales management, William finally answered the calling to share his incredible story.

William worked in construction and development management until 2005. He then sold his shares in the business he founded and began to concentrate fully on writing and other creative projects. One of those initiatives is The Imagination Project, an innovative non-profit organization that promotes, supports and encourages emerging young luminaries and writers involved in human rights, corporate social responsibility and personal development. To fund and kick-start this exciting project, William has managed to persuade leaders, change-makers and visionaries from across all sectors of change to write and submit short "vision statements" of hope for the future. These inspirational and positive quotes will form the foundation to a series of published books. The first title, *Visionaries for the 21st Century,* will be published by Red Wheel in 2010.

For more information: www.williammurtha.com

Lightning Source UK Ltd.
Milton Keynes UK
UKOW02f1830080916

282564UK00001B/127/P

9 780982 385081